THE SOCIAL WORKER'S GUIDE TO THE CARE ACT 2014

Other books you may be interested in:

Personal Safety for Social Workers and Health Professionals
By Brian Atkins ISBN 978-1-909330-33-7

Positive Social Work: The Essential Toolkit for NQSWs, 2nd ed
By Julie Adams and Angie Sheard ISBN 978-1-911106-76-0

Practice Education in Social Work: Achieving Professional Standards, 2nd ed
By Pam Field, Cathie Jasper and Lesley Littler ISBN 978-1-911106-10-4

Titles are also available in a range of electronic formats. To order please go to our website www.criticalpublishing.com or contact our distributor NBN International, 10 Thornbury Road, Plymouth PL6 7PP, telephone 01752 202301 or email orders@nbninternational.com

THE SOCIAL WORKER'S GUIDE TO THE CARE ACT 2014

Pete Feldon

First published in 2017 by Critical Publishing Ltd
Reprinted in 2017 (twice) , 2018 (twice) and 2019.

British Library Cataloguing in Publication Data
A CIP record for this book is available from the British Library

ISBN: 978-1-911106-68-5

This book is also available in the following e-book formats:
MOBI ISBN: 978-1-911106-69-2
EPUB ISBN: 978-1-911106-70-8
Adobe e-book ISBN: 978-1-911106-71-5

Cover design by Out of House
Text design by Greensplash Ltd
Project Management by Out of House Publishing
Printed and bound in Great Britain by 4edge, Essex

Critical Publishing
3 Connaught Road
St Albans
AL3 5RX

www.criticalpublishing.com

Paper from responsible sources

Contents

Figures

Meet the author

Pete Feldon is a freelance Care Act consultant and trainer. He has a background of working in many sectors of social care as a social worker, trainer, manager and policy developer. He was a member of the team that developed learning materials for the Care Act for Skills for Care. He currently provides Care Act training for local authorities and for BASW. He was previously a member of the board of Skills for Care (November 2012–November 2014). He has written articles on the Care Act published in *Professional Social Work*, and also *The A-Z of the Care Act 2014* for Community Care Inform.

Acknowledgements

I am very grateful for the help from social work colleagues whom I have met through my involvement with BASW (British Association of Social Workers). Peter Simcock, Geraldine Nosowska and Leire Agirre looked at the first few chapters that I wrote and helped me both with the detail and the overall shape. Particular thanks go to Pete Morgan, Chair of the Board of PASAUK (Practitioner Alliance for Safeguarding Adults), who worked with me on several versions of the safeguarding chapter. Thanks also to Helen Mitchell and Leire Agirre for their comments on the safeguarding chapter.

A key feature of the book is using case examples to explore the practical application of the Care Act. Thanks to Pete Morgan for providing me with outlines for the safeguarding cases, and to Jane Shears for her help with a mental health case example.

On matters of detail, my major concerns have been to ensure that the case examples are authentic and that what is written about the law is accurate, and while I have taken into account the suggestions of colleagues, the responsibility for any lack of authenticity or inaccuracy is mine.

Preface

The idea for this book derives from the submission made by BASW (British Association of Social Workers) on the draft of the Care and Support Statutory Guidance (published in June 2014), which proposed that the guide "would be improved through a specific section bringing together references to the role of the social worker". This didn't happen and in early 2016 with nothing of this nature in sight, I decided that I would write this book.

Since the Care Act was passed in April 2014 I have been involved in developing materials to assist people in their learning, and I have delivered training to social workers and other practitioners. I worked with IPC (Institute of Public Care) to produce the suite of learning materials for Skills for Care, and since then I have been providing training for local authorities and BASW. Through both of these sets of experiences I have been able to refine my ideas about what social workers want to know about the Care Act 2014 and the associated Regulations and the Care and Support Statutory Guidance.

My approach is intended to contribute to improving the 'legal literacy' of social workers, ie "the ability to connect relevant legal rules with professional priorities and objectives of ethical practice"*. The book aims to enable social workers to better understand the legal framework within which they make professional judgements and apply their expertise. Law requires interpretation when applied in complex situations, and while the statutory guidance provides some help with this by describing what social workers must take into consideration, when it comes to getting things right for adults with care and support needs and carers, it is social workers who must take the lead in balancing legal requirements with good social work practice in the context of the resources available from the local authorities that they work within.

* *Legal Literacy in Adult Social Care – Research in Practice for Adults* (2016)

Introduction

The implementation of the Care Act 2014 in April 2015 swept aside a patchwork of legislation that had developed over more than 50 years since the modern welfare state was established by the National Assistance Act 1948. The legislative framework of the Care Act 2014, the associated Regulations and the Care and Support Statutory Guidance, provides a revised mandate for social work with adults and a policy framework that embraces and supports the development of modern social care.

The Care Act provides the legislative mandate for the core social work tasks of assessment of needs, care and support planning and safeguarding. The accompanying Care and Support Statutory Guidance (revised 2017) is written for a generic audience and it is not always set out in a way that is coherent from a social work perspective. The intention of this book is to present the information from the Act, regulations and statutory guidance in a way that provides social workers with a good understanding of the legislation and how it applies to their role. In addition it highlights the circumstances where professional judgement is required and explores issues that need some interpretation through the use of case examples.

There are parts of the operational framework provided by the statutory guidance that require further interpretation before social workers can be confident about their application. Local authorities provide this to some extent by developing their own policies and procedures, and indeed they are required to do so in the key area of safeguarding. This book hopes to highlight and address those areas where there is a lack of clarity and detail by setting out the existing content in ways that focus on the role of the social worker, and additional detail is provided through the use of case examples to suggest interpretations that derive from practice. Although this book aims to be clear about what the law says, any interpretations that are suggested are in relation to social work practice and not on points of law.

The book is careful to distinguish between a local authority's duties and its powers, which simply put is the difference between 'must' or 'must not' and 'may' or 'may not', and to explain how the term 'should' is used to provide more detail about how the 'musts' are to be implemented. When using these terms in the book they are set out in the context of referenced quotations (from the Act, regulations and statutory guidance), and where sections are paraphrased the precise meaning of these terms is adhered to. It should be noted that the author reserves the term 'ought to' for where there is an implied requirement in the statutory guidance.

The changes in terminology introduced by the statutory guidance are used throughout. In particular, the term 'people with care and support needs' is used rather than 'service user'. This important change reflects the change in emphasis from providing services, to meeting needs.

This book differs from the statutory guidance in its use of terminology in two important respects, as follows:

- The statutory guidance uses the generic term of practitioner when referring to tasks that can be undertaken by either a social worker, occupational therapist or other professional. In most of the chapters of this book, where any task can potentially be undertaken by a social worker, this term is used.
- There is a distinction between the care and support needs of adults and the support needs of carers, and likewise a distinction between care and support plans for adults and support plans for carers. When referring to both adults and carers, the phrase 'care and/or support' is used.

In quoting from the Care Act and the Regulations in this book, the appropriate numeration and sub-numeration is used preceded by the word 'section', eg section 42 (a). When references from the statutory guidance are quoted, the term 'paragraph' is used, eg paragraph 6.125.

Social workers who are working towards achieving the requirements of the Knowledge and Skills Statement for Social Workers in Adult Services, ie to "be able to understand and work within the legal frameworks relevant to adult settings",[1] will hopefully find this book helpful. It can also provide a solid foundation for social work students who are aiming to achieve professional capability in demonstrating "a critical understanding of the legal and policy frameworks and guidance that inform and mandate social work practice, recognising the scope for professional judgement".[2] The content can also provide material for more experienced social workers seeking to apply the critical reflection necessary to develop professional judgement to "use appropriate assessment frameworks"[3] and "use assessment procedures discerningly".[4]

Readers should note that each local authority applies the operational framework provided by the statutory guidance in slightly different ways. This can be partly as a result of local decisions about how to apply local authority powers under the Care Act, but it can also be because of decisions taken about how to create an operational system that accords with local policies and priorities. This book provides social workers with a useful source of reference with which to evaluate their local systems and their associated policies and procedures.

The core of the book covers the key stages of the care and support journey, as set out in the Care and Support Statutory Guidance. In addition there are chapters that look at significant issues that cut across several stages of the journey, such as safeguarding and working with NHS (National Health Service) colleagues. In each chapter case examples are used to illustrate the application of the legislation, and to tease out issues that are particularly important and challenging for social workers. The emphasis is on the processes and practices that are a regular feature of the day-to-day professional lives of most social workers. Each chapter comprises three main sections, as follows:

1. summary of the legislation and how it differs from preceding legislation;
2. detailed description of the main points, set out in a way that focuses on the role of the social worker and their interaction with adults with care and support needs and carers with support needs;
3. the application of the Act, regulations and statutory guidance to case examples.

In addition there are three chapters in the book that simply provide straightforward summaries of what is in the statutory guidance without any case examples or analysis, as follows:

Chapter 9: Safeguarding – types of abuse, SABs and SARs

Chapter 11: Disputes

Chapter 13: Other modifications and additions

There are some chapters in the statutory guidance that social workers will want to refer to that are not included in this book, particularly those dealing with ordinary residence, and continuity of care and cross-border placements. Each of these chapters deals with different aspects of people moving between local authority areas, and the aim is to provide guidance on a range of circumstances where there can be uncertainty; they are best used for reference as and when required. In addition social workers may also wish to familiarise themselves with the chapters in the first section of the statutory guidance that set out the general responsibilities of local authorities.

This book focuses almost exclusively on what is stated in the Care Act, the associated Regulations and the Care and Support Statutory Guidance. Reference is made to additional guidance that has been provided by the Social Care Institute of Excellence and others, but as yet there has been little in the way of published research evaluating the implementation of the Care Act to draw upon. Consequently it would be premature to provide a critique of the legislation and how the statutory guidance could be improved, or to comment on the impact of the availability of local government funding on the implementation of the legislation. These issues will be considered at a later date when this book is updated.

The final chapter considers professional judgement in the context of duties, powers and good practice.

References

1. Knowledge and Skills Statement for Social Workers in Adult Services – Department of Health, 2016.
2. Professional Capabilities Framework*, knowledge domain, last placement onwards – www.basw.co.uk/pcf/.
3. Professional Capabilities Framework*, intervention and skills domain, ASYE.
4. Professional Capabilities Framework*, intervention and skills domain, social worker onwards.

* References are to the version prior to its review in 2017

Part I The care and support journey

This part of the book describes the social work role in the decisions made by local authorities in meeting the care and support needs of adults, and the support needs of carers.

These decisions are clustered together in a series of processes that set out what the Care and Support Statutory Guidance describes as "the journey through the care and support system" (paragraph 6.2). Each stage of the journey, as outlined in Figure P.1, is explored in a chapter in this part of the book.

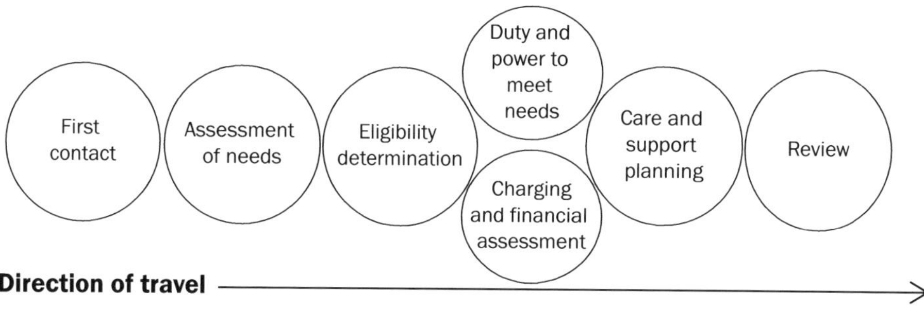

Figure P.1 *The care and support journey*

The model of the journey shown in Figure P.1 is very similar to the one set out following paragraph 6.12 of the Care and Support Statutory Guidance. The difference is in the addition of 'Duty and power to meet needs' and 'Charging and financial assessment'.

The content of this book is constructed to focus more closely on the role of social workers and hence it is important to highlight these two stages of the journey.

Each of the chapters in this part of the book describes what social workers need to know, and case examples are used to illustrate and analyse some of the key elements of the processes that are of particular relevance for social workers. The book follows the sequencing of the journey as described in the statutory guidance, but it is recognised that adults and carers will not experience their own individual journey in this way. The skilled social worker will use his or her expertise to apply these processes so that people with care and/or support needs experience them in a straightforward way.

Throughout the statutory guidance, mental capacity is referred to where relevant; however, the approach taken in this book is to consider it separately (in Chapter 10). This allows for a consideration of the differences that apply when someone lacks mental capacity, and to compare this with the new concept of 'substantial difficulty' and how this links with the role of the independent advocate.

There are additional factors to be taken account of in the application of the care and support journey to people in prisons and children in transition to adulthood; these are considered in Chapter 13.

Applying the duties of local authorities towards adults experiencing, or at risk of, abuse or neglect have distinctive requirements that are considered in Chapters 8 and 9.

1 First contact

Introduction

People will have their first contact with social care in a range of different ways. Sometimes it will be as a result of a crisis, or it could simply be an enquiry from someone anticipating that they might need help in the future. The contact might be directly with the local authority or the individual could be referred by another organisation, such as when someone is being discharged from hospital or where the individual has made an enquiry with a local voluntary organisation.

Where this first contact is in relation to someone who appears to have care and support needs or a carer who appears to have support needs, then a needs assessment or a carer's assessment must be offered. In addition to initiating the assessment, the first contact process must include steering people towards preventative services and sources of specialist advice and information.

This chapter focuses on the commencement of a needs or carer's assessment at the point of first contact, whether this is via a specialist first contact team or through other means such as planning for a discharge from hospital.

Although social workers are mostly not involved directly in the first contact process, they need to have a good understanding of how it works because they will be taking over cases either straight away, or after an intermediary stage such as reablement.

This chapter comprises the following sections:

- **First contact prior to April 2015**
- **Key terms and definitions**
- **The essential features of first contact**
- **The gateway to assessment**

- **First contact teams**
- **Initial assessment at first contact**
- **Applying the guidance using case examples**
- **Conclusion.**

There is a strong emphasis in the statutory guidance on enabling people to make well-informed decisions throughout the care and support journey, and this is particularly important during first contact. Staff responsible for the first contact have a role in making sure that individuals who contact them understand how the care and support system might apply to their circumstances, and signposting them to sources of specialist information.

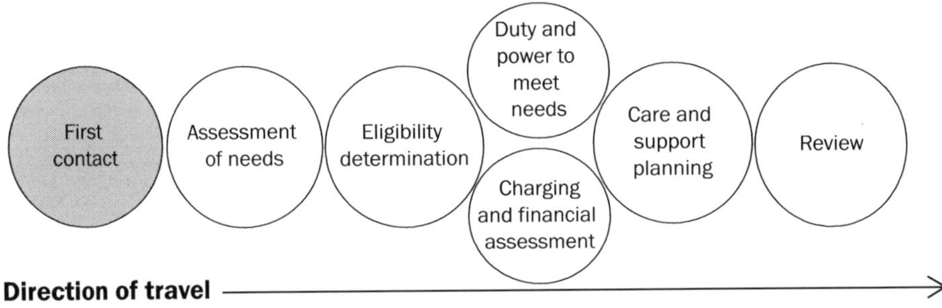

Figure 1.1 The care and support journey

First contact prior to April 2015

Section 47 (1) of the NHS and Community Care Act 1990 stated that "where it appears to a local authority that any person for whom they may provide or arrange for the provision of community care services may be in need of any such services, the authority – (a) shall carry out an assessment of his needs for those services".

Carers had a right to request an assessment of their needs under the Carers (Recognition and Services) Act 1995 and the Carers and Disabled Children Act 2000. Section 1 (1) of the former stated that where "an individual ('the carer') provides or intends to provide a substantial amount of care on a regular basis for the relevant person, the carer may request the local authority, before they make their decision as to whether the needs of the relevant person call for the provision of any services, to carry out an assessment of his ability to provide and to continue to provide care for the relevant person".

The previous statutory guidance was issued in 2010 in *Prioritising Need in the Context of Putting People First: A Whole System Approach to Eligibility for Social Care*. In paragraph 73 it stated that "before starting a community care assessment councils should first ascertain whether a person appears to be in need of community care services regardless of whether and how those needs are currently being met". This statutory guidance did not add anything in relation to the initial assessment of carers.

Key terms and definitions*

Key term	Care Act 2014	The Care and Support Statutory Guidance (revised 2017)
Appearance of need for care and support	The duty to assess is triggered where "it appears to the local authority that an adult may have needs for care and support" – section 9 (1)	Paragraph 6.13 states: "Local authorities must undertake an assessment for any adult with an appearance of need for care and support, regardless of whether or not the local authority thinks the individual has eligible needs or of their financial situation."
Appearance of need for support	The duty to assess is triggered where "it appears to the local authority that the carer may have needs for support" – section 10 (1)	Paragraph 6.16 states: "Where an individual provides or intends to provide care for another adult and it appears that the carer may have any level of needs for support, local authorities must carry out a carer's assessment."
First contact	No reference	This is described as a distinct process in 6.22–29. Paragraph 6.22 states: "From their very first contact with the local authority, the person must be given as much information as possible about the assessment process, as early as possible, to ensure a personalised approach to the assessment."
Refusal of assessment	Where an adult or a carer refuses an assessment, the local authority has no duty to assess. This does not apply where the adult lacks capacity and it is in their best interests, or the adult is experiencing (or is at risk of) abuse or neglect – section 11 (1) and (2).	Nothing further is added to the definition.
Urgent needs	The power to meet an adult's care and support needs that appear to be urgent is set out in section 19 (3).	Paragraph 5.26 clarifies that: "In this context, 'urgent' takes its everyday meaning, subject to interpretation by the courts, and may be related to, for example, time, severity etc."

* There is no reference to any of these terms in the Regulations

The essential features of first contact

1. The key factor in determining if a needs assessment must be considered for an adult, or a carer's assessment for a carer, is whether the individual has an appearance of need.
2. Once an appearance of need is determined, the duty to assess is triggered. The first contact is the initial part of the assessment process.
3. An assessment must be initiated regardless of whether the individual is thought to have eligible needs or to be a self-funder.
4. At this stage it must be ascertained whether the individual is able to be involved in their assessment, or whether they have substantial difficulty in doing so.
5. Once an assessment has commenced, it can be concluded only in one of two ways. Either the person being assessed declines further assessment, or the assessment continues until eligibility has been determined.
6. The first contact can often be at a time of crisis and the individual may have urgent needs for care and support.
7. Urgent needs can be met regardless of whether the individual meets the ordinary residence requirement.
8. This initial stage of the assessment can be undertaken through a telephone conversation or online.
9. At the conclusion of the first contact the person being assessed should be clear about the next steps and be given an indication of timescales.
10. Staff involved in first contact must have access to support from social workers and other professionally qualified staff, or be social workers or qualified professionals themselves.

The gateway to assessment

A needs assessment or a carer's assessment cannot take place unless it has been established that someone appears to have needs for care and support (or for support in the case of a carer).

The statutory guidance does not give any definition of 'appearance of need'. By using the term 'appearance' it sets a low threshold for assessment, and means that an assessment ought to be carried out for any adult who may have needs for care and support, and any carer who may have needs for support.

Appearance of need is the only criteria identified for a person to be considered for an assessment. The Care Act underscores this by identifying what cannot be taken into account in section 9 (3):

"The duty to carry out a needs assessment applies regardless of the authority's view of –

a) the level of the adult's needs for care and support, or

b) the level of the adult's financial resources."

Being ordinarily resident in a local authority area is not a requirement where a person has urgent needs, as specified in section 19 (3) of the Care Act. The only other reference to ordinary residence in relation to assessment is in paragraph 6.134 of the statutory guidance where it is set out what a local authority must do if an adult has eligible needs, and one of these requirements is to "establish whether the person meets the ordinary residence requirement".

Paragraph 6.16 clarifies that a carer is an individual who "provides or intends to provide care for another adult", and would qualify for an assessment where "it appears that the carer may have any level of needs for support". Someone who provides "care under contract (e.g. for employment) or as part of voluntary work" (paragraph 6.16) is not normally regarded as a carer in the sense that this term is used in the Act, regulations and statutory guidance.

First contact teams

Most local authorities have specialist teams that respond to people making contact with a local authority for the first time about social care. These teams also receive and process referrals from other organisations.

The revised statutory guidance endorses the setting up of specialist teams to get "the initial response right" (paragraph 6.24). This paragraph notes that "local authorities have found that putting in place a single access point for all new requests and people currently receiving care can speed up and simplify the process for people approaching the authority; and can also free up time for professional staff to focus on more complex cases".

Most local authorities have acted on the suggestion in paragraph 3.25 that the first point of contact is one means by which they can "provide – or signpost to – advice and information when people in need of care and support come into contact with them".

These teams are organised in a number of different ways, and have a range of different names ranging from the straightforward 'Access Team' to snappier titles such as 'Choices'. Some comprise both office-based staff who provide the initial response and social workers who undertake initial assessments. In other local authorities the staff providing the initial response are part of an information and advice team that makes the decision about whether there is an 'appearance of need'. Or in some cases there is a corporate call-handling team that does not make the 'appearance of need' decision and forwards on the request for assessment to the relevant team.

Where first contact teams do not include social workers, arrangements should be made so that staff "have the benefit of access to professional support from social workers, occupational therapists and other relevant experts as appropriate, to support the identification of any underlying conditions or to ensure that complex needs are identified early and that people are signposted appropriately" (paragraph 6.27).

For some people the route to assessment may not be via a first contact team, eg where potential care and support needs are first identified when someone is in hospital, social workers often manage all of the initial response. Also, for people whose most significant needs are because of mental illness or learning disability, the initial assessment of care and support needs may be part of a multi-disciplinary assessment. Carers will always be offered an assessment of their support needs in conjunction with the adult, but for some people the starting point could be the carer requesting an assessment, and this could come via a local carers organisation.

Initial assessment at first contact

Paragraph 6.22 is clear that the "assessment process starts from when local authorities start to collect information about the person".

The previous statutory guidance issued in 2010 in *Prioritising Need in the Context of Putting People First: A Whole System Approach to Eligibility for Social Care* distinguished between first establishing an individual's 'presenting needs' and then going on to determine if they had 'eligible needs'. But no such distinction exists in the Care Act 2014 or the statutory guidance.

In deciding how to organise the initial stage of assessments of need, either through a team specialising in first contact or through some other means such as hospital discharge, local authorities will have to make their own policy and practice decisions about how to apply the statutory guidance in relation to information and advice, appropriateness and proportionality, involvement, meeting urgent needs and ending an assessment.

Information and advice

It is specified in paragraph 6.22 that an individual "must be given as much information as possible about the assessment process, as early as possible". This information should include detail of what can be expected during the assessment process" and:

- the format and timescale of assessment;
- complaints processes;
- possible access to independent advocacy.

In addition paragraph 6.38 states "the local authority should provide in advance, and in an accessible format, the list of questions to be covered in the assessment... (to) help the individual or carer prepare for their assessment and think through what their needs are and the outcomes they want to achieve". Paragraph 6.22 also states that local authorities "must ensure that this information is in an accessible format for those to whom it is provided", eg in Braille for people who have a sight impairment.

Chapter 3 of the statutory guidance sets out the general duty placed on the local authority to provide information and advice in relation to care and support, some of which is particularly relevant to first contact. In paragraph 3.33 reference is made to research findings that "people 'don't know what they need to know' in relation to their care and support". Paragraph 3.35 states that in providing an information and advice service, local authorities should assist "people to navigate all points and aspects of their journey through care and support".

Paragraph 3.23 says that local authorities must ensure that information and advice is provided on "the care and support system locally – about how the system works", and that this will include an "outline of what the 'process' may entail and the judgements that may need to be made" and also "specific information on what the assessment process, eligibility, and review stage is, how to complain or make a formal appeal to the authority, what they involve and when independent advocacy should be provided".

An example is given in paragraph 6.101 of how the early provision of information and advice "would delay a person from developing needs which meet the eligibility criteria" and that this would also help individuals to "think more broadly about what support might be available in the local community or through their support network to meet their needs and support the outcomes they want to achieve".

Appropriateness and proportionality

Local authorities must ensure that an individual "receives a proportionate assessment which identifies their level of needs" (paragraph 6.28), and in doing so it may be appropriate for the assessment to be "carried out over the phone or online". A caveat is added that these methods may not be appropriate in some circumstances, particularly where "there is concern about a person's capacity to make a decision, for example as a result of a mental impairment such as those with dementia, acquired brain injury, learning disabilities or mental health needs". In these circumstances "a face-to-face assessment should be arranged".

Difficulties with involvement

The general duty of local authorities to consider whether individuals "would have substantial difficulty in engaging with the local authority care and support processes" (paragraph 7.10) will be applicable at first contact. Paragraph 6.23 states: "From this early stage local authorities should consider whether the individual would have substantial difficulty in being involved in the assessment process and if so consider the need for independent advocacy." The implications of having difficulties with involvement are considered in more depth in Chapter 10.

Meeting urgent needs

Staff who receive approaches from people with urgent needs or referrals from other organisations will be responsible for initiating the exercise of the local authority's power to "provide an immediate response and meet the individual's care and support needs" (paragraph 6.26). This can be done by making arrangements to meet these needs, or "an immediate referral may be the best way to meet a person's urgent needs" (paragraph 6.26). It may be that their urgent needs are best met by the NHS.

Urgent needs can be met without taking into account ordinary residence and finances (see paragraph 6.26).

Ending the assessment

Unless people choose to end their assessment, it ought to continue until it concludes with the determination of eligibility. The statutory guidance does not suggest any alternatives.

An individual "may choose not to have an assessment because they do not feel that they need care or they may not want local authority support" (paragraph 6.20), and in these circumstances the local authority is not required to undertake an assessment. However, section 11 (2) specifies that an assessment must take place where an adult says that he or she doesn't want one if either of the two following circumstances apply:

a) the adult lacks mental capacity and it would be in their best interests;

b) the adult is experiencing, or is at risk of experiencing, abuse or neglect.

Applying the guidance using case examples

What follows in this section are three examples that have been constructed to illustrate and analyse some of the typical aspects of first contact that are of particular relevance for social workers.

The cases used in this chapter will also be used in subsequent chapters of Part I to illustrate each person's journey through the care and support system.

Chapter 10 considers all stages of the care and support journey for people who lack mental capacity or have substantial difficulty, so examples are not given in this chapter and in subsequent chapters of Part I.

Each case, and the subsequent analysis, is set out using the following headings:

- **Commencing of an assessment;**
- **Concluding first contact.**

The first case also considers the following:

- **Meeting urgent needs.**

Mr K

Commencing an assessment

Ms K telephones the local authority First Contact team to find out if her father can get help with having meals prepared for him. She says that he is perfectly capable of making enquiries on his own behalf, but is a bit embarrassed about asking for help and has agreed that she can make enquiries on his behalf.

Mr K has COPD (Chronic Obstructive Pulmonary Disease) and arthritis. He lives alone in a house that he owns. Ms K has been cooking meals for Mr K for the past six months but is no longer willing to continue doing this, although she is willing to continue to do his shopping. Ms K mentions that her father pays a neighbour to help with the cleaning and laundry.

The First Contact team member concludes that Mr K appears to have needs for care and support and that Ms K appears to have needs for support.

Ms K is informed that the local authority can help Mr K to plan how to best meet his needs and may be able to help pay for what he requires, but the first step would be to undertake an assessment of what he can and cannot do in relation to looking after himself and working with him to help him maximise his abilities. She is also informed that the assessment would benefit from finding out more about how his healthcare needs are being managed.

It is agreed that Ms K will discuss this plan with her father and obtain his agreement (as he has the legal right to refuse an assessment). Ms K is advised that she can obtain more information from the local authority website about how the care and support system works.

Ms K is offered a carer's assessment, but she declines the offer. She says that all she wants is to not have to keep cooking meals for her father.

Concluding first contact

Ms K telephones back having had a discussion with her father. His view is that he can't see the point in having an assessment if he is going to have to pay for all of his care anyway. It turns out that both Mr and Ms K had wrongly concluded that the value of his home (that he owns) would be taken into account in providing him with the type of care and support that he wants.

Despite reassurance that the value of his home is not considered, Ms K believes that Mr K might still decline to have an assessment as he does have an occupational pension that will be taken into account.

Ms K agrees to try to persuade her father to have an assessment of his needs for care and support.

Ms K is also advised of where she can obtain information about alternative ways of her father buying in meals for himself.

Alternative scenario

If Mr K did not have COPD and his arthritis was less severe, and if it was clear that he could prepare his own meals if he wished to, he and his daughter might conclude that he would not meet the eligibility criteria (having read them on the local authority's website). So when Ms K rings back she might say that there is no point in Mr K having an assessment if he is not going to get any help because he doesn't meet the criteria.

In these circumstances Ms K ought to be made aware of the following:

- *An assessment for Mr K can help them both plan how to make the best use of what is available in the community and in their own support networks, and that this will be of value whether or not the eligibility criteria are met.*
- *Information about the local authority's policy on meeting non-eligible needs for care and support, as it is possible that some of his non-eligible needs could be met.*

If Ms K decided that she and her father wanted to make their own arrangements, she would be given advice about resources that can prevent and delay the development of needs and advised to make contact in the future.

Meeting urgent needs

If Mr K has a fall following the initial contact made by his daughter, and this resulted in him not being able to use the stairs to get to the toilet and his bedroom, and it also meant that he could not self-manage his personal care or use the toilet independently, an urgent response to meeting his needs might be required.

The extent of what would need to be provided would depend on what Ms K was willing and able to do. It might be the case that home care would be required to help meet his personal care needs. In any event he would probably require the provision of specialist equipment and some adaptations to his living arrangements, which would be determined by an OT.

Mr K and Ms K could choose to make their own arrangements and simply act on advice provided by the local authority. But if they wanted the local authority to make the arrangements, services would be provided and the assessment would then be completed at a later stage.

Ms W

Commencing an assessment

Ms W's GP has been contacted by the manager of the housing association who is concerned about potential fire risk because of the condition of Ms W's flat. The GP agreed to the housing manager's request that a referral is made to the Single Point of Access for Community Mental Health Services run by the NHS Mental Health Trust for her area. This referral route was chosen by the GP because the housing association had previous contact with mental health services about Ms W.

The manager believes that there is a potential fire risk because of the large amount of magazines and newspapers that Ms W has accumulated. Housing association staff have tried to get her to remove these but have had no success. Ms W has been advised of the plan to ask for help from the local mental health service.

The Mental Health Trust records provide the following information:

- *Ms W (aged 40) was diagnosed as having psychotic depression at the age of 25, and she was admitted to hospital in her early 30s.*
- *She was placed in her current housing association accommodation seven years ago, and at the time she was subject to a section 117 after-care order under the Mental Health Act 1983, following a hospital admission.*
- *The after-care order ceased five years ago and she was discharged to the care of her GP.*
- *A year before her hospital admission, she was made redundant from her administrative job in a university.*
- *Her mother died four years ago. She has limited contact with her father.*

The referral from the GP contained the following additional information:

- *The delusional aspects of her depression are being satisfactorily managed through medication. She has declined the offer of talking therapy.*
- *She says that she keeps herself busy by collecting old books and magazines from car boot sales. I was not able to determine whether she sells them as well, as she is reluctant to talk about it. I wonder whether she has Diogenes syndrome?*
- *In other respects she is healthy.*

The assessor at the Single Point of Access service passes the referral on for consideration for an assessment to be undertaken by the local Community Mental Health Team.

Concluding first contact

The Community Mental Health Team decide that the referral about Ms W will be followed up by an initial assessment to be undertaken by a social worker. This is because the description of her circumstances indicates at this stage that her primary needs are in relation to care and support.

Mrs O

Commencing an assessment

Mrs O emails the local carers centre requesting a carer's assessment. She has read on the local authority website that this organisation can arrange for this type of assessment and provide help for carers.

Mrs O outlines in her email that she wants help because her husband is a problem drinker and periodically has episodes where his heavy drinking results in him being incontinent. He is separated from Mrs O but lives close by to the family home. Mr O's father had provided him with a lot of support, but he has recently died.

Concluding first contact

The carers centre assessor concludes that Mrs O appears to have support needs, and so there is a telephone follow-up. The following information is obtained from Mrs O:

- *Following earlier advice from the local authority she has made use of Al-Anon Family Group meetings.*
- *She is worried that she doesn't have enough time for her children because of the help she gives to her husband.*
- *She doesn't think her husband will accept help from anyone else.*

Mrs O agrees to the offer of a face-to-face assessment, and gives permission for enquiries to be made about her previous contact with the local authority.

Comment and analysis

Readers should note that what is set out in this section and the previous section is intended to show how the statutory guidance might be applied, and in doing so, what would be complex situations in real life have had to be simplified.

Commencing an assessment

It is probable that the majority of people who make contact with their local authority for help with social care will meet the threshold criteria for the appearance of need. Those who don't will usually be people who have other needs, and can be given contact details for NHS services, benefits, police, and so on.

Many people who make contact on a planned basis, like Mr K and Mrs O, will have some idea of what social care can achieve. The individual, or their representative, may have made their own enquiries before deciding to make contact or they may have been recommended to make contact by a friend/neighbour or another professional. However, there will be many people where the first contact is made in an emergency, where they may not have had the opportunity to form a view about what social care can offer in their circumstances.

Ms W's situation demonstrates that the initiative for first contact may come from a 'referral', and also that first contact may not necessarily be with the local authority.

Having confirmed the appearance of need, the next step required of staff responsible for first contact is "to make the appropriate judgements needed to steer individuals seeking support towards information and advice, preventative services or a more detailed care and support assessment, or all of these" (paragraph 6.25). Some local authorities describe this process as 'screening'. Many local authorities choose to provide an online assessment that enables people to establish that they have the appearance of need, and it also 'steers' them through the various options. The examples given have not explored the practical application of the 'steering' process, as it is not part of the social work role.

For Mr K and Ms W a social worker, another professional or a suitably trained local authority employee would complete the subsequent assessment of needs. But for Mrs O the local authority has contracted out carers' assessments to a specialist organisation, and usually such assessments are not undertaken by social workers.

Concluding first contact

In addition to making the decision to either end an assessment at first contact or pass it on for a full assessment and eligibility determination, there is the option of pausing the assessment. Whatever the decision, it should be with the agreement of the adult and/or the carer.

Local authorities have to balance the right of an individual to have an assessment with their duty to encourage people to make use of what is available in the community and in their own support networks to prevent or delay needs developing (see sections 9 (6) and 10 (8) of the Care Act).

In ensuring that people who present with an appearance of need consider what resources they can access, local authorities must provide them "with targeted, personalised information and advice that can support them to take steps to prevent or reduce their needs, connect more effectively with their local community, and delay the onset of greater needs to maximise their independence and quality of life" (paragraph 2.53). To give people time to act on this advice and to achieve the benefits of prevention, it may be appropriate to defer the decision about whether to continue with the assessment. Paragraph 6.25 states how this should be managed: "Early or targeted interventions such as universal services, a period of reablement and providing equipment or minor household adaptions can delay an adult's needs from progressing. The first contact with the authority, which triggers the requirement to assess, may lead to a pause in the assessment process to allow such interventions to take place and for any benefit to the adult to be determined."

In addition to receiving information about steps that can be taken to prevent or delay needs developing during the process of first contact, people should receive information about eligibility criteria and charging. Some people may conclude that they are not likely to have eligible needs and as a result may decide that they do not wish to proceed with an assessment of their needs. Or it may be that they see no point in being assessed, having realised that they will get no financial help because they are a self-funder. However, any information given about eligibility ought to include the advice that assessment "should not just be seen as a gateway to care and support, but should be a critical intervention in its own right, which can help people to understand their situation and the needs they have, to reduce or delay the onset of greater needs, and to access support when they require it" (paragraph 6.2).

Conclusion

As a result of these arrangements for first contact, people ought to have a good idea about what the care and support journey entails before their first encounter with the social worker who is going to undertake the assessment of their needs. Some people will get their information from the local authority's first contact team (or other organisations that have a first contact role), and they may have also looked at the local authority website or have been advised by other professionals. Others will have already had the experience of making their own arrangements to prevent, reduce or delay their needs, based upon the advice and information given to them when they previously had contact with the local authority.

It is important that social workers are familiar with the information that is provided about the care and support journey on the local authority website, as this information will have been used by first contact staff, as well as by those individuals who are due to receive a needs assessment or a carer's assessment. In addition to being alert to any misunderstandings that people may have developed from what they have read, social workers can use this information to help people to build on their knowledge of the care and support system and to use this constructively throughout their journey. For example, during the early stages of an assessment the social worker will not be able to tell an individual whether his or her needs are going to meet the eligibility criteria, but the social worker can give the individual information about the eligibility criteria so that they can start considering how this might apply.

Social workers ought to understand how judgements are made at the point of first contact about steering individuals towards alternatives to a needs assessment. In many local authorities this 'steering' is undertaken by first contact teams that comprise staff who are not professionally qualified; in some local authorities their websites are constructed to encourage people to make use of what is available in the community and in their own networks before requesting an assessment.

First contact is the only part of the care and support journey where social workers usually do not have a lead role. In the remaining chapters of this book the focus is on the role of the social worker.

2 Assessment of needs

Introduction

In the context of the Care Act 2014, assessment is about both needs and outcomes. The purpose of an assessment is to identify an adult's care and support needs (and/or a carer's support needs), and what outcomes can maintain or improve their wellbeing.

When people come into contact with social care for the first time they are often seeking help to manage their lives better and be more independent. A needs assessment is about helping people to identify and clarify what could be improved and what steps to take to achieve these improvements.

A needs assessment is both the gateway to care and support and a means by which people can be helped to take an active role in addressing their needs. During an assessment, people will develop a better understanding of their needs and how their desired outcomes could be achieved, so that they can take steps to reduce or delay greater needs developing – and this can involve people making better use of their own abilities, networks and community resources.

Once a person's needs have been assessed it can then be determined which of these needs the local authority is required to or chooses to meet, and this may lead to a care and/or support plan being developed to maintain or improve their wellbeing.

This chapter aims to set out those parts of the Act, regulations and statutory guidance relevant to social workers in a way that helps with their practical application.

The chapter comprises the following sections:

- **Assessment of needs prior to April 2015**
- **Key terms and definitions**
- **The essential features of a suggested assessment framework**

- **The components of a needs assessment**
- **What must be considered when undertaking an assessment**
- **Methods of assessment**
- **The outputs of assessment**
- **Recording formats and duties**
- **Knowledge and skills needed to undertake assessments**
- **Applying the guidance using case examples**
- **Conclusion.**

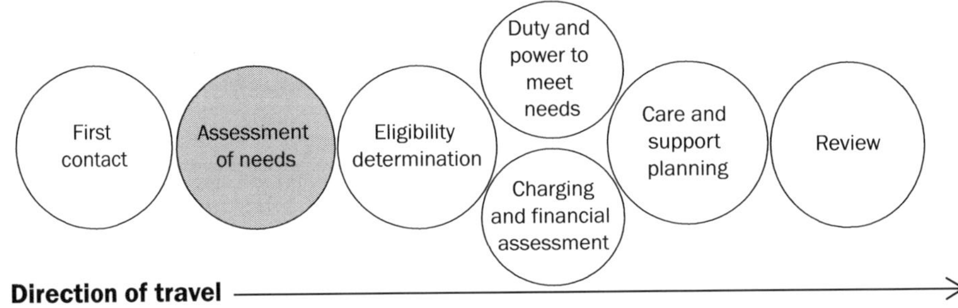

Figure 2.1 *The care and support journey*

Assessment of needs prior to April 2015

The purpose of an assessment as set out in section 47 (1) of the NHS and Community Care Act 1990 was to determine whether an adult was in need of any of the services that the local authority had a duty to provide under sections 42 and 46. Elements of the Chronically Sick and Disabled Persons Act 1970 and the Disabled Persons (Services, Consultation and Representation) Act 1986 were also relevant.

The Carers (Recognition and Services) Act 1995 and the Carers and Disabled Children Act 2000 conferred the right for carers to request an assessment of their needs as carers. The focus of the assessment was the carer's "ability to provide and to continue to provide care for the relevant person".

Good practice evolved in the two decades following the NHS and Community Care Act 1990, culminating in the person-centred approach that was evident in the statutory guidance issued in 2010 in *Prioritising Need in the Context of Putting People First: A Whole System Approach to Eligibility for Social Care*. In paragraph 79 it stated: "The purpose of a community care assessment is to identify and evaluate an individual's presenting needs and how these needs impose barriers to that person's independence and/or wellbeing. Information derived from an individual's assessment should be used to inform decisions on eligibility. Where eligible needs have been identified, an appropriate support plan can then be put together in collaboration with the individual, describing the support they will draw upon to overcome barriers to independence and wellbeing, both immediately and over the longer term."

The 2010 statutory guidance described carers' assessments as having two main purposes: "The first is to consider the sustainability of the caring role. The second is to consider whether or not the carer works or wishes to work and whether or not the carer is undertaking or wishes to undertake education, training or leisure activity, and the impact that their caring role might have on these commitments or aspirations."

Although guidance on assessment evolved, it still had to operate within the constraint of the service-focused approach of the NHS and Community Care Act 1990. The Care Act has changed this as eligibility now applies to needs and not to services. The emphasis is now on identifying needs for care and support and determining eligible needs, as opposed to determining whether an adult was in need of any of the services that the local authority had a duty to provide. The local authority now has no duties to provide specific services.

Also, assessment now has a more active role to play by helping individuals to prevent, reduce and delay the development of needs, and also to assist with the achieving of outcomes by means other than through the provision of care and support.

Assessment of the needs of carers has changed significantly because they are now entitled to an assessment in their own right, and they no longer have to request an assessment.

Key terms and definitions

The following have been selected because they appear in either the Care Act and/or the Regulations.

Key term	Care Act 2014	The Care and Support (Assessment) Regulations 2014	The Care and Support Statutory Guidance (revised 2017)
Appropriate and proportionate	Section 12 specifies that the Regulations must include what must be considered to ensure that an assessment is appropriate and proportionate.	Carrying out an assessment in an appropriate and proportionate manner means local authorities must have regard to: (a) the person's wishes and preferences (b) the outcomes they seek from the assessment (c) the severity and overall extent of the person's needs – sections 3 (1–2)	Paragraph 6.4 describes how an assessment will vary depending on the circumstances, and that "it could range from an initial contact or triage process which helps a person with lower needs to access support in their local community, to a more intensive, ongoing process which requires the input of a number of professionals over a longer period of time".

Key term	Care Act 2014	The Care and Support (Assessment) Regulations 2014	The Care and Support Statutory Guidance (revised 2017)
Assessment	Section 9 states that an assessment is of an adult's needs for care and support. Section 10 states that a carer's assessment is of their needs for support. Sections 58, 60 and 64 set out that assessment also applies respectively to the following: (a) a child's needs for care and support (after they reach 18) (b) a child's carer's needs for support (c) a young carer's needs for support	The scope of an assessment is specified in sections 3 (1–2).	The glossary at the end of the statutory guidance states that assessment "is what a local authority does to find out the information so that it can decide whether a person needs care and support to help them live their day-to-day lives". In addition to identifying needs, an assessment also includes identifying for a person "outcomes and how these impact on their wellbeing" (paragraph 6.85).
Fluctating needs	No reference	Section 3 (3) specifies that account must be taken of where the level of a person's needs fluctuate over a period of time.	Paragraph 6.58 emphasises that "the condition(s) of the individual at the time of the assessment may not be entirely indicative of their needs more generally". Paragraph 6.132 adds that that the "level of a carer's need can also fluctuate irrespective of whether the needs of the adult for whom they care, fluctuate".
Supported self-assessment	No reference	Section 2 (1) makes provision for supported self-assessment, which is an assessment carried out jointly by the local authority and the individual to whom it relates.	Paragraph 6.44 clarifies that "the duty to assess the person's needs... remains with the local authority".

Key term	Care Act 2014	The Care and Support (Assessment) Regulations 2014	The Care and Support Statutory Guidance (revised 2017)
Whole family approach	Section 12 specifies that the Regulations must include what must be considered to ensure that an assessment has regard to the needs of the family of the adult.	When considering the impact of the needs of the individual being assessed on others section 4 (1) (b) broadens the scope to include: • any person who is involved in caring for the individual • any person the local authority considers to be relevant.	Paragraph 6.65 defines the 'whole family approach' as taking a "holistic view of the person's needs and to identify how the adult's needs for care and support impact on family members or others in their support network".

The essential features of a suggested assessment framework

The approach taken in this chapter is to present the material in the Act, regulations and statutory guidance in terms of inputs and outputs. It identifies what social workers (and other assessors) must make sure takes place in any needs assessment, and what the end products should be.

How an assessment proceeds will depend to some extent on how the first contact was concluded. For example, a particular intervention such as reablement may have been initiated, or a person's urgent needs may have been met.

Figure 2.2 sets out a suggested pathway for the assessment process after first contact as set out in the statutory guidance. Each of the elements are outlined in more detail and then fully described in the following sections of this chapter.

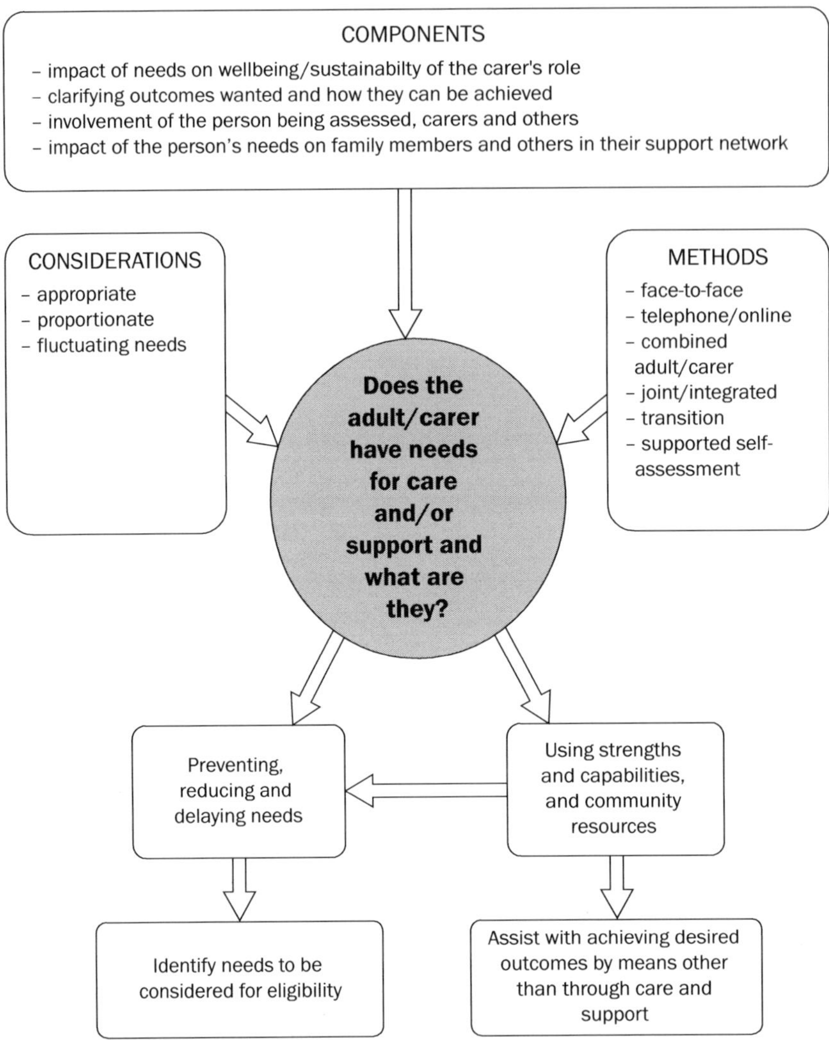

Figure 2.2 *Assessment pathway*

The assessment must aim to establish the total extent of an individual's care and/or support needs before eligibility is determined. Assessment also has a critical role to play in preventing, reducing and delaying needs prior to the eligibility determination. To apply this holistic approach to assessment the assessor has to ensure the following:

a) *all of the mandatory components of the assessment are applied;*

b) *the assessment must be undertaken in a person-centred way;*

c) *appropriate methods are used.*

The main components are as follows:

a) *assessing the impact of the person's needs on their wellbeing, and for carers this includes the sustainability of the caring role;*

b) *clarifying what outcomes a person wants to achieve in their day-to-day life, and engagement in work and recreational activity;*

c) *involvement of the person being assessed, carers and relevant others;*

d) *considering how the person's needs impact on family members and others in their support network.*

In undertaking the assessment the following must be considered:

a) *it must be appropriate to the individual's circumstances and preferences, particularly in relation to their communication needs;*

b) *it must be proportionate to their circumstances and preferences, eg more complex needs will require a more detailed assessment;*

c) *whether the person's needs for care and support fluctuate.*

The following methods of assessment are to be used where appropriate:

a) *a face-to-face assessment between the person and an assessor;*

b) *an online or phone assessment, eg where the person's needs are less complex;*

c) *a combined assessment of an adult and the carer, where each agrees that their assessments can be combined;*

d) *a joint or integrated assessment, where relevant agencies work together to avoid the person undergoing multiple assessments;*

e) *a transition assessment applies to young people who may have care and support needs when they reach the age of 18;*

f) *every person has the right to a supported self-assessment, except for people who lack capacity to make the necessary decisions.*

In addition to providing the basis for eligibility determination, the assessment should achieve the following:

a) *identify and take steps to prevent, reduce or delay needs;*

b) *identify and consider what else, other than the provision of care and support, can assist in meeting desired outcomes.*

The determination of eligibility is based on a person's remaining care and support needs that have not been met through preventive interventions. Because of this it may be necessary to pause the assessment to allow time for the benefits of prevention to be realised.

The components of a needs assessment

Sections 9 (4) and (5) of the Care Act 2014 specify the following requirements for the assessment of an adult.

It must include:

a) the impact of the adult's needs for care and support on their wellbeing;

b) the outcomes that the adult wishes to achieve in day-to-day life;

c) whether the provision of care and support could contribute to the achievement of those outcomes.

It must involve:

a) the adult;

b) any carer that the adult has;

c) any person whom the adult asks the authority to involve or, where the adult lacks capacity to ask the authority to do that, any person who appears to the authority to be interested in the adult's welfare.

Sections 10 (5), (6) and (7) of the Care Act 2014 specify the following conditions for assessment of a carer.

It must include:

a) whether the carer is able, and is likely to continue to be able, to provide care for the adult needing care;

b) whether the carer is willing, and is likely to continue to be willing, to do so;

c) the impact of the carer's needs for support on their wellbeing;

d) the outcomes that the carer wishes to achieve in day-to-day life;

e) whether the provision of support could contribute to the achievement of those outcomes.

It must have regard to:

a) whether the carer works or wishes to do so;

b) whether the carer is participating in or wishes to participate in education, training or recreation.

It must involve:

a) the carer;

b) any carer that the adult has;

c) any person whom the carer asks the authority to involve.

The impact of needs on wellbeing

The starting point is what the adult identifies as "a need or any challenges or difficulties" (paragraph 6.14) and establishing the impact on their day-to-day life. But to establish the impact on their wider wellbeing the assessment has to go "beyond the ways identified by the individual" (paragraph 6.14), and it has to take into account anything that might apply that falls within the description of wellbeing in paragraph 1.5 as follows:

- personal dignity (including treatment of the individual with respect);
- physical and mental health and emotional wellbeing;
- protection from abuse and neglect;
- control by the individual over day-to-day life (including over care and support provided and the way it is provided);
- participation in work, education, training or recreation;
- social and economic wellbeing;
- domestic, family and personal;
- suitability of living accommodation;
- the individual's contribution to society.

All of the adult's care and support needs must be considered, regardless of whether they are already being met. Paragraph 6.15 specifies that this includes "any support being provided by a carer".

A carer's assessment must include the "impact of caring responsibilities on a carer's desire and ability to work and to partake in education, training or recreational activities" (paragraph 6.19).

Clarifying desired outcomes and how they can be achieved

In addition to identifying the individual's needs, it is essential to identify "what outcomes they are looking to achieve to maintain or improve their wellbeing" (paragraph 6.5).

In addition to enabling people to express their desired outcomes, the assessment process is intended to support their "understanding how the provision of care and support may assist the adult in achieving their desired outcomes" (paragraph 6.9). This will not only involve giving people information and advice about what type of care and support could be provided if they have eligible needs, but also a consideration of "how the adult, their support network and the wider community can contribute towards meeting the outcomes the person wants to achieve" (paragraph 6.10).

Paragraph 6.19 states: "The carer's assessment must also consider the outcomes that the carer wants to achieve in their daily life, their activities beyond their caring responsibilities, and the impact of caring upon those activities."

Involvement of the person being assessed, carers and others

Paragraph 6.30 states: "Putting the person at the heart of the assessment process is crucial to understanding the person's needs, outcomes and wellbeing, and delivering better care and support." This paragraph emphasises that the person being assessed is "best placed to judge their own wellbeing".

Paragraph 6.30 also clarifies that in the case of an assessment of an adult that any person who is a carer must be involved, and that where the person being assessed requests the involvement of any other person, the local authority must involve them.

The statutory guidance makes a point of stating that local authorities "should have... suitably trained staff to ensure the involvement of these parties" (paragraph 6.30).

In circumstances where "an adult is unable to engage effectively in the assessment process independently" (paragraph 6.31), local authorities should involve somebody who can assist the adult.

Paragraph 6.31 also identifies that a local authority may need to provide an assessment "tailored to their circumstances, their needs and their ability to engage".

Assessments "must be person-centred throughout" (paragraph 6.35), and this is to be achieved by enabling an individual to be involved as they want to be in the assessment, and in addition it "should be a collaborative process" (paragraph 6.36).

It is essential that the process is "transparent and understandable" (paragraph 6.36) and this means that the individual is able to achieve the following:

a) develop an understanding of the assessment process;

b) develop an understanding of the implications of the assessment process on their conditions and situation;

c) understand their own needs, the outcomes they want to achieve and the impact of their needs on their own wellbeing to allow them to engage effectively with the assessment process;

d) start to identify the options that are available to them to meet those outcomes and to support their independence and wellbeing;

e) understand the basis on which decisions are reached.

Impact of the person's needs on family members and others in their support network

What is described as the "whole family approach" is set out in paragraphs 6.65–71.

Paragraph 6.66 states: "During the assessment the local authority must consider the impact of the person's needs for care and support on family members or other people the authority may feel appropriate."

It may be the case that there are children carrying out a caring role. If this is the case, consideration has to be given as to whether there should be a referral for "a young carer's assessment or needs assessment under the Children Act 1989" (paragraph 6.68).

There may also be people who don't require an assessment, but nevertheless the person's care and/or support needs may have some impact on them. In these circumstances "the local authority must consider whether or not the provision of any information and advice would be beneficial to those people they have identified" (paragraph 6.67).

Sustainability of the carer's role

Paragraph 6.18 identifies that a carer's assessment must include the following:

a) the carer's need for support;

b) the sustainability of the caring role;

c) the outcomes that the carer wants to achieve in their daily life.

Paragraph 6.18 describes sustainability as including the following:

a) the practical and emotional support provided by the carer for the adult;

b) the carer's potential future needs for support;

c) the carer's willingness and ability to continue caring.

What must be considered when undertaking an assessment

Achieving the person-centred requirement includes ensuring that assessments establish the individual's communication needs and take into account each individual's circumstances. The assessment process has to be flexible enough to achieve this.

To support this the statutory guidance specifies that assessments must be appropriate, proportionate and take into account fluctuating needs.

Appropriate assessment

The assessment "should establish the individual's communication needs and seek to adapt the assessment process accordingly" (paragraph 6.37). For example, a person may be deaf or blind and need an interpreter.

Also, to help ameliorate any worries that individuals may have about the assessment process, paragraph 6.40 states that consideration should be given "to the preferences of the individual with regards to the timing, location and medium of the assessment."

Proportionate assessment

Some circumstances will merit a more detailed assessment than others and this will often be related to the complexity of a person's needs. But there can be circumstances where the individual does not want all of their needs met, eg "an individual who pays for their own care may wish to receive local authority support with accessing a particular service, but may not want the same interaction with the authority as someone who wants greater support" (paragraph 6.42).

In circumstances where a detailed assessment is not required and where the local authority uses an assessment tool, it should consider "which elements of the assessment tool it should use and which are not necessary" (paragraph 6.43).

Fluctuating needs

Paragraph 6.58 states: "As the condition(s) of the individual at the time of the assessment may not be entirely indicative of their needs more generally, local authorities must consider whether the individual's current level of need is likely to fluctuate and what their ongoing needs for care and support are likely to be."

This involves taking into account both the frequency and degree of fluctuation, and the past history of these fluctuations. It is important that the approach taken is comprehensive and can include taking into account "what fluctuations in need can be reasonably expected based on experience of others with a similar condition" (paragraph 6.58).

Methods

The statutory guidance describes a number of ways that an assessment can be undertaken, ranging from a telephone assessment in straightforward circumstances to a complex assessment where there is a need for co-operation between agencies.

In all of these circumstances the individual is entitled to undertake a supported self-assessment (except where the person lacks capacity to make relevant decisions).

Face-to-face versus online/telephone

Online and telephone contact can often take place during first contact (see Chapter 1), but this could also take place "where the person is already known to the local authority and it is carrying out an assessment following a change in their needs or circumstances" (paragraph 6.3).

In listing a face-to-face assessment as an option in paragraph 6.3, the statutory guidance takes the opportunity of specifying that such an assessment should be undertaken by someone whose professional role and qualifications are appropriate for the circumstances.

Combined assessment

An assessment of an adult and the carer can be combined, if they both agree. The purpose of this is "so that interrelated needs are properly captured and the process is efficient as possible" (paragraph 6.3)

Joint or integrated assessment

The descriptions of joint and integrated assessments are very similar. But whatever terminology is used the overriding consideration is stated in paragraph 6.77: "Where more than one agency is assessing a person, they should all work closely together to prevent that person having to undergo a number of assessments at different times, which can be distressing and confusing."

A joint assessment is described as taking place "where relevant agencies work together to avoid the person undergoing multiple assessments" (paragraph 6.3).

An integrated assessment takes place where people "may have needs that are met by various bodies" (paragraph 6.75). Paragraph 6.76 gives examples of what an integrated assessment may involve, as follows:

- a needs or carer's assessment is undertaken jointly with another body carrying out any other assessment in relation to the person concerned;
- [the integration or alignment of the] assessment processes in order to better fit around the needs of the individual;
- working together with relevant professionals on a single assessment;
- putting processes in place to ensure that the person is referred for other assessments such as an assessment for after-care needs under the Mental Health Act 1983.

Where such a joint or integrated assessment takes place it is necessary that the person concerned agrees to this approach.

Transition assessment

This applies to young people who may have care and support needs when they reach the age of 18.

Sections 58 (1), 60 (1) and 63 (1) of the Care Act 2014 specify the following types of transition assessment:

- a child's needs assessment, for young people who appear likely to have care and support needs on turning 18;
- a child's carer's assessment for carers of children who appear likely to have support needs when the child turns 18;
- a young carer's assessment, for those who appear likely to have needs for support on turning 18.

Supported self-assessment

Paragraph 6.44 states: "A supported self-assessment is an assessment carried out jointly by the adult with care and support needs or carer and the local authority... [and it] places the individual in control of the assessment process to a point where they themselves complete their assessment form." Paragraph 6.44 specifies that this type of assessment must be offered to adults and carers, except where they lack capacity to undertake it.

It is clarified in paragraph 6.44 that "the duty to assess the person's needs, and in doing so ensure that they are accurate and complete, remains with the local authority". However, it goes on to say in paragraph 6.46 that "a local authority should not look to repeat the full assessment process again".

The outputs of assessment

All assessments of need must proceed to the next step of eligibility determination unless an individual with capacity chooses to withdraw from the process. The needs to be considered for eligibility will be those that remain after steps have been taken to prevent, reduce or delay them.

The legislative authority for prevention is set out in section 2 (1) of the Care Act 2014 whereby a local authority must facilitate the following:

a) prevent or delay the development by adults of needs for care and support;

b) prevent or delay the development by carers of needs for support;

c) reduce the needs for care and support of adults;

d) reduce the needs for support of carers.

In addition the local authority has a duty to consider how someone could be helped other than through the provision of care and support. This duty is set out in sections 9 (6) and 10 (8) of the Care Act 2014 and it says that the local authority must consider the following:

a) whether matters other than the provision of care and support could contribute to the achievement of the outcomes that the adult or carer wishes to achieve in day-to-day life;

b) whether the adult or carer would benefit from the provision of anything under section 2 (prevention) or 4 (information and advice) or of anything which might be available in the community.

Preventing, reducing and delaying needs

Paragraph 6.60 states: "It is during the assessment where local authorities can identify needs that could be reduced, or where escalation could be delayed, and help people improve their wellbeing by providing specific preventive services, or information and advice on other universal services available locally."

Paragraph 2.49 adds that as part of the process of prevention "the local authority should also take into account the person's own capabilities, and the potential for improving their skills, as well as the role of any support from family, friends or others that could help them to achieve what they wish for from day-to-day life".

Paragraph 6.61 gives examples of how needs can be reduced or met through the universal services available in the community, as follows:

- directing people to services such as community support groups which ensure that people feel supported, including an ability to participate in their local community;
- helping the person to access services which the local authority provides as part of its universal offer on prevention.

Paragraph 6.61 also states that individuals should be enabled to make use of their existing support network to understand "other types of support available to them" (paragraph 6.61). An example is given of accessing "appropriate employment, education or training".

Chapter 2 of the statutory guidance also has examples of prevention in case studies that illustrate the following:

- reducing social isolation of an older person to lessen the impact of caring on his daughter (see paragraph 2.19);
- use of reablement following hospital discharge thus avoiding institutional care (see paragraph 2.31);
- a rehabilitation plan, including physiotherapy and occupational therapy, for an older person following a stroke and hip replacement, which resulted in the person ceasing to have any eligible needs (see paragraph 2.63).

Eligibility determination is "based on the remaining needs which have not been met through such interventions" (paragraph 6.62), so it is important that any benefits of prevention are realised where possible before considering whether the person has any eligible care and/or support needs. This may require that the assessment be 'paused' "to allow time for the benefits of such activities to be realised" (paragraph 6.62).

The duty to consider what else can assist in meeting outcomes

The local authority has a duty to "consider what else other than the provision of care and support might assist the person in meeting the outcomes they want to achieve" (paragraph 6.63).

To achieve this, similar types of resources to those considered for prevention could be accessed. Paragraph 6.63 refers to support that "might be available from their wider support network or within the community to help" and also "authorities should consider the person's own strengths and capabilities".

The following examples of how "the person's own strengths and capabilities" can be utilised are given in paragraphs 6.63–64:

- co-production of services with people who are receiving care and support to foster mutual support networks;
- encouraging people to use their gifts and strengths in a community setting could involve developing residents' groups and appropriate training to support people in developing their skills;

- a person's cultural and spiritual networks can support them in meeting needs and building strengths;
- support could be available from family and friends.

No examples are given in the statutory guidance about how this might apply to carers, although section 10 (8) of the Care Act is clear that this duty does apply to carers as well as adults.

Recording formats and duties

Many local authorities use a single format to record both the person's care and/or support needs and also to record eligibility determination. Some local authorities use formats devised by specialist companies and often they are customised to reflect local preferences.

The needs assessment part of these formats is often set out as a questionnaire with questions such as 'do you have any difficulties with breathing?'. Where a supported self-assessment takes place, the person being assessed "should be asked to complete a similar assessment questionnaire" (paragraph 6.48).

Paragraph 6.98 states: "Following their assessment, individuals must be given a record of their needs or carer's assessment." This is often combined with the record of eligibility determination, for which there is a similar duty.

Knowledge and skills needed to undertake assessments

Local authorities have a duty to ensure that assessors are competent to undertake assessments, whether this is a first contact assessment or a complex assessment requiring a high level of expertise. In addition there is a duty placed on assessors to consult experts where relevant.

Paragraph 6.28 states: "Local authorities must ensure that assessors have the skills, knowledge and competence to carry out the assessment in question, and this applies to all assessments regardless of the format they take."

In circumstances where the assessor does not have the necessary knowledge or experience in a particular condition or circumstances "they must consult someone who has relevant expertise" (paragraph 6.88).

Paragraph 6.83 identifies that the following elements must be included in an assessment to ensure that it is of the highest quality:

a) identify the person's needs, outcomes and how these impact on their wellbeing;

b) consider the person's strengths and capabilities;

c) consider what universal services might help the person improve their wellbeing.

There is an emphasis on ensuring that assessors are "appropriately trained and competent" (paragraph 6.86) and that they "undergo regular, up-to-date training on an ongoing basis" (paragraph 6.86).

There is a duty to ensure that staff have the necessary expertise "to carry out an assessment of needs that relate to a specific condition or circumstances requiring expert insight, for example when assessing an individual who has autism, learning disabilities, mental health needs or dementia" (paragraph 6.86). Paragraph 6.28 makes reference to the importance of the Department of Health guidance on both "people who are deafblind and people with autism". In addition paragraphs 6.91–97 set out a number of requirements in relation to people who are deafblind, as follows:

- local authorities must ensure that an expert is involved in the assessment of adults who are deafblind;
- the person carrying out the assessment must have suitable training and expertise;
- during an assessment if there is the appearance of both sensory impairments, even if when taken separately each sensory impairment appears relatively mild, the assessor must consider whether the person is deafblind;
- local authorities should recognise that adults may not define themselves as deafblind;
- where necessary a qualified interpreter with training appropriate for the deafblind adult's communication should be used.

Applying the guidance using case examples

This section continues with the three examples developed in the previous chapter to illustrate and analyse some of the typical aspects of assessment that are of particular relevance for social workers.

The statutory guidance states that it sets out "how a local authority should go about performing its care and support responsibilities" (paragraph 1.1). The aim of the case examples in this and other chapters is to take this guidance further and illustrate how the legal requirements and powers must, should and can be applied by social workers, and how this relates to professional judgement.

Each part of the care and support journey is presented as a separate process in the Care Act and the statutory guidance, and each segment of the process is also presented separately, but in real life this degree of separation will be less pronounced and in many cases non-existent. Many people will experience assessment as everything that takes place prior to a care and support plan being formulated (or not, in the case where the local authority decides that it is not going to meet a person's needs), and although social workers have to distinguish between a needs or carer's assessment, eligibility determination, charging and financial assessment, and applying the duty/power to meet needs – the person being assessed ought to experience these parts of the care and support journey as seamlessly as possible.

The analysis and case examples are set out under the following headings:

- **Summary of first contact**
- **Impact of needs and clarifying outcomes**
- **Person-centredness and methods of assessment**
- **Concluding the assessment – prevention and making use of networks and resources in the community.**

Mr K

Summary of first contact

Mr K has COPD (Chronic Obstructive Pulmonary Disease) and arthritis. He lives alone in a house that he owns. Ms K has been cooking meals for Mr K but is no longer willing to continue doing this, although she is willing to continue to do his shopping. Ms K mentioned that her father pays a neighbour to help with the cleaning and laundry.

Mr K has agreed to have a needs assessment following telephone enquiries made by Ms K. He had previously taken the view that there was no point in having an assessment as he thinks he may be a self-funder, but has now agreed to meet with someone to find out what is available. Ms K has declined to have a carer's assessment. Mr K has said that he is not sure whether he wants to do a supported self-assessment; he wants to meet with someone first and then decide.

Impact of needs and clarifying outcomes

During the home visit Mr K says that what he wants is to reduce what he describes as "annoying difficulties with the basics of day-to-day life" and to be able to pursue his musical interests with his friends. Keeping in regular contact with his daughter is also very important to him.

As a consequence of having COPD (Chronic Obstructive Pulmonary Disease) and arthritis, Mr K experiences some problems with daily living because of restricted mobility, difficulty in lifting and not being able to handle safely things such as kettles. Mr K says that he has no problems using the toilet, shower and getting in and out of bed, and he dismissed the concerns of his daughter that he is not able to do all of these things safely.

Ms K has been cooking meals for Mr K but is no longer willing to continue doing this. She started coming in every day to do this six months ago when Mr K was unwell with a cold, and has continued as he much prefers this arrangement to having to prepare the basic meals for himself. Ms K wants to stop having to come in every day because she wants more time for herself, and believes that a good alternative would be for the neighbour to cook meals as well as doing the cleaning and laundry, although she doesn't know if the neighbour is willing to do this. Mr K's view is that he can't afford the additional cost, and he is adamant that he will not go back to 'living out of a microwave'. Ms K is willing to continue to do her father's shopping.

Person-centredness and methods of assessment

Initially Mr K had not wanted to proceed with a full assessment. He said he just wanted advice about where he could buy the services that he wants, as he thinks that he is not going to get any financial help. However, he has now agreed that he might benefit from giving more thought to the detail of what he can and cannot do, and how this relates to what is most important to his wellbeing, before deciding on what care and support services he wants to buy.

All contact prior to the home visit had been with Ms K. She had put forward her father's views as she saw them, and has been clear that she does not want to be assessed as a carer. In light of this the first task for the social worker would be to assess whether Mr K wants and requires his daughter's ongoing assistance to engage in the assessment process. It could be that the social worker concludes that such assistance was not required as Mr K did not have substantial difficulty in involvement, but regardless of this Mr K may want his daughter actively involved in his assessment and to be present during the home visit. Whether or not Ms K is present, the social worker would want to find some way of assessing the impact on her of Mr K's needs.

The social worker proposed that in order to complete the assessment the following should take place:

- *Mr K to receive 'reablement'. The aim of this would be to get a more detailed understanding of what Mr K can and cannot do, and to help him maximise his independent living skills. It is explained that after this process is completed a decision can then be made about whether Mr K has any eligible needs, and if so whether he will receive any financial assistance from the local authority. Mr K agrees to the assessment element of reablement but is doubtful about acquiring independent living skills.*
- *Mr K to complete a self-assessment of what he currently can and cannot do in preparation for reablement. This is proposed to enable Mr K to have the control over how his abilities and inabilities are described, particularly in relation to his 'good' days and 'bad' days. This self-assessment would also give him the opportunity to describe how his desired outcomes of pursuing his musical interests with his friends and keeping in contact with his daughter are affected.*
- *The social worker to contact the GP to get a better idea of how Mr K's COPD is being treated. Ms K said she says that the GP was going to look into a scheme to help Mr K to learn how to breathe better, but hadn't heard back from her.*
- *The social worker to talk to the neighbour who does the cleaning and laundry about what she is willing to do. It was suggested that Mr K or Ms K do this, but they prefer that this be done by the social worker, as they think the neighbour will speak more freely.*

Mr K and Ms K are disappointed that they don't know whether Mr K will get any help from the local authority until the social worker completes the eligibility determination. The social worker outlines how eligibility criteria and financial assessment work and explains how they can get more information online if they wish to know more at this stage. The social worker also outlines the other elements of the care and support journey.

Concluding the assessment

The plan for Mr K to receive reablement could potentially improve his wellbeing by enabling him to learn some independent living skills, thus preventing or reducing difficulties he has with the activities of daily living.

Mr K may benefit from a pulmonary rehabilitation course, the aim of which is to help people breathe more efficiently and to cope better with feeling out of breath. This may also improve his general fitness and thus his ability to undertake the activities of daily living. This would have to be explored with his GP.

Mr K used to play the saxophone, but this is now not possible because he doesn't have the strength to blow or the dexterity to work the keys. He does have friends who still play at the local jazz club and he likes to go there to listen and chat. Mr W identified that his main difficulty is that he needs help in getting to and from the local jazz club, and when he is there he needs help with getting drinks and using the toilet. He can get friends to give him a lift and buy drinks for him, but he doesn't feel comfortable with asking them to help him to the toilet – so he has stopped going. The social worker suggests that the local personal assistant agency could provide someone to help Mr K with using the toilet, but payment would be required. Because of the cost it is decided to look at this later, once Mr K knows whether he is going to get any financial help from the local authority.

Mr K may benefit from help in using his ability to play music in some other way, and if Mr K is interested the assessment conversation should address how this could be pursued, as this could help meet some of his needs by means other than providing care and support.

Ms W

Summary of first contact

Ms W's GP has been contacted by the manager of the housing association who is concerned about potential fire risk because of the condition of Ms W's flat. Following a referral to the Community Mental Health Team it is decided that the referral about Ms W will be followed up by an initial assessment to be undertaken by a social worker. This is because the description of her circumstances indicates at this stage that her primary needs are in relation to care and support.

The following is known about Ms W:

- *Ms W (aged 40) was diagnosed as having psychotic depression at the age of 25, and she was admitted to hospital in her early 30s.*

- *She was placed in her current housing association accommodation seven years ago, and at the time she was subject to a section 117 after-care order under the Mental Health Act 1983, following a hospital admission.*
- *The after-care order ceased five years ago and she was discharged to the care of her GP.*
- *A year before her hospital admission she was made redundant from her administrative job in a university.*
- *Her mother died four years ago. She has limited contact with her father.*

The referral from the GP contained the following additional information:

- *The delusional aspects of her depression are being satisfactorily managed through medication. She has declined the offer of talking therapy.*
- *She says that she keeps herself busy by collecting old books and magazines from car boot sales. I was not able to determine whether she sells them as well, as she is reluctant to talk about it. I wonder whether she has Diogenes syndrome?*
- *In other respects she is healthy.*

Impact of needs and clarifying outcomes

At the beginning of the visit, the social worker emphasises that although the visit has been prompted by the concerns of the housing association about a perceived fire risk, the purpose of the visit is to find out whether Ms W could benefit from the changes that have taken place to the ways that social workers and mental health services support people with mental ill-health.

The social worker observes that the main room of the flat and the hallway have numerous stacks of books, booklets and magazines. Ms W collects books and other written material about ancient Rome and the Middle Ages. Her collection includes numerous guide books to most of Europe. She visits car-boot sales to add to her collection. This interest in collecting started in a small way when she studied history at university. Ms W acknowledged that her flat has a lot of books and magazines and that she hasn't got around to sorting them all out – but she didn't agree that there is a fire risk.

The social worker refers to Ms W's previous diagnosis of depression. Ms W confirmed that she wasn't keen on talking therapies. She says that she is OK if she takes her medication, gets lots of exercise and keeps busy. Ms W says she has tried jogging but finds it hard to get motivated. She feels that she might benefit from going to a gym and getting professional help in developing an exercise programme. She has not discussed exercise with her GP.

She acknowledged that she might benefit from more contact with other people. She has never had close friends, but enjoyed being with people when she was at university and during her brief period of working as an administrator. She sees her father a few times a year and he telephones occasionally.

Person-centredness and methods of assessment

The social worker explains that it is now normal practice to offer people the option of taking a lead role in setting out their assessment in what is described as a 'supported self-assessment'. Ms W decides that she is happy for the social worker to do the writing, in the knowledge that she will receive a copy of the written assessment and be able to comment on it.

The social worker suggests that a three-way meeting with the manager of the housing association would enhance the assessment, but Ms W does not agree to this. Ms W says that she doesn't want anyone else involved and volunteers that she will not give permission for her father to be contacted.

The social worker outlines how it will be decided whether she has any eligible care and support needs and tells Ms W how she can get information about the process online. The social worker also outlines the other elements of the care and support journey, and explains that if Ms W has eligible needs she would not have to pay anything towards the cost of care and support as she is on basic benefits.

It is thought unlikely that Ms W would be diagnosed as having Diogenes syndrome as there is no sign of her living in squalor. Her flat is very congested as a result of her large collection of magazines and books, but the social worker concludes that there is no evidence of self-neglect.

An assessment of whether she would benefit from some form of 'talking therapy' may well help with her overall assessment, but she is not agreeable to this at present.

Concluding the assessment

Ms W is agreeable to developing a plan to improve her social interaction and thinks that going to a gym and getting help from a personal trainer would be a good way of doing this, and at the same time this would enable her to exercise more effectively.

This proposal has the merits of making use of resources in the community to achieve her desired outcomes, and doing so in a way that she believes she will enjoy. However, Ms W cannot afford to pay for this; it would only be possible if it was meeting a health or social care need.

The social worker decides to proceed with exploring eligibility with Ms W during this first visit as she doesn't want to run the risk of not being able to see Ms W again, and also the social worker believes that she is more likely to be able to engage Ms W in the future by using this process to demonstrate how she could be helped.

Mrs O

Summary of first contact

Mrs O emails the local carers centre requesting a carer's assessment. She has read on the local authority website that this organisation can arrange for this type of assessment and provide help for carers.

Prior to the assessment she had been in contact with the centre by email and telephone, and the following was established:

- *She is worried that she doesn't have enough time for her three children (aged 11, 15 and 19) because of the help she gives to her husband.*
- *Her husband is a problem drinker and periodically has episodes where his heavy drinking results in him being incontinent.*
- *Mrs O is separated from Mr O but he lives close by to the family home.*
- *Mr O's father had provided him with a lot of support, but he has recently died.*
- *Following earlier advice from the local authority she has made use of Al-Anon Family Group meetings.*
- *She doesn't think her husband will accept help from anyone else.*

Impact of needs and clarifying outcomes

Mrs O receives a carer's assessment from a Care Navigator employed by the local carers centre. She was aware of the option of a supported self-assessment, but preferred a face-to-face assessment.

Enquiries made about her previous contact with the local authority (for which she gave her permission) established that she had brief contact in the past with Learning Disability Services because her youngest child has Down's syndrome. Nine months ago the child's school was concerned about the impact of Mr O's drinking problem, so they made a referral to the Children and Families service. No concerns about Mrs O's abilities to care for her children were identified as a result of this. The main outcome of this contact was that Mrs O was advised to make use of Al-Anon.

In the face-to-face assessment Mrs O says that she is willing to continue to support her husband emotionally and to help him cope with the consequences of his episodes of heavy drinking (ie meeting personal care needs), but she is worried that there may be times when there will be simply too much for her to do and her children may be neglected, and the stress will be too much for her. She says she would find it helpful to be able to talk through her problems with someone on a regular basis.

The Care Navigator proposes that the assessment of Mrs O is paused so that Mr O can have a needs assessment to determine whether the impact of his needs on his wife can be reduced. Mrs O agrees that she would find it less stressful if she had some help with meeting Mr O's personal care needs, but doubts whether he would accept outside help.

Person-centredness and methods of assessment

Mrs O has chosen to obtain an assessment from the local carers centre. She had read on the local authority website that this organisation can arrange for this type of assessment and provide help for carers on behalf of the local authority. In making this choice she was aware that the carers centre did not offer a combined assessment of a carer's needs with the cared for person's needs.

In the case of a carer there is no requirement to consider whether there are any difficulties with involvement, although if Mrs O had requested that someone else be involved in the assessment the carers centre should agree to this.

Concluding the assessment

Mrs O does get support from attending Al-Anon meetings, but she has not found this to be sufficient to meet her needs, hence her request for one-to-one support.

Mrs O acknowledged that her request for help was prompted by the death of her father-in-law who had provided Mr O with a lot of support. She said that there are no other friends and family that she feels comfortable with about asking for support, but she agreed it might be possible for her 19-year-old son to become more involved in caring for his younger siblings when there is a crisis with her husband. It was agreed that she would discuss this with her son and let him know that he could have his own carer's assessment if he wished.

The next step is for Mrs O to ask her husband if he will agree to the local authority undertaking an assessment of his needs. Once the outcome of this proposed assessment is known, the Care Navigator can complete the carer's assessment and make a recommendation to the local authority about whether Mrs O has eligible needs.

Comment and analysis

Readers should note that what is set out in this section and the previous section is intended to show how the statutory guidance might be applied, and in doing so, what would be complex situations in real life have had to be simplified.

Impact of needs on wellbeing and clarifying outcomes

The first step in any assessment is identifying the individual's needs. However, there is no definition of needs in the Act, the regulations or the statutory guidance. Section 2 (1) (b) of the Care and Support (Eligibility) Regulations clarifies that in considering the first condition of the eligibility criteria for an adult, needs have to "arise from or are related to a physical or mental impairment or illness", and for carers section 3 (1) (b) similarly clarifies that needs have to arise "as a consequence of providing necessary care for an adult".

The nearest that the statutory guidance gets to a definition of needs is in a case study on eligibility determination (paragraph 6.112), where the needs of an adult on the autistic spectrum are described as follows: "Dave struggles severely in social situations leading to difficulties accessing work and cooperating with other people. He only has transactional exchanges with others and cannot maintain eye contact. Dave knows that others feel uneasy around him and spends a lot of his time alone." From this brief description it could be deduced that a care and support need is any difficulty in the activities of daily living, maintaining independence and social interaction experienced by an adult that derive from impairment or illness, which the individual may need help with. Mr K describes his needs as the "annoying difficulties with the basics of day-to-day life" which limit his independence and desired social interactions. Ms W's perceptions of her needs are exclusively in relation to the lack of social interaction, although her landlord believes she is also not able look after her accommodation satisfactorily.

There is nothing in the statutory guidance from which a definition of the support needs of carers can be easily deduced. Paragraph 6.129 has a case study where the carer is described as seeming "stressed and anxious" because of the care (which is deemed as necessary) he is providing for his mother who has dementia, and it is implied that this has an impact on the outcomes that the carer wants to achieve. Therefore it seems reasonable to conclude that a support need is any difficulty experienced by a carer in maintaining wellbeing that derives from providing necessary care to an adult, which the individual may need help with. Mrs O's needs are in relation to the stress she experiences in looking after her children when her husband has a crisis.

In the assessment stage a key task is having a conversation with people about the difficulties that they are experiencing, and the impact these difficulties have on their wellbeing. In considering the impact on the wider family and others in the support network, it would be reasonable to conclude that the impact on them would be in relation to their wellbeing, although the statutory guidance doesn't actually say this – except in relation to young carers.

The evaluation of the impact of these difficulties takes place in the next stage when eligibility is being determined.

The conversations with Mr K, Ms W and Mrs O clarify the nature of the difficulties that they are experiencing, and while there is discussion about outcomes, conclusions are not yet reached. Mr K and Ms W are clear about some of the things that they don't want to happen, but it is only Mrs O who has a clear idea about what she wants.

Person-centredness and methods of assessment

The person-centred approach is at the heart of the Care Act and it is built into all of the processes set out in the statutory guidance. Therefore a person's wishes and preferences are of paramount importance in any assessment of needs.

It may not always be possible to determine the individual's preferences for the method of assessment at the outset. The choice as to whether there should be a combined assessment with a carer can be made in advance, although circumstances could change, eg in the assessment conversation it may become apparent that the adult and carer have different priorities, therefore a planned combined assessment may no longer be feasible.

The amount of support an individual needs for a supported self-assessment can vary, and it will often require a conversation to determine how much help a person wants. Also the individual may not be able to decide whether they want this option until they have had the chance to discuss how it could work, as was the case with Mr K.

Often the assessment can benefit from the involvement of other professionals. Mr K was agreeable to this, but Ms W wasn't.

The requirement on the local authority to "seek to involve somebody who can assist the adult in engaging with the process and helping them to articulate their preferred outcomes and needs" (paragraph 6.31) doesn't just apply to people who lack capacity and people who meet the criteria of substantial difficulty in involvement. The statutory guidance states that people who may need assistance "will include some people with mental impairments who will nevertheless have capacity to engage in the assessment alongside the local authority" (paragraph 6.31). Implicit in this guidance is that the social worker will need to make a judgement early on in the process about whether a person needs assistance, and whether this might be informal support from a relative or friend, or from an independent advocate or an Independent Mental Capacity Advocate. (The roles of an independent advocate and Independent Mental Capacity Advocate are considered in Chapter 10).

Mr K, Ms W and Mrs O did not require assistance as none of them has substantial difficulty in being involved. Examples of how this applies to individuals are given in Chapter 10.

Decisions about whether there needs to be a joint or integrated assessment could be made from the outset, eg where the assessment is undertaken in the context of a hospital discharge. But in other circumstances the need for this may emerge only during the assessment conversation. Examples of joint and integrated assessments are given in Chapter 12.

Concluding the assessment

Developing a sound understanding of the impact of needs on wellbeing is an essential building block of an assessment and a task that requires professional knowledge and skills. But just as important is enabling people to express their desired outcomes, and to understand how these outcomes can be achieved by the provision of care and support. The professional task is to identify what needs to change that is in accord with the wishes and feelings of the individual, and how this change can potentially be achieved both through the provision of care and support and other means (eg making use of networks and resources in the community).

The adult or carer will not always experience the assessment as concluding in a single interview. In Ms W's case the social worker undertook both the assessment and eligibility determination in a single interview. But for both Mr K and Mrs O the assessment was paused.

Mr K's assessment was paused so that it could be enhanced by input from other professionals and to get a better idea of which of his needs could be prevented, delayed or reduced. But the pause was also to allow him to have more control over the process, and to give him time to reflect on his needs in relation to social interaction and to explore how his friends may be able to help him.

Mrs O's assessment was paused to see whether her needs could be prevented. If the cared-for person (ie her husband) would agree to receive services, she might no longer have potentially eligible needs.

In practice people will often experience the decision making about prevention as a pause in the assessment, but they ought to be made aware that the eligibility determination can be contingent upon the elimination of potential eligible needs where this is possible. Where prevention is successful in eliminating all of a person's eligible needs, then the care and support journey might come to a close.

There may be resources available in the community and in the person's own networks that can be used both for prevention and achieving desired outcomes, and deciding how to make use of these resources is an important part of the assessment process. In the same way it is also important to make use of the individual's strengths and capabilities.

It is important for Mr K's wellbeing that he is able to have an active involvement with jazz music, and while it is not possible to help him regain his ability to play the saxophone, he can potentially be helped to go to venues where he can hear live music and meet like-minded people. The assessment conversation would have helped shape his feelings about the loss of his musical ability into an achievable outcome, and one that could potentially fit within the eligibility determination framework. It is also a requirement that consideration is given to achieving desired outcomes by means other than through the provision of care and support, hence the discussion with him about using his ability to play a musical instrument in other ways.

Making use of the individual's strengths and capabilities and resources in the community is well-illustrated in Mr K's case, but not with the other two. However, these considerations are applicable throughout the care and support journey, and readers will see how they are utilised for Ms W in her care and support plan and for Mrs O's support plan, in a later chapter.

Conclusion

The Care Act has broadened the scope of what is required from assessment to formally include preventing, reducing and delaying needs. It has also signaled a move towards placing more emphasis on the context of family and social networks, and utilising the person's strengths and capabilities and community resources.

To successfully deliver the significant changes to the way that needs assessments and carers' assessments are now undertaken has required major changes to the way that social workers and other staff apply their professional knowledge and skills. But as with all parts of the care and support journey, the statutory guidance provides a framework that will benefit from being added to. To fully realise the potential of assessment to promote wellbeing, it is likely that the way this process is applied will continue to evolve for several years to come.

The statutory guidance sets out in detail what social workers need to know about how to undertake some aspects of assessments, but not others. For example, there is a lot of guidance about how to identify needs that must be determined as eligible or otherwise, but there is very little about applying a strengths-based approach and integrated assessment. Over time good practice will emerge and become documented. For example, the Social Care Institute of Excellence (SCIE)[1] has produced a comprehensive guide to the strengths-based approach in its suite of materials on the Care Act.

The way that assessment takes place in each local authority is evolving in a number of different ways. In the previous chapter reference was made to the different approaches to steering individuals towards alternatives to a needs assessment. Further different approaches are evident in those local authorities who believe that to ensure there is an effective conversation about prevention, social workers must be involved at a very early stage. In a number of local authorities all assessments are now undertaken by registered social workers and/or occupational therapists, so as to maintain this emphasis on prevention and ensuring that full use is made of people's strengths and capabilities.

The next two chapters explore how the information about an adult's care and support needs and a carer's support needs are used to determine eligibility and to decide what needs are going to be met by the local authority.

Reference

1. www.scie.org.uk/care-act-2014/assessment-and-eligibility/strengths-based-approach

3 Eligibility determination

Introduction

One of the main purposes of the assessment process is to provide information to determine whether a person has needs that meet the eligibility criteria. Some or all of the care and support needs identified and agreed during the assessment process may qualify as eligible needs.

This chapter considers the application of the national eligibility criteria for people with care and support needs and national eligibility criteria for carers with support needs.

Determining the impact of what the individual cannot do (or has difficulty with) on their wellbeing is at the heart of the eligibility process. Where an individual has eligible needs and other conditions are met, they are entitled to receive funding for care and support from the local authority.

It is intended that the eligibility criteria bring clarity and consistency to the application of this gateway to local authority resources for care and support. To achieve this the Care and Support (Eligibility) Regulations 2014 set out a detailed framework for eligibility determination. Although the framework itself is very prescriptive, professional judgement is required to apply it. This chapter considers each element of the framework, as described in both the regulations and the statutory guidance, and provides case examples to assist social workers in interpreting and applying the criteria.

The chapter comprises the following sections:

- **The eligibility framework prior to April 2015**
- **Key terms and definitions**
- **The essential features of eligibility criteria**
- **The National Eligibility Criteria for Adults and National Eligibility Criteria for Carers**

- **Recording formats and duties**
- **Applying the eligibility criteria using case examples**
- **Conclusion.**

Where a person has eligible needs the local authority has a duty to meet them – subject to certain conditions being met. The following chapter will consider these conditions and how to apply them, as well as a local authority's duties and powers in relation to non-eligible needs.

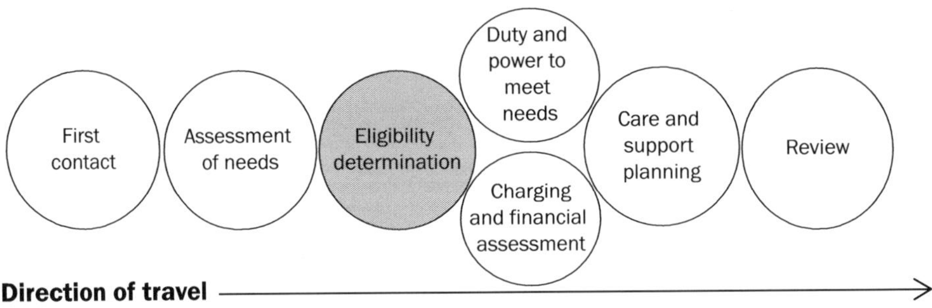

Figure 3.1 *The care and support journey*

Eligibility framework prior to April 2015

Under section 47 of the NHS and Community Care Act 1990 local authorities had a duty to meet the needs of any person who may have been in need of any of the community care services that the local authority had a duty to provide. The Carers (Recognition and Services) Act 1995 required local authorities to take account of the sustainability of the caring role when deciding what community care services it was necessary to provide.

In the previous statutory guidance issued in 2010 in *Prioritising Need in the Context of Putting People First: A Whole System Approach to Eligibility for Social Care*, eligibility was graded into four bands – critical, severe, moderate and low. Each of these described "the seriousness of the risk to independence and wellbeing or other consequences if needs are not addressed" (paragraph 54).

The major difference is that the local authority no longer has a duty to provide certain services and to determine whether people are in need of these services. Eligibility now applies only to needs – and not to services.

Key terms and definitions

The following have been selected because they appear in either the Care Act and/or the Regulations.

Key term	Care Act 2014	The Care and Support Regulations 2014	The Care and Support Statutory Guidance (revised 2017)
Eligibility criteria (adults)	Section 13 (6–8) provides for eligibility criteria to be set out in regulations.	The three conditions which must apply for an adult's needs to meet the eligibility criteria are specified in section 2 (1) of the Care and Support (Eligibility) Regulations 2014 as follows: (a) the adult's needs arise from or are related to a physical or mental impairment or illness; (b) as a result of the adult's needs the adult is unable to achieve two or more of the outcomes specified in section (2); and (c) as a consequence there is, or is likely to be, a significant impact on the adult's wellbeing.	Provides further definition and guidance on interpretation for the three conditions, in paragraphs 6.100–114.
Eligibility criteria (carers)	Section 13 (6–8) provides for eligibility criteria to be set out in regulations.	The three conditions which must apply for an carer's needs to meet the eligibility criteria are specified in section 3 (1) as follows: (a) the needs arise as a consequence of providing necessary care for an adult; (b) the effect of the carer's needs is that any of the circumstances specified in section (2) apply to the carer; and (c) as a consequence of that fact there is, or is likely to be, a significant impact on the carer's wellbeing.	Provides further definition and guidance on interpretation for the three conditions, in paragraphs 6.115–134.

The essential features of eligibility criteria

1. A person's needs must be assessed before eligibility can be determined.
2. There are separate eligibility criteria for adults and carers.
3. Each of these two sets of eligibility criteria comprise three conditions specified in the regulations, and all three must apply for the criteria to be met.
4. The term 'eligible needs' is used to describe needs that meet the eligibility criteria.
5. Eligibility determination has to be 'carer-blind', ie all needs must be included, regardless of whether they are being met by a carer.
6. A carer may meet the eligibility criteria for carers even if the cared for person does not meet the eligibility criteria for adults.
7. The decision to undertake a safeguarding enquiry does not depend on an individual having eligible care and support needs.
8. The final decision regarding eligibility rests with the local authority.
9. Having eligible needs does not necessarily mean that these will be met by the local authority. There are further factors that must be taken into account to determine whether there is a duty to meet an individual's needs.
10. Local authorities have the power to meet needs that are not eligible.

The national eligibility criteria for adults and national eligibility criteria for carers

The eligibility criteria "set a minimum threshold" (paragraph 6.100) with which all local authorities must comply. This emphasis on a minimum threshold and compliance contrasts with the statutory guidance on eligibility prior to the Care Act, where there was some discretion. It is intended that these criteria provide "more transparency on what level of need is eligible" (paragraph 6.101).

This section sets out the key components which are then explored in more detail later in this chapter in their application to case examples.

Eligibility criteria for adults

Paragraph 6.103 sets out the three conditions of the eligibility criteria (replicating what first appears in the Care and Support (Eligibility Criteria) Regulations 2014 in section 2):

- the adult's needs arise from or are related to a physical or mental impairment or illness;
- as a result of the adult's needs the adult is unable to achieve two or more of the specified outcomes;
- as a consequence of being unable to achieve these outcomes there is, or there is likely to be, a significant impact on the adult's wellbeing.

Paragraph 6.103 also clarifies that all three conditions have to be met.

The content in Figure 3.2 is taken from paragraphs 6.103–6.106 of the statutory guidance. Some of the examples shown in italicised text have been modified for brevity.

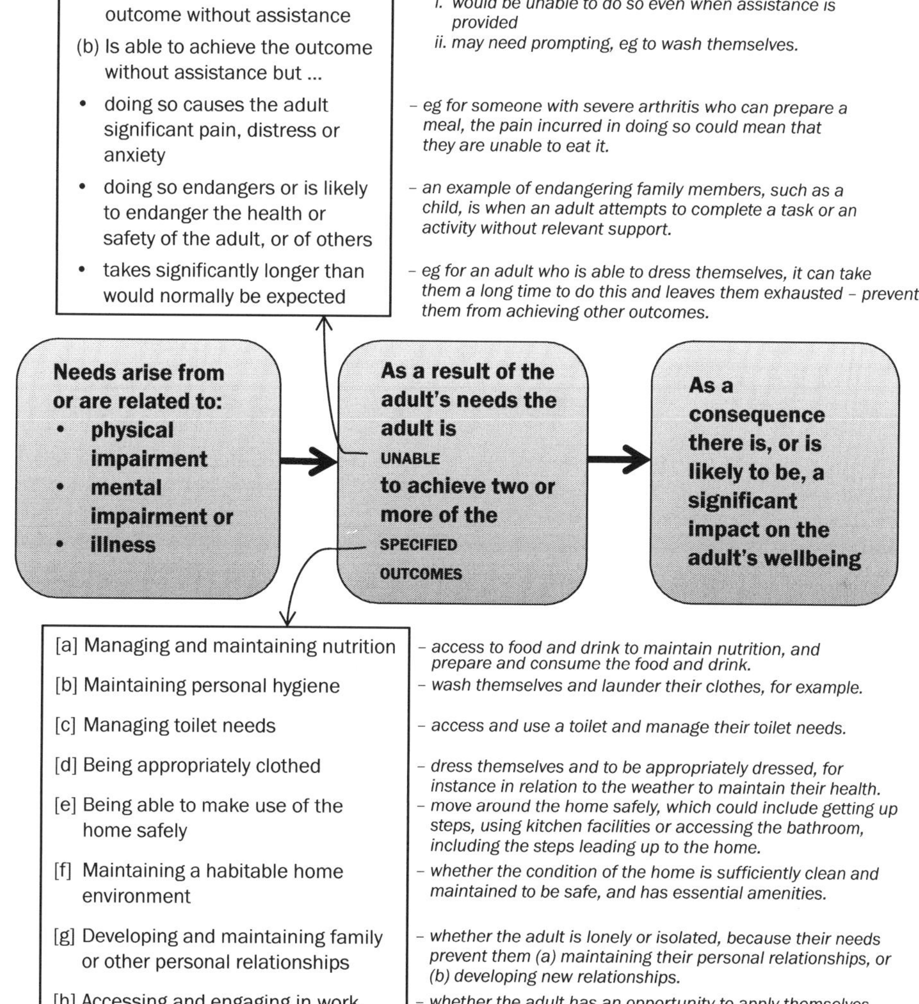

Figure 3.2 *Eligibility criteria for adults*

Physical or mental impairment or illness

Paragraph 6.104 clarifies that this first condition of the eligibility criteria applies for needs that are as a result of either:

- physical, mental, sensory, learning or cognitive disabilities;
- illnesses;
- substance misuse;
- brain injury.

Paragraph 6.104 makes it clear that a "formal diagnosis of the condition should not be required" and that the judgement of whether an adult's needs arise from or are related to physical or mental impairment or illness should be based on the assessment of their care and support needs.

Specified outcomes

These ten specified outcomes are set out in section 2 (2) of the Care and Support (Eligibility Criteria) Regulations 2014. The explanatory sentences reproduced in Figure 3.2 are from paragraph 6.106 of the statutory guidance.

Some of these outcomes are relatively straightforward to assess. Others are more complex and may require the knowledge and skills of registered social workers or occupational therapists to interpret and apply them, because of the degree of judgement that is required. Examples of how to apply these outcomes are provided later in this chapter.

Unable to achieve an outcome

To meet the second condition an adult has to be unable to achieve at least two of the specified outcomes.

There are four different ways that an adult could be unable to achieve a specified outcome, and these are set out in section 2 (3) of the eligibility regulations. The first is "unable to achieve the outcome without assistance" but the other three of these commence with the statement "is able to achieve the outcome without assistance but…". The additional guidance added in Figure 3.2 is from paragraph 6.105 of the statutory guidance.

The circumstances where a person can qualify even though they are able to achieve an outcome are where it takes the individual significantly longer than would normally be expected, or causes them significant pain, distress or anxiety, or endangers themselves or others. For example, a person may be able to wash themselves but it causes them significant pain or it puts them at significant risk of falling (using a bath or a shower).

Significant impact on wellbeing

Having met the first two conditions of being unable to achieve at least two of the specified outcomes that are a result of needs that arise from impairment or illness, the third and final condition to be considered is the impact that this has on their wellbeing. To qualify, the impact has to be judged as significant.

Wellbeing is defined in section 1 (2) of the Care Act. The statutory guidance slightly reframes the description of wellbeing in paragraph 6.111 as "including the following":

- personal dignity (including treatment of the individual with respect);
- physical and mental health and emotional wellbeing;
- protection from abuse and neglect;
- control by the individual over day-to-day life (including over care and support provided and the way it is provided);
- participation in work, education, training or recreation;
- social and economic wellbeing;
- domestic, family and personal relationships;
- suitability of living accommodation;
- the individual's contribution to society.

Paragraph 6.108 identifies two ways in which significant impact can be considered:

- the adult's inability to achieve the outcomes above impacts on at least one of the areas of wellbeing (as described in section 1 of the Act and Chapter 1 of this guidance) in a significant way;
- the effect of the impact on a number of the areas of wellbeing mean that there is a significant impact on the adult's overall wellbeing.

Eligibility criteria for carers

Paragraph 6.117 of the statutory guidance reiterates what is set out in the regulations, that the three conditions of the eligibility criteria are:

a) needs arise as a consequence of providing necessary care for an adult;

b) the effect of the carer's needs is that any of the circumstances specified in the Eligibility Regulations apply to the carer;

c) as a consequence of that fact there is, or there is likely to be, a significant impact on the carer's wellbeing.

Paragraph 6.117 also clarifies that all three conditions have to be met.

The circumstances specified in the eligibility regulations in relation to the second condition are restated and added to in paragraph 6.120. The condition is met in the following circumstances:

- either "the carer's physical or mental health is either deteriorating or at risk of doing so";

- or, alternatively, it can be met in the same way as for adults, ie "the carer is unable to achieve any of a list of other outcomes which may apply".

There is a list of specified outcomes and a description of inabilities that are both very similar to those for adults. However, the carer has to have inabilities with only one of the specified outcomes.

The content in Figure 3.3 is taken from paragraphs 6.116–128 of the statutory guidance.

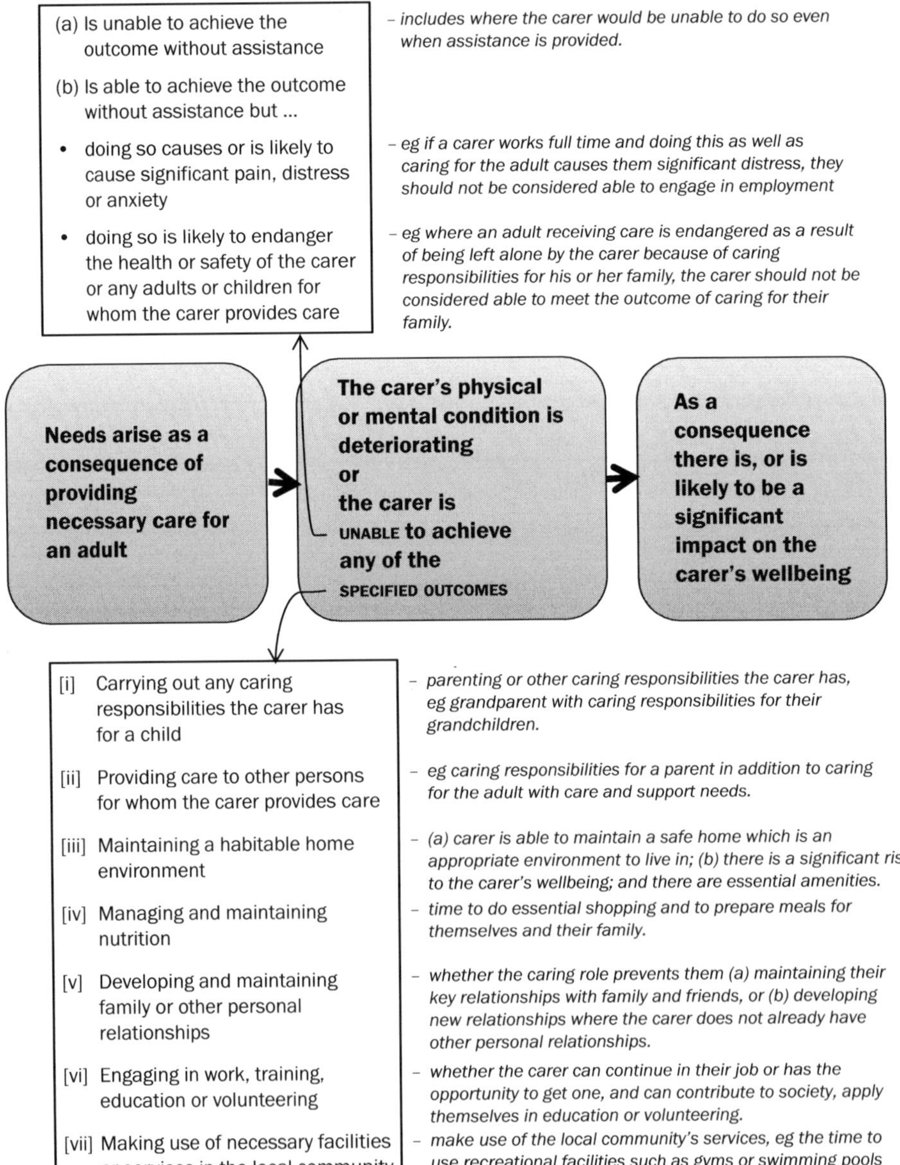

***Figure 3.3** Eligibility criteria for carers*

Needs that arise as a consequence of providing necessary care

The statutory guidance only defines 'necessary care' by stating what it isn't, ie "If the carer is providing care and support for needs which the adult is capable of meeting themselves, the carer may not be providing necessary support" (paragraph 6.119).

The carer's physical or mental condition

The second condition of the eligibility criteria is met where the carer's physical or mental health is "either deteriorating or is at risk of doing so" (paragraph 6.120). If this is clearly the case, then there is no need to consider the alternative of whether or not he or she is unable to achieve any of the specified outcomes.

Specified outcomes

Of the eight specified outcomes listed in paragraph 6.123 as part of the second condition, three are identical in their description in the regulations to the specified outcomes for adults, and four are very similar. However, these identical and similar specified outcomes apply in a different way, eg with item "[vi] managing and maintaining nutrition" the emphasis is on considering "whether the carer has the time to do essential shopping and to prepare meals for themselves and their family".

There is one specified outcome that is distinctly different: "[ii] providing care to other persons for whom the carer provides care".

Unable to achieve an outcome

This part of the second condition set out in paragraph 6.121 is virtually the same as for adults, with the exception that the 'takes significantly longer than would normally be expected' clause does not apply.

There is a slight difference in the wording of the clause about endangering health or safety. For adults it states "doing so endangers or is likely to endanger..." whereas for carers it states "doing so is likely to endanger...".

Significant impact on wellbeing

The third and final condition to be considered is the actual or likely impact of the carer's deteriorating health, or their inability of achieving one of the specified outcomes, on their wellbeing. To qualify, the impact has to be judged to be significant.

Paragraph 6.124 identifies two ways that significant impact can be considered:

- the carer's needs and inability to achieve the outcomes impact on an area of the carer's wellbeing in a significant way;
- the impact on a number of the areas of wellbeing is such that they have a significant impact on an adult's overall wellbeing.

The statutory guidance sets out wellbeing in paragraph 6.128 as "including the following":

- personal dignity (including treatment of the individual with respect);
- physical and mental health and emotional wellbeing;
- protection from abuse and neglect;
- control by the individual over day-to-day life (including over care and support provided and the way it is provided);
- participation in work, education, training or recreation;
- social and economic wellbeing;
- domestic, family and personal relationships;
- suitability of living accommodation;
- the individual's contribution to society.

Note that this is the same as listed for adults in paragraph 6.111 as it follows what is set out in section 1 (2) of the Care Act.

Needs met by a carer

When determining whether an adult meets the eligibility criteria, any activity undertaken by a carer to meet care and support needs must be discounted. The statutory guidance is clear that "the determination must be based solely on the adult's needs". The SCIE guidance describes this as the eligibility determination having to be 'carer blind', ie that "any impact on wellbeing that would be reduced or minimised by what carers are currently doing must be ignored for the sake of the determination".[1]

Safeguarding

Paragraph 6.55 states that the "decision to carry out a safeguarding enquiry does not depend on the person's eligibility", although in taking action to protect the adult this paragraph states that "safeguarding enquiries may result in the provision of care and support". The eligibility/safeguarding relationship is considered further in Chapter 8.

Non-eligible needs

Where a person has no eligible needs the local authority "must provide advice and information on what services are available in the community that can support the person in meeting those needs" (paragraph 6.53).

The statutory guidance also says that such information and advice must be provided in respect of "any needs that are not eligible" with regard to young people and prisoners (paragraphs 16.54 and 17.24).

However, a local authority can use its powers to meet an individual's non-eligible needs. This duty is considered in more detail in the next chapter.

Urgent need

Under section 19(3) of the Care Act, a local authority may meet an adult's needs for care and support which appear to it to be urgent, without having undertaken an eligibility determination.

Chapter 2 has provided more detail of the statutory guidance in relation to responding to urgent need.

The final decision

Paragraph 6.53 states unequivocally that "the final decision regarding eligibility will rest with the local authority", and that "this may include taking into account the person's own view" where this is appropriate.

Recording formats and duties

As noted in the Chapter 2:

- many local authorities use a single format to record both the person's care and/or support needs and also to record eligibility determination;
- specialist companies have devised these formats and some have been customised to reflect local preferences.

These formats usually conclude with an eligibility determination that records how each of the three conditions applies to the individual being assessed. To ensure that every specified outcome is fully considered, many of the formats include a yes/no question for each of them. This question will be something similar to "Are you able to do this by yourself without it taking an unreasonably long time or causing you significant pain, distress or anxiety, or endangering the health and safety of yourself or others?".

For the final condition as to whether there is significant impact on wellbeing, there is usually no set format. This is the point in the record where the social worker provides a written summary of their professional judgement about eligibility.

Some of the formats include a summary of what information and advice has been given about how to prevent or delay care and support needs that have not met the eligibility criteria. The duty to provide this type of information and advice is considered in the next chapter.

While these formats will closely follow the wording of the statutory guidance, they may paraphrase in ways that reflect the local interpretation of what constitutes user-friendly language. Some local authorities have developed formats that significantly reframe the process of assessment and eligibility determination, particularly where there are local criteria for meeting non-eligible needs.

Paragraph 6.132 states: "When the eligibility determination has been made, local authorities must provide the person to whom the determination relates (whether that is an adult with care and support needs, or a carer with support needs) with a copy of their decision." There is also a duty to explain it as set out in paragraph 6.53: "In all cases, the authority must inform the person of their eligibility judgement and why the local authority has reached the eligibility determination that it has." In practice this duty to inform is combined with the duty to give individuals "a record of their needs or carer's assessment" (paragraph 6.98).

The recording formats can be utilised to deliver the duty to inform, but some local authorities send a letter setting out the eligibility determination.

Applying the eligibility criteria using case examples

This section illustrates and analyses some of the typical aspects of eligibility determination that are of particular relevance for social workers.

These examples have been considered in the previous two chapters, so this section commences with a summary of where things are at the point where the needs assessment is moving on to eligibility determination. There can rarely be a clear separation between needs assessment and eligibility determination, and people will experience both of these processes as part of the overall process of assessment.

There is a danger that the prescriptive nature of the eligibility criteria framework could result in its application being process driven, and consequently being less person-centred than it should be. To act as a counterweight to this, many of the assessment and eligibility formats used by local authorities have as the starting point the recording of what is important for the individual's wellbeing and what they enjoy and value in their lives. Accordingly, each of the three examples starts with what the individual states as being most important to them, before going on to consider how each element of the three eligibility conditions might apply.

In considering these cases it is important for the reader to appreciate that the term 'outcomes' takes on a narrow and precise meaning when used in the context of the second condition of eligibility determination. The key characteristic is that these outcomes are specified, ie the eligibility criteria specify ten types of outcome for adults and eight for carers. This differs from the concept of desired outcomes introduced in previous chapters, where the focus is on identifying the outcomes that people with care and support needs want "to achieve in their day-to-day life" (paragraph 6.9).

In exploring the interrelationship between the three conditions it is important to be aware that meeting the first condition is more than simply identifying that an adult has needs that derive from an impairment or illness, or a carer providing necessary care. In the table that follows paragraph 6.111 in the statutory guidance it states: "As a result of the needs, the adult is unable to achieve 2 or more of the following (outcomes)." Similarly in the table that follows paragraph 6.128 it states: "The needs arise as a consequence of providing necessary care to an adult, and the carer is 'unable' to achieve the following (outcomes)." In practice this means the consequential link ought to be demonstrated between the first and second conditions.

The case examples and analysis are set out under the following headings:

- **Summary of assessment**
- **Desired outcomes and specified outcomes**
- **Fluctuating needs**
- **Needs deriving from physical or mental impairment or illness**
- **Relationship between impairment/illness and specified outcomes**
- **Needs deriving from providing necessary care**
- **Relationship between necessary care and carer health or specified outcomes**
- **Applicability of the specified outcomes**
- **Determining if the 'unable' condition is met**
- **Significant impact on wellbeing**
- **Excluding what the carer is doing**
- **The final decision: involvement of the adult and carer, explaining the eligibility determination and next steps.**

Mr K

Summary of assessment

Mr K has COPD (Chronic Obstructive Pulmonary Disease) and arthritis. His daughter has been cooking meals for him but is no longer willing to continue, although she is willing to do her father's shopping. Ms K does not want a carer's assessment. Mr K pays a neighbour to help with the cleaning and laundry.

After receiving reablement it has been concluded that he is independent in all aspects of his personal care but that there are a number of things that he finds difficult that he wants help with (ie his desired outcomes):

- *He wants someone to come in every day and prepare him a home-cooked meal in the way that his daughter has been doing – he is unable to safely use any cooking devices.*
- *Cleaning and laundry – he finds this difficult because of his arthritis and COPD and he would rather employ someone to do this.*
- *He likes to go the local jazz club, but has stopped going because he is embarrassed to ask for help with going to the toilet and he also finds using public transport difficult.*

Mr K wants to know if he is eligible for a 'home-help' to do his cooking, cleaning and laundry, and if he can get financial help to pay for a taxi to go to the jazz club and pay for someone to help him use the toilet.

Desired outcomes and specified outcomes

All of Mr K's desired outcomes can be considered in relation to the specified outcomes:

- *He may be able to get help with having a home-cooked meal if he is unable to achieve specified outcome "[a] managing and maintaining nutrition".*
- *If it can be established that he has qualifying inabilities in achieving "[b] maintaining personal hygiene", then he may be able to get help with his laundry.*
- *Similarly, if it can be established that his breathing difficulties are exacerbated by environmental factors he may qualify under "[f] maintaining a habitable home environment", and may be able to get help with cleaning.*
- *An important desired outcome for Mr K is to be able to go to the jazz club. If he cannot use the toilet without assistance, and if it is too difficult for him to use a bus – then specified outcome "[i] making use of necessary facilities or services in the community including public transport and recreational facilities or services" may apply.*

Fluctuating needs

Mr K has COPD. This is a condition that results in variable breathing difficulties, and this can be exacerbated by environmental factors. On the information thus far there is no indication of the nature and degree of any fluctuation of needs.

Needs deriving from physical or mental impairment or illness

Mr K is physically impaired because he has COPD (Chronic Obstructive Pulmonary Disease) and arthritis. His needs, as he describes them, are the "annoying difficulties with the basics of day-to-day life", and these limit his independence and desired social interactions.

Relationship between impairment/illness and specified outcomes

It is relatively straightforward to establish the link between the needs that derive from his physical impairment and both of the specified outcomes of "[a] managing and maintaining nutrition" and "[b] maintaining personal hygiene". Mr K is physically impaired because of his COPD and arthritis, and this can result in him being breathless with any exertion. Also certain types of activity can be painful, thus restricting his mobility and ability to grip things properly. It was concluded during his period of reablement that he could not use cooking devices safely enough to cook himself a meal, and would experience significant pain in lifting clothing in and out of the washing machine and it could also take him longer than would normally be expected.

In considering "[f] maintaining a habitable home environment", in order to determine whether doing his own housework would endanger his health, it would need to be established that his breathing difficulties are likely to be exacerbated by environmental factors, ie dust. There is no actual evidence that this has happened because he is not doing any housework as he has a cleaner, so in order to conclude on the likelihood of this happening, specialist medical opinion may be required.

There are two aspects of his difficulties with achieving specified outcome "[i] making use of necessary facilities or services in the community including public transport and recreational facilities or services". He cannot use a bus because of his arthritis and this means he cannot get to the jazz club. He can manage taxis (with help) but he says he would find it difficult to use the toilet without help because of his poor mobility, ie it would take him longer than would normally be expected.

Needs deriving from providing necessary care

Should Ms K change her mind and request a carer's assessment she would qualify for this only if it could be concluded that she is providing necessary care. Ms K does her father's shopping for him, but if it was established that he could arrange to have his shopping delivered without needing any assistance to place an order, then she would not be providing necessary care and would not meet the first eligibility condition for a carer.

Applicability of the specified outcomes

With Mr K we know that his daughter has been cooking meals for him, so one of the specified outcomes that the eligibility determination should consider is "[a] managing and maintaining nutrition". The statutory guidance says this comprises two elements: i) access to food and drink to maintain nutrition and ii) ability to prepare and consume the food and drink.

The application of "[b] maintaining personal hygiene" is straightforward as the guidance states that this includes laundering of clothes.

To establish that "[f] maintaining a habitable home environment" applies might require a series of causal links to be established to determine if his breathing difficulties are exacerbated by environmental factors (see further pages).

There is no further relevant clarification in the guidance in relation to "[i] making use of necessary facilities or services in the community including public transport and recreational facilities or services" that apply to Mr K's circumstances.

Determining if the 'unable' condition is met

Mr K qualifies as being unable to achieve outcome "[a] managing and maintaining nutrition" without assistance. He cannot cook a meal because he cannot safely use cooking devices to prepare food. He is not able to go out and shop for food, although he could have it delivered – so in considering 'access' it would need to be determined whether he is able to order food without any assistance.

He is able to achieve outcome "[b] maintaining personal hygiene" without assistance, but he qualifies because lifting clothing in and out of the washing machine causes him significant pain and it takes him significantly longer than would normally be expected.

He is able to do his own housework and keep the house clean; however, in achieving the outcome of "[f] maintaining a habitable home environment", doing the dusting and the exertion of housework could exacerbate his breathlessness and result in a hospital admission to stabilise his condition. Therefore it could be considered that cleaning his house endangers his health.

He qualifies with regard to "[i] making use of necessary facilities or services in the community including public transport and recreational facilities or services" because he cannot use buses to get to the jazz club. Walking to the nearest bus stop unaided takes significantly longer than would normally expected, and he could injure himself after boarding a bus as he sometimes cannot sit down safely before the bus pulls away. He is able to get there by taxi, but says that he cannot afford it. Also he says he cannot use the toilet facilities at the jazz club unaided.

Significant impact on wellbeing

Let us assume that the second condition is met for Mr K because he is unable to achieve the following outcomes:

- *[a] "managing and maintaining nutrition" – he needs assistance because he cannot safely use cooking appliances;*
- *[b] "maintaining personal hygiene" – lifting clothing in and out of the washing machine causes him significant pain and it takes him longer than would normally be expected;*
- *[f] "maintaining a habitable home environment" – cleaning the house and dusting in particular endangers his health;*
- *[i] "making use of necessary facilities or services in the community including public transport and recreational facilities or services" – it is too difficult for him to use public transport to get to the jazz club and he has problems using the toilet in public places.*

The effect of Mr K being unable to cook for himself and do his laundry and cleaning could be considered as having a significant impact on his physical wellbeing and also control over his day-to-day-life. The eligibility criteria are therefore met as two of the specified outcomes apply and there is significant impact.

Not being able to go to the jazz club could be considered as having a significant impact on his wellbeing in relation to participation in recreational activities. During the needs assessment conversation he had spoken of his love of playing and listening to music, and that his friendships revolved around the jazz club that he no longer attends. Even though the eligibility threshold has already been reached, the significance of the impact of this inability ought to be determined so that it can be decided whether this is included in the list of eligible needs.

Alternative scenario

If Mr K did not have COPD and his arthritis was less severe each of the specified outcomes may be marginal in relation to the inability test. However, it might be possible to argue that the cumulative effect of difficulties with day-to-day living and getting to the jazz club, and the fact that he would not see his daughter so often (as she would not need to do his shopping or cooking), are leading to him becoming lonely and socially isolated, and thus there is a significant impact on his wellbeing.

Excluding what the carer is doing

The eligibility determination has to set aside the fact that his daughter is doing Mr K's food shopping and is cooking meals for him.

However, although it has been established that he cannot safely cook for himself and it is difficult for him to go out and shop for food, he may have the ability to order food for delivery without any assistance.

Involvement of the adult and carer, explaining the eligibility determination and next steps

The way that Mr K has expressed what he wants help with gives a good indication of what his view is about how his wellbeing could be maintained. For example, having a cooked meal is very important to him and the eligibility determination would most likely conclude that not having this would have a significant detrimental impact on his wellbeing. However, the social worker would need to be clear that agreeing that the third condition is met does not mean that Mr K would necessarily be considered for the funding for someone to come in every day and prepare him a home-cooked meal in the way that his daughter has been doing.

In the early stages of the eligibility determination during the discussion of specified outcome "[b] maintaining personal hygiene", Mr K might think that he would qualify under this outcome because he is already paying someone to do the laundry as he finds this very time consuming. It is appropriate to be guided by Mr K in considering his ability to manage this task, but he ought to be made aware that the funding that the local authority decides is sufficient to meet his needs may not equate with what he is currently paying.

Ms W

Summary of assessment

Ms W reluctantly agreed to a visit from a social worker from a Community Mental Health Team. This visit was prompted by a referral from the manager of the housing association flat that Ms W lives in, who is concerned that there is a fire risk because of the large number of books and magazines in the house.

The following is known about Ms W:

- *Ms W (aged 40) was diagnosed as having psychotic depression at the age of 25, and she was admitted to hospital in her early 30s.*
- *She was placed in her current housing association accommodation seven years ago, and at the time she was subject to a section 117 after-care order under the Mental Health Act 1983, following a hospital admission.*
- *The after-care order ceased five years ago and she was discharged to the care of her GP.*
- *A year before her hospital admission she was made redundant from her administrative job in a university.*
- *Her mother died four years ago. She has limited contact with her father.*

The referral from the GP contained the following additional information:

- *The delusional aspects of her depression are being satisfactorily managed through medication. She has declined the offer of talking therapy.*
- *She says that she keeps herself busy by collecting old books and magazines from car boot sales. I was not able to determine whether she sells them as well, as she is reluctant to talk about it. I wonder whether she has Diogenes syndrome?*
- *In other respects she is healthy.*

The social worker concluded the following:

- *It is unlikely that Ms W would be diagnosed as having Diogenes syndrome as there is no sign of her living in squalor. Her flat is very congested as a result of her large collection of magazines and books, but there is no evidence of self-neglect.*
- *Ms W will not agree to a three-way meeting with the manager of the housing association, and she doesn't want anyone else involved and will not give permission for her father to be contacted.*
- *An assessment of whether she would benefit from talking therapies may well help with her overall assessment, but she is not agreeable to this at present.*
- *Ms W is agreeable to developing a plan to improve her social interaction and thinks that going to a gym and getting help from a personal trainer would be a good way of doing this, and at the same time this would enable her to exercise more effectively.*

The social worker decides to proceed with exploring eligibility with Ms W during this first visit as she doesn't want to run the risk of not being able to see Ms W again.

Desired outcomes and specified outcomes

Ms W has never had close friends but enjoys having 'arms-length' contact with other people. It would therefore appear that specified outcome "[g] developing and maintaining family or other personal relationships" is applicable.

The social worker may also conclude that specified outcome "[f] maintaining a habitable home environment" applies. However, as Ms W is not willing to accept help at present to make her home safer she is unlikely to agree with this. Nevertheless, the decision about which outcomes apply is up to the social worker, so this can be included in the eligibility determination.

It is possible that at a later stage other specified outcomes may apply. Ms W may not initially articulate that she has any desired outcomes that link with specified outcome "[h] accessing and engaging in work, training, education or volunteering", but this could be considered at a later stage if her circumstances change.

Fluctuating needs

There are indicators that her circumstances could deteriorate in the future such that she may not be able to maintain a habitable home. It could be argued that the more she continues to fill her flat with newspapers and magazines, the greater the potential fire risk.

Needs deriving from physical or mental impairment or illness

Ms W meets the description of mental impairment as she has been formally diagnosed as having psychotic depression. Ms W's perceptions of her needs are exclusively in relation to the lack of social interaction, although her landlord believes she is also not able look after her accommodation satisfactorily.

Relationship between impairment/illness and specified outcomes

There is a known association between social isolation and depression; therefore the consequential link can be made with specified outcome "[g] developing and maintaining family or other personal relationships".

There is some evidence of hoarding behaviour and this can be associated with depression, and thus a link could be made with "[f] maintaining a habitable home environment".

Applicability of the specified outcomes

It is relatively straightforward to apply "[g] developing and maintaining family or other personal relationships" to Ms W's circumstances. It is not necessary to consider the additional clarification of the meaning of these terms that is provided in the statutory guidance.

However, in considering "[f] maintaining a habitable home environment" the determining factor is whether she is able to keep the flat "sufficiently clean and maintained to be safe", and in this case there is a safety consideration in relation to the potential fire risk.

Determining if the 'unable' condition is met

Ms W has become socially isolated and will be unable to achieve the specified outcome "[g] developing and maintaining family or other personal relationships" without assistance.

If it is accepted that there is a fire risk then it could be concluded that by not achieving specified outcome "[f] maintaining a habitable home environment", Ms W is likely to endanger her own safety and the safety of others.

Significant impact on wellbeing

Let us assume that the second condition is met for Ms W because she is unable to achieve the following two outcomes:

- *"[g] developing and maintaining family or other personal relationships" – she needs assistance to develop social networks and thus reduce her social isolation;*
- *"[f] maintaining a habitable home environment" – she is not able to keep the house sufficiently well maintained to minimise fire risk.*

It is possible that her social isolation is not regarded as having a significant impact on her wellbeing. It is difficult to correlate the relationship between the fact that she does not have much contact with people and her mental health and emotional wellbeing. A case could be made by citing research evidence for people in similar circumstances.

If the fire risk is thought to be high, then the impact of [f] could definitely be regarded as significant. This may be less clear-cut where the fire risk is deemed to be low.

However, even if each of them is only partially established, by taking all of the outcomes together it might be possible to conclude that the cumulative impact on her wellbeing is significant. This could be demonstrated by considering the interrelationship between her social isolation and her hoarding behaviour.

Involvement of the adult, explaining the eligibility determination and next steps

With Ms W, there is likely to be a significant difference between her view of the specified outcomes she has difficulty in achieving and that of the social worker responsible for the eligibility determination.

She agrees that she is socially isolated, and that this is connected with her depression.

She doesn't appear to agree that there are any risks posed by what could be described as hoarding behaviour, so while the social worker may conclude that outcome "[f] maintaining a habitable home environment" applies, this is likely to be something that she wouldn't accept.

The fact that Ms W doesn't agree with the way that [f] has been interpreted by the social worker does not prevent it being applied, because the local authority makes the final decision. However, her views will have an important impact on the subsequent decisions about if and how this need is to be met by the local authority.

Mrs O

Summary of assessment

Mrs O has had her needs assessed by a Care Navigator from the local carers centre. This organisation is also contracted to undertake eligibility determinations on behalf of the local authority.

Mr O is a problem drinker and periodically has episodes where his heavy drinking results in him being incontinent. He is separated from his wife but lives close by to the family home. Mr and Mrs O have three children aged 11, 15 and 19. The youngest child has Down's syndrome. Mrs O works part time in a supermarket. Mr O's father had provided him with a lot of support but he recently died.

Mrs O says that she is willing to continue to support her husband emotionally and to help him cope with the consequences of his episodes of heavy drinking (ie meeting personal care needs), but she is worried that there may be times when there will be simply too much for her to do and her children may be neglected, and the stress will be too much for her.

Nine months ago the youngest child's school was concerned about the impact of Mr O's drinking problem, so they made a referral to the Children and Families service. No concerns were recorded about Mrs O's abilities to care for her children. Mrs O was advised to make use of Al-Anon.

Mr O agreed to discuss an assessment of his needs by the local authority, but when contact was made he said that he didn't need any help, and in effect he declined to be assessed. He said that he is quite happy with the care and support he gets from his wife when he needs it.

Mrs O says she finds it helpful to talk about her problems to a 'professional' and wants to know if she can get help with this. Ideally she would like to talk to a social worker, and speak to the same one each time.

Desired outcomes and specified outcomes

It could be concluded that when Mrs O is caring for Mr O during a bout of heavy drinking she may have difficulties in achieving specified outcome "[i] carrying out any caring responsibilities the carer has for a child". She has articulated her concern that her children could be neglected. It is an outcome that she particularly desires to avoid.

Mrs O sometimes has to take time off work to respond to her husband and agrees with the Care Navigator's observation that she doesn't have much time for herself. The Care

Navigator notes that the specified outcomes "[vi] engaging in work, training, education or volunteering" and "[viii] engaging in recreational activities" might apply.

Fluctuating needs

Mr O is sometimes not able to meet all of his personal care needs after a bout of heavy drinking and it is during these periods that the coping ability of his wife is going to be particularly stretched. So the eligibility determination ought to be based on this fluctuation in needs.

Needs deriving from providing necessary care

It appears from what Mrs O describes that the personal care she provides for Mr O is necessary care, ie that this is care and support that Mr O is not capable of providing for himself. As a consequence of providing this necessary care, Mrs O has developed needs in relation to the stress she experiences in looking after her children when her husband has a crisis.

Relationship between necessary care and carer health or specified outcomes

There is no evidence that Mrs O has deteriorating health, but she anticipates having difficulty achieving specified outcome "[a] carrying out any caring responsibilities for a child". This difficulty could occur when Mr O is drinking heavily and needs help with his personal care. Mrs O is able to care for her children and her husband, but in doing so it is possible that the health and safety of either her husband or her younger children could be endangered.

The demands of providing care for her husband impact on specified outcomes "[vi] engaging in work, training, education or volunteering" and "[viii] engaging in recreational activities".

Mrs O also provides Mr O with emotional support as well as personal care when he is drinking heavily. This could also be regarded as necessary care and support that Mr O is not capable of providing for himself.

Applicability of the specified outcomes

It has been identified that Mrs O periodically has difficulty in achieving outcome "[a] carrying out any caring responsibilities for a child". The guidance given in the example for this outcome includes a consideration of "any parenting or other caring responsibilities the carer has for a child in addition to their caring role for the adult". This clearly applies.

Mrs O's job is not at risk and her employer is very helpful in allowing her to work flexibly, so the specified outcome "[vi] engaging in work, training, education or volunteering" doesn't apply. But she certainly has no leisure time, so specified outcome "[viii] engaging in recreational activities" applies.

Determining if the 'unable' condition is met

Mrs O would qualify under this condition for outcome "[a] carrying out any caring responsibilities for a child", because she is likely to endanger the health and safety of her husband or her children in trying to care for them both at the same time.

She is unlikely to qualify for outcome "[viii] engaging in recreational activities", because she could engage in leisure activities without assistance and she would not experience "significant pain, distress or anxiety" or "endanger the health or safety of the carer or any adults or children for whom the carer provides care".

Significant impact on wellbeing

Let us assume that the second condition is met for Mrs O because she is unable to achieve outcome "[a] carrying out any caring responsibilities for a child". She expresses this as a worry that there may be times when there will be simply too much for her to do and her children may be neglected, and the stress will be too much for her.

There is a plausible link between the potential difficulty in her achieving this outcome and her view of the impact of this on her wellbeing. The stress element can be related to her emotional wellbeing.

As the incidents where Mrs O experiences stress are periodic, the consideration would be about whether there is significant impact on the carer's wellbeing following each incident, or whether the most significant impact is as a result of worrying what might happen.

Involvement of the adult and carer, explaining the eligibility determination and next steps

Mrs O has expressed her concern that her children may be neglected and that the stress will be too much for her. So in this case her view is likely to closely match how the social worker describes the significant impact on wellbeing. However, the social worker would need to be clear that this does not mean that Mrs O would necessarily be considered for the funding for the solution that she has identified, ie having a named social worker with whom she can talk through her problems.

If it is concluded that Mrs O's needs do not meet the first condition of the eligibility criteria because it is decided that she is not providing necessary care, the local authority would need to set out why it had decided that the care and support that Mrs O is providing is something that Mr O is capable of providing for himself, and inform Mrs O of this in the eligibility judgement.

Comment and analysis

Readers should note that what is set out in this section and the previous section is intended to show how the statutory guidance might be applied, and in doing so, what would be complex situations in real life have had to be simplified.

Desired outcomes and specified outcomes

With the case examples, it is mostly the individuals' desired outcomes that are shaping which of the specified outcomes are considered. Although, as we can see with Ms W, some specified outcomes apply where they are contrary to the outcomes that the individual desires. The identifying of desired outcomes will be led by the adult or carer, but because of the preciseness of the specified outcomes it is the professional expertise of the social worker that ought to determine whether they apply.

Where an individual lacks capacity, the task of aiming for the specified outcomes to be driven by their desired outcomes may be more challenging. This will be considered in more detail in Chapter 10.

Fluctuating needs

In Chapter 2 it was noted that assessment of needs "must consider whether the individual's current level of need is likely to fluctuate and what their on-going needs for care and support are likely to be", and that this can include taking into account "what fluctuations in need can be reasonably expected based on experience of others with a similar condition" (paragraph 6.58).

This duty applies to the whole care and support planning process, and it is referenced in relation to eligibility determination for adults and carers in sections 2 (4) and 3 (4) of the Care and Support (Eligibility) Regulations 2014 where it states "the local authority must take into account… circumstances over such period as it considers necessary to establish accurately the… level of need".

Local authorities have a duty to consider what the nature of the adult's/carer's needs have been over an appropriate period to get a complete picture of the level of need when determining eligibility, because individuals "may have needs which are not apparent at the time of the assessment, but may have arisen in the past and are likely to arise again in the future" (paragraph 6.113).

The following examples are given in paragraphs 6.113 and 6.130:

- an adult with a mental illness, which has been managed in the past eight months but which could deteriorate if circumstances in the adult's life change;
- a carer could be caring for an adult with a mental illness, which has been managed in the past eight months, but which could deteriorate if circumstances in the adult's life change.

The fluctuation in Mrs O's needs is a very significant element in her eligibility determination. This derives from the unpredictable nature and frequency of the needs of the cared-for person. For Ms W there are no fluctuating needs to consider. She has a mental illness but this has been successfully managed for the past five years. Mr K has a condition that could be exacerbated by environmental factors, and although there is no evidence of this actually happening he could have breathing difficulties if he exerted himself and was exposed to dust, ie if he did his own housework.

Needs deriving from physical or mental impairment or illness

Mr K has needs that derive from his physical impairments and Ms W has needs that derive from a mental impairment.

In many cases it will be almost self-evident that this first condition is met. But there can be circumstances where someone has needs for care and support that were caused wholly or partly by "other circumstantial factors" (paragraph 6.104), which may mean that the first condition is not met. For example, an individual could have care and support needs that derive from financial hardship because they have no access to public funds.

Relationship between impairment/illness and specified outcomes

Establishing this relationship can sometimes be a straightforward matter of applying the statutory guidance on the specified outcomes to the individual's circumstances as they have described them. For example, identifying the relationship between Mr K's arthritis on getting a bus to the jazz club and the specified outcome "[i] making use of necessary facilities or services in the community including public transport and recreational facilities or services".

But it can often be more complex and require a good understanding of the nature of the individual's impairment. For the case to be made for Mr K in relation to the specified outcome "[f] maintaining a habitable home environment" that he would have breathing difficulties if he exerted himself and was exposed to dust, the social worker would need to know enough about COPD to consider whether this was the case and/or whether medical opinion was necessary.

In considering the specified outcomes of "[g] developing and maintaining family or other personal relationships" and "[f] maintaining a habitable home environment" for Ms W, the social worker would have to rely on his/her knowledge of depression, social isolation and hoarding behaviour to make the necessary links.

Needs deriving from providing necessary care

For a carer to meet the first condition, their need for support must arise "because they are providing care to an adult" (paragraph 6.118). This need must be as a consequence of the carer also providing "necessary care" (paragraph 6.119), ie meeting some of an adult's care and support needs that the adult is not capable of meeting for himself or herself.

Mrs O is providing care and support for Mr O that he is not capable of providing for himself, and as a result she experiences stress in looking after her children when her husband has a crisis. If the circumstances were similar but Mr O was not thought to have care and support needs, and he was very demanding of attention from Mrs O in other ways, Mrs O would not meet the eligibility criteria as a carer – even if she was experiencing stress for similar reasons.

If Ms K requested a carer's assessment she may not meet the first condition because Mr K may be able to do online shopping without her help. But if he needed her help to use a computer or other device, she might qualify. The guidance provided by SCIE suggests that it means "activities that the individual requiring support should be able to carry out as part of normal daily life but is unable to do so".[1]

Relationship between necessary care and carer health or specified outcomes

A causal link has to be demonstrated by either describing the effect (actual or anticipated) of providing necessary care on the carer's health, or their difficulty in achieving one of the specified outcomes.

In Mrs O's case there is no indication that her "physical or mental health is either deteriorating or is at risk of doing so" (paragraph 6.120), so the route requiring a link with a specified outcome was followed. But with a less resilient person, their mental health could be at risk.

Applicability of the specified outcomes

SCIE suggests that the specified outcomes should be considered as "indications of what would normally be said to constitute a full life", and that they should be thought of simply as the "usual domains in a person's life".[1] The task for the social worker is to consider these 'domains', and discern whether the inabilities or difficulties described by the adult or carer fall within the scope of the outcomes specified in the statutory guidance.

Sometimes it will be self-evident that whatever the adult or carer cannot do or has difficulties with will be within scope. Where this is not the case a professional judgement has to be made; paragraphs 6.106 and 6.123 give "examples of how local authorities should consider each outcome" (see Figures 3.2 and 3.3). There is a caveat added in 6.106 that states that these examples "do not constitute an exhaustive list".

Some examples are straightforward to apply. For outcome "[b] managing toilet needs", paragraph 6.104 states: "Local authorities should consider the adult's ability to access and use a toilet and manage their toilet needs." This helps to clarify the scope of this outcome as including the ability to access a toilet – as well as being able to use it.

With Mr K, Ms W and Mrs O, deciding on which specified outcomes to consider was relatively straightforward. The exception being in relation to "[f] maintaining a habitable home environment", for Mr K and Ms W.

The guidance for [f] is set out as follows:

> Adults –
>
> Local authorities should consider whether the condition of the adult's home is sufficiently clean and maintained to be safe. A habitable home is safe and has essential amenities. An adult may require support to sustain their occupancy of the home and to maintain amenities, such as water, electricity and gas.

> Carers –
>
> Local authorities should consider whether the condition of the carer's home is safe and an appropriate environment to live in and whether it presents a significant risk to the carer's wellbeing. A habitable home should be safe and have essential amenities such as water, electricity and gas.

This guidance can be broken down and analysed, as follows:

- For adults a judgement has to be made about "whether the condition of the home is sufficiently clean and maintained to be safe". The implication is that safety comprises two necessary components – cleanliness and maintenance.
- For carers the judgement is similar, except instead of "sufficiently clean and maintained to be safe" the judgement rests on "whether the condition of the carer's home is safe and an appropriate environment to live in and whether it presents a significant risk to the carer's wellbeing".
- A key factor both for adults and carers appears to be whether the home is safe. For carers there is the added factor of the home being "an appropriate environment to live in", and whether both the lack of safety and inappropriateness of the environment poses a risk to the carer's wellbeing which is judged to be significant.
- For both carers and adults there is reference to a habitable home having essential amenities, as well as being safe.

The application of specified outcome [f] alongside the 'unable' element of this second condition is explored in the next section.

Applying the 'unable' criteria

For each of the four different definitions of 'unable', examples are given in the statutory guidance to help with interpretation. These are set out in Figures 3.2 and 3.3.

Of the four different ways that an adult could be 'unable' to achieve a specified outcome, three commence with the statement "is able to achieve the outcome without assistance but…". In other words they are about difficulties or inabilities in achieving outcomes.

Four of the specified outcomes apply to Mr K and he is able to achieve most of them without assistance, but safety is a factor for cooking and housework, and with his laundry this takes him significantly longer than would normally be expected. With regard to the jazz club he has difficulties getting there by public transport that are in relation both to safety and taking significantly longer than would normally be expected, and he cannot make use of this recreational facility because he cannot use the toilet without assistance.

Ms W is unable to achieve one of the two specified outcomes that are applicable, ie she cannot develop the social networks she needs without some help. In relation to [f] she is able to maintain her home, but because of the way that she does so this is perceived as a fire risk and could be seen as endangering the health and safety of others.

It is worth noting that the term 'endanger' is used rather than the more general term of 'risk', ie an adult may be "able to achieve the outcome without assistance, but doing so endangers or is likely to endanger the health or safety of the adult, or of others" (paragraph 6.105).

The application of 'endangering' is relatively straightforward when considering Ms W's inability to maintain her home safely, but more nuanced reasoning is required for Mr K. Mr K needs to keep the house sufficiently clean to minimise the build up of dust, but left to his own devices the exertion of doing housework could cause him to become dangerously breathless. He would be able to do housework, but maintaining his home to a habitable standard is likely to endanger his health.

Additional guidance[1] provided by SCIE suggests there may not be a habitable home environment if:

- the home is damp or in very poor repair;
- the adult is unable to clean the kitchen, leading to infestation;
- the adult is hoarding excessively.

The SCIE guidance[1] offers some further examples to help with the interpretation of the habitable home outcome for carers as follows:

- If the carer's role means that they are unable to pay their bills, or do not have time to deal with the maintenance of their home, eg if there is a damp problem, they may not be maintaining a habitable home.
- If the carer is caring for somebody in their own home, and there is not enough space in the home, it may not be a habitable environment.

If the carer and the adult with care and support needs share a home, and the adult's condition means that they have high expectations about the home maintenance that the carer 'struggles' to meet, the carer may not be meeting this outcome.

For carers the application of the 'unable' part of the second condition is virtually the same as for adults, with the exception that the 'takes significantly longer than would normally be expected' clause does not apply. However, this part of the second condition does not need to be considered where the carer's physical or mental health is "either deteriorating or is at risk of doing so" (paragraph 6.118), because in these circumstances there is no need to consider whether or not he or she is unable to achieve any of the specified outcomes.

Mrs O experiences difficulty in achieving outcome "[a] carrying out any caring responsibilities for a child". The difficulty that she has is that in trying to care for both her husband and her children (particularly her 11-year-old child who has Down's syndrome), she is likely to endanger the health and safety of her husband or her children.

Significant impact on wellbeing

Having explored all the component parts of eligibility, the final part of the eligibility determination is where "local authorities must consider whether the adult's needs and their inability to achieve the outcomes above cause or risk causing a significant impact on their wellbeing" (paragraph 6.107).

The judgement about the significant impact on an adult's or carer's wellbeing has to demonstrate a consequential link with a person's inabilities to achieve outcomes. This is set out in sections following paragraph 6.111 and 6.128, as follows:

- As a consequence there is, or there is likely to be, a significant impact on the adult's wellbeing.
- As a consequence of that fact there is, or there is likely to be, a significant impact on the carer's wellbeing.

This section considers what is meant by each of the four terms, ie 'significant', 'impact', 'wellbeing' and 'consequential', and what they mean when combined.

In deciding what is 'significant' for the individual, paragraph 6.110 clarifies that in "making this judgement, local authorities should look to understand the adult's needs in the context of what is important to him or her" (paragraph 6.126 repeats this for carers). However, there is relatively little guidance on what else to consider when making this professional judgement, and this is underscored by the fact that the term 'significant' is not defined and that paragraph 6.109 states that it "must therefore be understood to have its everyday meaning".

There will be areas of case law that will bring clarity to some aspects of the Care Act, although this is unlikely to happen with the meaning of 'significant' because the courts have been reluctant to define this word in other areas of law according to Cornerstone Barristers.[2] For example, in *re B (A Child) (Care Proceedings: Threshold Criteria)* [2013] the Supreme Court when considering 'significant' in the context of the threshold of 'significant harm', Lord Wilson stated, "...in my view this court should avoid attempting to explain the word 'significant'. It would be a gloss; attention might then turn to the meaning of the gloss and, albeit with the best of intentions, the courts might find in due course that they had travelled far from the word itself."

Readers may wish to know that the definition for 'significant' in the *Oxford Living Dictionary* is "sufficiently great or important to be worthy of attention".[3]

The key factor in considering the 'impact' is whether either of the following applies, as set out in paragraph 6.108:

a) the adult's inability to achieve the outcomes impacts on at least one of the areas of wellbeing in a significant way;

b) the effect of the impact on a number of the areas of wellbeing mean that there is a significant impact on the adult's overall wellbeing.

The third element of 'wellbeing' is set out in section 1 (2) of the Care Act. Although the scope would appear to be slightly broader than just wellbeing, because in paragraphs 6.109 and 6.125 there is reference to the consequential effect of the inability of adults and carers to achieve outcomes, "on their daily lives, their independence and their wellbeing".

On the SCIE web page 'What does significant impact mean?',[2] they reframe the statutory guidance by saying that significant impact could be as a consequence of either of the following:

> A single effect – "The inability to achieve two or more outcomes affects at least one of the areas of wellbeing in a significant way."
>
> A cumulative effect – "The individual may have needs across several of the eligibility outcomes, perhaps at a relatively low level, but as these needs affect the individual in various areas of their life, the overall impact on the individual is significant."

SCIE also suggests an additional category described as a 'domino effect', whereby "the individual may have needs in relation to few eligibility outcomes, but it can be anticipated that in the near future other outcomes will be affected, causing a significant impact on the individual's wellbeing".[1]

The consequence of Mr K being unable to cook for himself and do his laundry and cleaning could be considered as having a significant impact on his physical wellbeing and also control over his day-to-day-life, and in addition his inability to access his preferred recreational activity would lead to him becoming lonely and isolated. He could possibly survive by taking taxis to the local shops and preparing himself cold food, and struggling to do his laundry and keep his house clean – but living like this would soon have a negative effect on his health and his quality of life. On top of this he may not be able to afford to go to the jazz club as this might require taxis, and in any event he may not be fit enough.

The decision about whether Ms W's inabilities can be regarded as having a significant impact on her wellbeing could go either way, depending on the circumstances. She has been socially isolated for a significant period of time and there is no observable deterioration in her wellbeing, and although her flat is very cluttered with paper she shows no signs of being careless to the extent that there is a high risk of fire. Alternatively it may be thought likely that she will develop more extreme hoarding behaviour and may end up living in squalor, unless steps are taken to mitigate this potential 'domino effect'. Or it could be that there is evidence that there is a very real risk of fire, and because the two outcomes test is met, her needs would be determined as eligible.

The impact on Mrs O's wellbeing of her having too many caring responsibilities is less tangible than with Mr K and Ms W, because much of the stress is about what might happen. The impact is on her emotional wellbeing, which in turn has an impact on her relationship with her children. Mrs O believes that without support she will not be able to manage. The decision on significance would very much depend on how Mrs O presents, and therein lies the skill of the social worker in making this judgement.

It should be emphasised that none of these suggestions from SCIE carry the same legal weight as the statutory guidance. SCIE provides an interpretation, which social workers should apply only where they believe it accords with the statutory guidance.

Excluding what the carer is doing

"The eligibility determination must be made based on the adult's needs and how these impact on their wellbeing" (paragraph 6.115). As referred to earlier in this chapter, this is about the determination being 'carer blind'.

In practice this means establishing what the adult would be unable to do if the carer were not providing any care and support. Where an adult is receiving assistance with a number of outcomes from a carer, it may require specialist assessment to determine whether or not they are unable to achieve the outcome without assistance or if they experience significant pain, endanger themselves or it takes a significantly longer time than normally expected. This may require the provision of a reablement service to determine this, or assessment from an OT.

With Mr K the eligibility determination has to set aside anything that his daughter is doing for him that he is unable to do for himself or can only do with difficulty, ie shopping.

Involvement of the adult and carer, explaining the eligibility determination and next steps

Paragraph 6.53 states unequivocally "that the final decision regarding eligibility will rest with the local authority", and adds that "this may include taking into account the person's own view". There is no guidance on circumstances where this would not apply, so it is reasonable to assume that the person's view ought to be taken into account unless there is a very good reason for not doing so.

In making the judgement about what is of significance in relation to an individual's wellbeing, paragraph 6.110 states that "local authorities should look to understand the adult's needs in the context of what is important to him or her". This is in line with the general principle set out in paragraph 1.14 where it is stated that "the local authority should assume that the person themselves knows best their own outcomes, goals and wellbeing".

The concluding of the eligibility determination can be an important opportunity to unravel assumptions the individual may have made about how their needs are going to be met. Often people will perceive a strong link between what they see as improving or maintaining their wellbeing, and what should be included in a care and support plan to meet their needs. However, it is important for social workers to be clear that meeting the eligibility criteria is simply conferring a status, and that the next steps are first to consider whether there is a duty to meet an individual's needs, and then to identify how they can be met and what level of resources the local authority will make available.

For those people whose needs do not meet the eligibility criteria the local authority has a duty to consider whether to use its discretionary power to meet them. This duty is explored in the next chapter.

Mr K is hoping that he can have a hot meal cooked for him every day in the way that his daughter is currently doing. It is important to acknowledge this preference, but explain that any funding agreed by the local authority to meet his need for a hot meal would not be sufficient for him to meet his need in this way.

Similarly, Mrs O has a particular preference for how her needs would be best met, ie the allocation of a named social worker, and this may not be agreed as the most appropriate and cost-effective way of meeting her needs.

Ms W's concerns are likely to be of a different nature. The social worker would need to reassure her that although this perceived fire risk is part of the rationale for concluding that specified outcome "[f] maintaining a habitable home environment" applies, that eligibility is only a gateway to care and support planning, and that nothing would be included in her plan without her agreement.

Where the individual disagrees with the eligibility determination and wishes to challenge the decision, the first step would be for them to make a complaint in accordance with the Local Authority Social Services and NHS Complaints Regulations 2009. Disputes are considered in more detail in Chapter 11.

Conclusion

Social workers play a vital role in interpreting the eligibility framework both in terms of the day-to-day application and developing what constitutes good practice. Although the eligibility framework is elaborate, the essential features are relatively straightforward to understand, but the circumstances of adults and carers to which it is being applied can be complex. The skill of the social worker lies in ensuring that the complexities of an individual's circumstances are reflected in the application of the framework.

Local authorities have developed recording formats that rightly seek to make the framework as easy as possible to comprehend and use, both for staff and people with care and support needs, and to ensure that there is a satisfactory level of consistency. Although there are boxes to be ticked and filled out, the capturing of the complexities of the eligibility determination process requires input from skilled and knowledgeable social workers. For example, social workers ought to make sure that they use the free text boxes to show how they have developed plausible causal links between the three eligibility conditions, and demonstrate that they have taken into account the person's own view about the application of each element, particularly about whether their inabilities and difficulties result in significant impact on their wellbeing.

This chapter has focused on the principal role of eligibility criteria as the gateway to local authority resources for care and support. Consequently, the emphasis has been on how social workers can use what they have learned from an assessment of a person's needs to determine eligibility. But an equally important application of the description of a person's assessed needs and how these do and don't meet the eligibility criteria is in the formulation of the care and support plan (or support plan for a carer), which is considered in a later chapter.

References

1. www.scie.org.uk/care-act-2014/assessment-and-eligibility/eligibility/
2. Eligibility for Care and Support and the Care Act 2014 – ADASS/DoH/LGA (no longer available)
3. https://en.oxforddictionaries.com/definition/significant

4 The duty and power to meet needs

Introduction

Before it is concluded whether adults and carers are going to receive help from the local authority to meet their eligible needs, there are a number of conditions and constraints to be considered. In addition the local authority has to decide whether it wishes to use its powers to meet any non-eligible care and/or support needs the individual may have.

The adult and/or carer has to decide whether they want their needs met by the local authority, and this may depend on the extent of their financial contribution. Also, the duty of a local authority to meet needs is affected by whether or not the individual is a self-funder. So for both these reasons the decision to charge and the outcome of a financial assessment is intertwined with this decision-making process.

This chapter describes those parts of the care and support journey that enable adults and carers to understand if and how their needs might be met, and whether they are going to have to pay anything. The statutory guidance sets out each element of the decision making in a logical sequence, but in practice it will rarely make sense to adults and carers to proceed in a step-by-step way. There will often need to be some iteration between the steps, and this chapter demonstrates this.

Reference will be made to the conditions that have to be met before adults and carers can be considered for help to meet their needs, as set out in paragraphs 6.130–132 in the statutory guidance. Reference will also be made to Chapters 10 and 19 of the statutory guidance to describe how local authorities must apply their duty to meet eligible needs and their power to meet non-eligible needs, and also the circumstances where the local authority is constrained in what it can do for adults.

This chapter comprises the following sections:

- **Making decisions about meeting needs prior to April 2015**
- **Key terms and definitions**
- **Essential steps**
- **Limitations on meeting eligible needs**
- **Conditions and constraints on meeting eligible needs**
- **The power to meet non-eligible needs**
- **Requirements that apply when needs are not going to be meet**
- **The timing of the financial assessment**
- **Applying the statutory guidance using case examples**
- **Conclusion.**

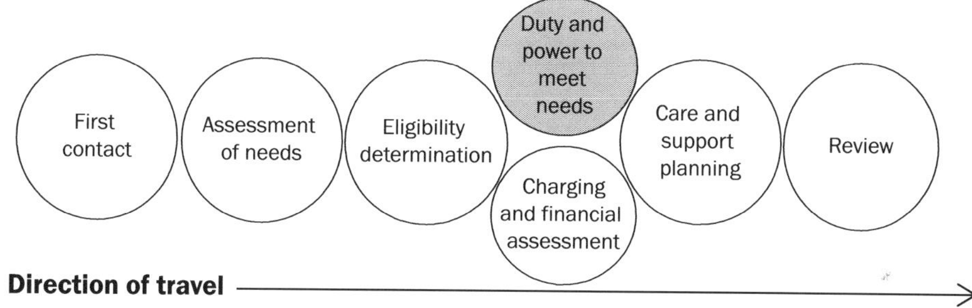

Figure 4.1 The care and support journey

Making decisions about meeting needs prior to April 2015

Previously there was no separation between the determination of eligible needs and the decision about whether there is a duty to meet them.

In the previous statutory guidance issued in 2010, *Prioritising Need in the Context of Putting People First: A Whole System Approach to Eligibility for Social Care*, it states that eligibility criteria "describe the full range of eligible needs that will be met by councils, taking their resources into account". Local authorities were able to make a policy decision about what level of needs to meet.

Key terms and definitions

The following have been selected because they appear in the Care Act. There are no references in the Care and Support Regulations.

Key term	Care Act 2014	The Care and Support Statutory Guidance (revised 2017)
Agreement to meet eligible needs	Section 13 (3) identifies that the local authority must ascertain whether the adult wants to have their needs met by the local authority.	Paragraph 6.134 provides some examples of the application of this section. These are where the individual... • "may not wish to have support in relation to all their needs"; • may "intend to arrange alternative services themselves to meet some needs".
Duty to meet needs	Section 18 sets out that this duty applies where an adult meets the eligibility criteria, subject to certain conditions. Section 20 sets out that this duty applies where a carer meets the eligibility criteria, subject to certain conditions. These conditions are in relation to the following: • ordinary residence; • charging; • lack of capacity. Sections 21, 22 and 23 set out the circumstances where a local authority cannot meet a person's needs in relation to the following: • immigration status; • health care needs; • housing needs.	Paragraph 6.134 provides some guidance on the application of sections 18 and 20, as follows: • ordinary residence – adults "must be ordinarily resident in the authority's area", whereas for carers, "the person for whom they care must be ordinarily resident in the authority's area"; • charging – there should be "early consideration of the potential support options, in order to determine whether some of those may be services for which the local authority makes a charge", and where this applies, "the local authority must carry out a financial assessment. Paragraphs 10.21–25 provide some guidance on the application of sections 21, 22 and 23, and set out additional circumstances where there is no duty to meet needs, as follows: • needs already being met; • services to which a person is entitled under other legislation.
Power to meet non-eligible needs	Local authorities have the power to meet the care and support needs of adults that they are not required to meet, under section 19. They also have the power to meet support needs of carers that they are not required to meet, under sections 20 (6) and (7).	Paragraphs 10.28–30 describe the circumstances where this power may be used and outlines how it must be applied. Examples given are as follows: • needs which do not meet the eligibility criteria; • where the person has eligible needs but is ordinarily resident in another area.

Essential steps

1. The first thing to establish is whether there are any reasons why a local authority may not meet an adult's care and support needs or a carer's support needs. To do this, steps must be taken to determine whether:

a) the ordinary residence requirement is met for the adult with care and support needs;

b) the adult with care and support needs is subject to immigration controls and has been excluded from receiving welfare benefits.

2. Having established that there is no reason why the local authority may not meet a person's needs, the following steps have to be taken (not necessarily in this order) in relation to eligible needs, to determine whether:

a) the adult wants the local authority to meet their care and support needs;

b) any needs are being met by a carer;

c) any care and support needs are being met by other services;

d) any of the services that may be provided are those for which the local authority charges.

3. Where a person has non-eligible care and support needs, the local authority has to decide whether it wishes to use its power to meet any of them.

4. Local authorities should provide people with an early indication of what they might be charged, to help them to decide whether they want the local authority to meet their needs.

5. For any care and support needs that are not going to be met, the following must be provided in writing:

a) an explanation about why the local authority is not going to meet these needs;

b) information and advice about reducing and delaying needs.

Limitations on meeting eligible needs

Application of the ordinary residence requirement

After eligibility has been determined, one of the first steps to be taken is to establish whether the adult meets the ordinary residence requirement, as specified in section 13 (4) the Care Act. This requirement applies only when eligibility has been determined.

Section 18 (1) (a) of the Care Act specifies that the local authority is required to meet needs only in respect of an adult who "is ordinarily resident in the authority's area or is present in its area but has no settled residence". For carers there is an identical specification in section 20 (1) (a).

There is no definition of ordinary residence in the Care Act. The statutory guidance states in paragraph 19.12 that the term should be given its "ordinary and natural meaning".

Paragraph 19.14 states that local authorities must have regard to the case of *Shah v London Borough of Barnet* (1983) in relation to people who have capacity, in which Lord Scarman set out the following definition of ordinary residence: "a man's abode in a particular place or country which he has adopted voluntarily and for settled purposes as part of the regular order of his life for the time being, whether of short or long duration".

Paragraph 19.15 elaborates the meaning of this as follows: "Local authorities should in particular apply the principle that ordinary residence is the place the person has voluntarily adopted for a settled purpose, whether for a short or long duration. Ordinary residence can be acquired as soon as the person moves to an area, if their move is voluntary and for settled purposes, irrespective of whether they own, or have an interest in a property in another local authority area. There is no minimum period in which a person has to be living in a particular place for them to be considered ordinarily resident there, because it depends on the nature and quality of the connection with the new place."

People who lack capacity (and children transitioning into adult social care services) "are not able to voluntarily adopt a particular place of residence" (paragraph 19.16). The relevant judgement specified in the statutory guidance is the case of R (on the application of Cornwall Council) Secretary of State & Ors [2015] UKSC46 (Cornwall).

In most cases, as the statutory guidance says in paragraph 19.13, "establishing the person's ordinary residence is a straightforward matter". Where circumstances are not clear-cut, social workers should refer to Chapter 19 in the statutory guidance.

The guiding principle set out in paragraph 19.11 is that the "determination of ordinary residence must not delay the process of meeting needs".

Adults subject to immigration controls

Local authorities may not meet the care and support needs of an adult subject to immigration controls and who is excluded from receiving benefits, where these needs arise solely because the adult is destitute or because of the physical effects of destitution. This limitation is set out in section 21 of the Care Act in relation to people subject to section 115 of the Immigration and Asylum Act 1999.

It should be noted that there will be individuals subject to immigration controls to whom this limitation does not apply, ie if they have care and support needs for reasons other than being destitute, then the Care Act applies.

Conditions and constraints on meeting eligible needs

Agreement by the individual to needs being met

This agreement is part of what the statutory guidance describes in paragraph 1.21 as the "genuine conversation about people's needs for care and support and how meeting these can help them achieve the outcomes most important to them".

Section 13 (3) (b) states that following the determination of eligible needs the local authority must "ascertain whether the adult wants to have those needs met". Paragraph 6.134 of the statutory guidance elaborates on this by stating that if an adult has some eligible needs the local authority must:

a) agree with the adult which of their needs they would like the local authority to meet; and

b) consider how the local authority may meet those needs.

The statutory guidance envisages there being some circumstances in which a "person may not wish to have support in relation to all their needs" (paragraph 6.134). So before initiating the processes necessary to meet a person's needs, it is important that social workers clarify with people whether there are any of their eligible needs that they don't want help in meeting. Paragraph 6.134 gives the example of where a person may "intend to arrange alternative services themselves to meet some needs". It is reasonable to assume from this that a local authority is not required to meet needs, when an individual is clear that he/she does not want them to be met.

In deciding with an adult and/or carer about how to proceed, paragraph 6.134 requires local authorities to give "early consideration of the potential support options". The purpose of this is to determine whether any of these might be "services for which the local authority makes a charge". Where there is going to be a charge, the local authority must carry out a financial assessment under section 17 of the Care Act. The impact of charging on the duty to meet needs is considered later in the chapter.

Charging and agreement to meet needs are interrelated, because how much the individual is going to be charged may well affect their decision about whether there are any eligible needs that they don't want the local authority to meet. This is considered further later in the chapter.

Needs being met by a carer

Section 18 (7) of the Care Act states that the duty to meet the needs of an adult does "not apply to such of the adult's needs as are being met by a carer".

Paragraph 10.26 of the statutory guidance clarifies that "any eligible needs met by a carer are not required to be met by the local authority, for so long as the carer continues to do so". In paragraph 10.40 it is stated that it is important that the "carer remains willing and able to continue caring".

Care and support needs being met by other services

There are two sets of circumstances in which local authorities have no duty to meet eligible needs and nor do they have the power to do so.

Section 22 (1) of the Care Act prevents local authorities from meeting any care and support needs by providing healthcare services that are the responsibility of the NHS.

Paragraph 15.31 of the statutory guidance provides for an exception for this rule, "where the services provided are 'incidental or ancillary' (that is, relatively minor, and part of a broader package)".

In meeting care and support needs, section 23 of the Care Act clarifies that local authorities may not do anything they or other local authorities are required to do under the Housing Act 1996.

The meeting of healthcare needs and housing needs are considered in more detail in Chapter 12 of this book.

There are also circumstances where the local authority may not have to meet needs that are already being met by other organisations. Paragraph 10.24 of the statutory guidance makes reference to "other services to which a person is entitled under other legislation (but which could also be provided as part of the provision of care and support), which a local authority is not specifically prohibited from providing under the Act", and in these circumstances "2 different organisations may be under a duty to provide a service in relation to the same needs". Where there is such an overlap of entitlements, the guidance is clear that "local authorities should take steps to support the individual to access the support to which they are entitled under other legislation", eg "helping the person to access some disability-related benefits and allowances".

For adults, where their eligible needs are being met by means other than via the local authority, the local authority remains under a duty to meet the person's eligible needs but "may not actually have to arrange or provide any services to comply with that duty" (paragraph 10.21). The examples given are where "needs may be met by a carer, in an educational establishment or by another institution other than the local authority".

Charging and the duty to meet eligible needs

Subject to being within the parameters of these considerations, the duty to meet eligible needs applies in all circumstances where there is no charge for meeting needs. Where there is a charge, the duty to meet the needs still applies as a matter of course, except for self-funders who have the capacity to make decisions about their care and support.

The duty is set out in sections 18 (1–6) and 20 (1–5) of the Care Act.

For both adults and carers, for whom there will be a charge, there is a duty to meet needs where the person's resources are "at or below the financial limit", ie the individual is not a 'self-funder'. This is specified in section 18 (2) of the Care Act. This section also specifies that the local authority has to be satisfied of the adult's financial resources "on the basis of the financial assessment it carried out".

For adults there is an alternative condition set out in section 18 (4), which states that the duty to meet needs applies where "the adult lacks capacity to arrange for the provision of care and support, but there is no person authorised to do so under the Mental Capacity Act 2005 or otherwise in a position to do so on the adult's behalf".

Where a carer's needs are being met by providing a service to the adult (with the agreement of the adult), eg respite care, section 20 (4) specifies that the duty to meet needs will apply where "the financial resources of the adult needing care are at or below the financial limit". It is the financial circumstances of the adult that are assessed, and not those of the carer.

Section 18 (3) sets out that there is a duty to meet the needs of an adult who is a 'self-funder', where the adult asks that the local authority meets their eligible needs. The same duty to respond to a request applies to carers who are self-funders, as set out in section 20 (3). Paragraph 8.56 of the statutory guidance adds a caveat that this duty does not currently apply to adults where it is anticipated that their needs will be met by a care home placement, and that in these circumstances "the local authority may choose to meet their needs, but is not required to do so". Paragraph 8.57 adds that steps should be taken "to make people aware that they have the right to request the local authority to meet their needs, in certain circumstances even when they have resources above the financial limits".

The power to meet non-eligible needs

Non-eligible needs are those needs that have been identified during an assessment, which the local authority is not required to meet in relation to both adults and carers.

Section 19 of the Care Act states that a local authority has the power to meet any needs, subject to the requirements of ordinary residence and the other constraints described. Paragraph 10.28 of the statutory guidance states that these needs may be either "needs which are not 'eligible' (for example, those which do not meet the eligibility criteria)" or "eligible needs in circumstances where the duty does not apply (for example, where the person is ordinarily resident in another area)".

Section 19 (4) clarifies that this power also applies where "the adult is terminally ill".

Under section 19 (3) of the Care Act, a local authority may meet an adult's needs for care and support that appear to it to be urgent, without having carried out a needs assessment or a financial assessment, or having made an eligibility determination.

Section 20 (7) allows for a local authority to meet a carer's needs through the provision of care and support to an adult "even if the authority would not be required to meet the adult's needs for care and support under section 18".

Requirements that apply when needs are not going to be met

In section 13 (5) of the Care Act it is specified that where none of an adult's needs meet the eligibility criteria, the "local authority must give him or her written advice and information" about how their needs can be otherwise met or prevented. In paragraph 10.29 the statutory guidance says that before this happens the local authority must first decide whether it is going to use its power to meet any needs, and if it decides not to what is written to the individual must also explain why.

The information and advice on how the person can reduce or delay their needs in future "should be personal and specific advice based on the person's needs assessment and not a generalised reference to prevention services or signpost to a general web-site" (paragraph 10.29).

These requirements also apply to circumstances where "a local authority is meeting some needs, but not others" (paragraph 10.30). So the individual must be given this written explanation and advice, in addition to receiving a "care and support plan for the needs the local authority is required, or decides to meet" (paragraph 10.30).

Section 13 (5) of the Care Act specifically refers to adults, and there is no corresponding section for carers. However, the references in paragraphs 10.29 and 10.30 do not specifically exclude carers from the requirement to provide a written explanation.

The timing of the financial assessment

The statutory guidance says in paragraph 11.4 that local authorities should provide "a clear upfront indicative (or 'ballpark') allocation at the start of the planning process", the purpose being to "help people to develop the plan and make appropriate choices over how their needs are met". The final allocation will differentiate between the amount the person must pay and the amount that the authority will pay, because a financial assessment will have been completed. However, at this early stage the individual will only know how much it might cost to meet their needs, but not how much they will have to contribute.

Applying the statutory guidance using case examples

This section illustrates and analyses some of the key elements of the processes described in this chapter that are of particular relevance for social workers.

The analysis and case examples are set out under the following headings:

- **Ordinary residence**
- **Agreeing whether and how eligible needs might be met by the local authority**
- **Needs being met by a carer**
- **Care and support needs being met by other services**
- **Charging and the duty to meet eligible needs**
- **Meeting non-eligible needs**
- **Requirements that apply when needs are not going to be met**
- **The timing of the financial assessment.**

Mr K

Summary of assessment and eligibility determination

Mr K has COPD (Chronic Obstructive Pulmonary Disease) and arthritis. His daughter (Ms K) has been cooking meals for him but is no longer willing to do so, although she is willing to do her father's shopping. Mr K pays a neighbour to help with the cleaning and laundry. He is unable to go to a jazz club that he used to attend regularly, because he cannot use public transport and he cannot use the toilet without someone's help. Ms K has declined to have a carer's assessment so she will not receive a carer's support plan.

Eligible needs	• *The effect of Mr K being unable to cook for himself and do his cleaning and laundry has a significant impact on his physical wellbeing and also control over his day-to-day life.* • *Not being able to go to the jazz club because he cannot use public transport and he cannot use the toilet without someone's help, has a significant impact on his wellbeing in relation to participation in recreational activities.*
Desired outcomes	• *He wants someone to come in every day and prepare him a home-cooked meal in the way that his daughter has been doing.* • *Cleaning and laundry – he wants to continue to employ his neighbour to do this.* • *Attending the local jazz club regularly.*
Eligible needs that the carer has agreed to meet	*Shopping (note that it has not been conclusively determined that Mr K could not do online shopping by himself).*

Ordinary residence

Mr K appears as being ordinarily resident at his current address. However, if Mr K decided to move in with his daughter and remain living with her for an indefinite period, because she lives in another local authority, it could be considered that there is a duty upon the local authority where his daughter is resident to meet his needs.

Agreement by the individual to needs being met

Mr K has a particular preference about one aspect of how he could be helped with obtaining a cooked meal – he wants someone to come into his house and cook it for him.

It is likely that his preferred method would cost more than the local authority would allocate for this, and all that would be on offer is a home meals service. He may respond to this offer by saying that he doesn't want this service and he will make alternative arrangements; however, this doesn't mean that he is necessarily saying that this is an eligible need that he doesn't want the local authority to meet. He could employ someone to cook him a meal at his home, by him accepting what the local authority would allocate (in the form of a direct payment) and finding a way of adding funding to pay for what he wants.

Needs being met by a carer

Mr K's daughter is partly helping him to achieve specified outcome "[a] managing and maintaining nutrition" by getting his shopping for him. If it was established that he was not able to order a shopping delivery by himself, it would be considered that she is meeting an eligible need. If the daughter is willing to continue doing this the local authority would not be under any duty to meet this aspect of his needs.

Charging and the duty to meet eligible needs

To improve Mr K's wellbeing he will require care and support to enable him to have a cooked meal, do his laundry, essential cleaning and facilitate attendance at the jazz club. Local authorities are permitted to charge to provide this type of care and support, and most choose to do so.

If it is determined that he is a self-funder, the local authority would only have a duty to meet his needs if he asked them to do so. Should his circumstances deteriorate to the extent that a care home is being considered, the local authority does not have a duty to meet his needs if he is a self-funder, but may choose to do so.

If his circumstances were such that he lacked the mental capacity to arrange services to meet his needs and his daughter was not able to do this for him, then the local authority would have to make the necessary arrangements – even if he is a self-funder.

Meeting non-eligible needs

In describing his desired outcomes Mr K has said that he likes to go to the local jazz club, but finds using public transport difficult. It may have been concluded that this was not an eligible need because either a) he did not meet the inability test in achieving the specified outcome "[i] making use of necessary facilities or services in the community including public transport and recreational facilities or services", or b) it was not considered to have a significant impact on his wellbeing. In either of these circumstances the local authority could decide to use its power to meet this care and support need, if it is within the scope of the local policy on meeting such needs.

Requirements that apply when needs are not going to be met

If Mr K did not have eligible needs in respect of going to the local jazz club for example, and the local authority decides that it will not use its power to meet these needs, then this decision would need to be explained in writing and information and advice given.

Information and advice would need to be given about how more use could be made of local facilities (possibly voluntary groups) and how Mr K could make more use of his own network to facilitate him attending the jazz club.

The explanation of why his needs are not going to be met could include the following reasons:

- *The time it takes to use public transport to get to the jazz club is not longer than would normally be expected and he is able to use the toilet when he gets there (because it can be suitably adapted).*
- *The local authority will not use its power to pay for a taxi (his preferred mode of transport), as an alternative is available.*

The timing of the financial assessment

There were early indications that Mr K may not be a self-funder. He said that he could not afford a taxi to the jazz club and that he is concerned that he will not be able to afford to pay someone to cook him a hot meal.

Because it is likely that the way that his care and support needs would be met would be chargeable, and he is concerned about what he can afford, the financial assessment ought to be initiated at the earliest opportunity after his needs assessment commenced, with the aim of finalising it immediately after the eligibility determination. He would then be able to make an informed decision about whether he wants the local authority to meet his eligible and non-eligible needs, or make private arrangements.

Ms W

Summary of assessment and eligibility determination

Ms W (aged 40) has psychotic depression and is socially isolated. The manager of the housing association flat where Ms W lives is concerned that there is a fire risk because of what is believed to be hoarding behaviour.

Desired outcomes	• *She feels regular exercise will improve her mental health and wellbeing.* • *She would like the type of casual social contact with people that she had when she had a job.* • *She does not want help with managing her collection of books and magazines.*
Eligible needs	*The cumulative impact on her wellbeing of her social isolation and her hoarding behaviour.*

Ordinary residence

She was placed in her current housing association accommodation seven years ago, when she was subject to a section 117 after-care order under the Mental Health Act 1983, following a hospital admission. At the time of the admission she was living in a neighbouring local authority. The after-care order now no longer applies.

In these circumstances she is ordinarily resident in the local authority where she is living. However, if the after-care order was still in force, the duty to meet her needs would fall to the local authority where she lived at the time of her hospital admission.

Agreement by the individual to needs being met

Although the fire risk to Ms W's home was identified as a key element in the eligibility determination, Ms W is unlikely to agree to receive any care and support to address this. In considering which of her needs are to be met she is likely to say that she does not want help with her hoarding behaviour.

Assuming that she has mental capacity in this matter, the local authority has to accept that she is not in agreement to having needs met that are framed in terms of fire risk and hoarding behaviour.

Care and support needs being met by other services

Ms W may benefit from interventions such as the Increasing Access to Psychological Therapy programme (IAPT) for her depression and hoarding behaviour, which is available from the NHS. She could possibly be referred for this treatment – if she was suitably motivated.

In some parts of the country it is possible to receive exercise on prescription (EOP). This is for people with medical conditions including depression, who are not normally active. It provides a supported time-limited exercise programme with the help of a specialist adviser. If Ms W could obtain this and it serves to improve her social interaction (as well as helping with her depression), this could result in her no longer having an eligible need in respect of "[g] developing and maintaining family or other personal relationships". In light of this, a decision would need to be taken whether to pause the assessment until she has undertaken EOP, or to go ahead and complete a care and support plan and subsequently consider the impact of the EOP at the review stage.

If Ms W is potentially eligible for exercise on prescription but refuses to discuss this with her GP, and thus would not obtain the benefits that this would provide in enhancing her social interactions, the duty upon the local authority to meet her eligible needs in relation to reducing social isolation remains.

Ms W was provided with a tenancy in her current housing association flat several years ago, following a hospital admission. At the time there was concern that her existing old and dilapidated accommodation combined with her hoarding behaviour posed a serious fire risk. By meeting some of her needs under the Housing Act 1996, this risk was diminished. Although this was prior to the Care Act, the same would apply if this were the case now.

Charging and the duty to meet eligible needs

Ms W will not be charged as she is on benefits.

Meeting non-eligible needs

A possible scenario with Ms W is that she does not meet the eligibility criteria because she has inabilities only in relation to one specified outcome. For example, this would be the case if it was concluded that her limited social contact did not have a significant impact on her wellbeing. In these circumstances the only specified outcome that applied would be "[f] maintaining a habitable home environment". This means she would not meet the eligibility criteria. However, the local authority may want to find a way of continuing to work with her and keep her engaged, and to do so it could use its power to meet her single need to develop social contact.

Requirements that apply when needs are not going to be met

A possible scenario is that the care and support need she doesn't want met is determined as non-eligible. It could be concluded that she is unable to keep the flat "sufficiently clean and maintained to be safe" in the sense that she is in danger of tripping over or books falling on her, but there is no reason to believe that there is a fire risk and consequently the impact on her wellbeing is not significant. In these circumstances where Ms W does not want this need met, there would be no reason for the local authority to exercise its power to meet this need.

A written explanation is technically required but the general principle of proportionality ought to apply in relation to the reasons for not meeting the need. However, clear information and advice about minimising hazards arguably ought to be given. Ms W may not follow the advice, but it could be useful to refer to should Ms W need to be reassessed in the future.

The timing of the financial assessment

A financial assessment would probably not be initiated at an early stage for Ms W. Her circumstances indicate that she is living on sufficiently low income for her to not be charged, and therefore she would meet the qualifying conditions for care and support from the local authority in this respect.

Mrs O

Summary of assessment and eligibility determination

Mrs O provides necessary care to her husband who is a problem drinker and periodically has episodes where his heavy drinking results in him being incontinent. She is separated from her husband who lives in a neighbouring borough. She also has three children to care for.

Eligible needs	*There are times when Mrs O will have difficulty in caring for her children and the stress of this has a significant impact on her emotional wellbeing.*
Desired outcomes	*Mrs O wants to continue to help her husband.*

Ordinary residence

The local authority responsible for meeting Mrs O's eligible needs is where Mr O is ordinarily resident.

Agreement by the individual to needs being met

Mrs O's preferred way of meeting her needs is through the allocation of a named social worker to talk through her problems with.

It may be suggested to her that the local authority would only offer her contact with the 'duty social worker', ie not by a named individual. If Mrs O doesn't agree to this, it doesn't mean that she is necessarily saying that this is an eligible need that she doesn't want the local authority to meet.

Charging and the duty to meet eligible needs

The local authority may decide not to charge Mrs O as she is a carer.

Meeting non-eligible needs

If Mrs O did not meet the eligibility criteria because it was concluded that she was not providing necessary care for Mr O, the local authority might conclude that it has no power to act, as under the Care Act as she would not have any support needs.

Requirements that apply when needs are not going to be met

If Mrs O did not meet the eligibility criteria because it was concluded that she was not providing necessary care, and the local authority decided that it had no power to respond to Mrs O under the Care Act, it could be concluded that there is no duty to provide a written explanation and information and advice. However, there is a general duty to provide information and advice about prevention and Mrs O should receive this.

Comment and analysis

Readers should note that what is set out in this section and the previous section is intended to show how the statutory guidance might be applied, and in doing so, what would be complex situations in real life have had to be simplified.

Ordinary residence

Although in most cases establishing ordinary residence should be straightforward, there is such a variety of circumstances that social workers are not expected to have all of the information at their fingertips. The statutory guidance provides help on what to do in most of the commonly encountered circumstances in Chapter 19 and Annex H, as follows:

- Persons of no settled residence – paragraph 19.44–46;
- Arranging care and support in another area, eg in a care home – paragraphs 19.47–59;
- Where a person goes into hospital, or other NHS accommodation – paragraphs 19.60–62;
- People who qualify for mental health after-care under section 117 of the Mental Health Act 1983 – paragraphs 19.63–69;
- People who are temporarily away from the local authority in which they are ordinarily resident – paragraphs 19.70–71;
- People with more than one home – paragraphs 19.72–74;
- Self-funders who move into residential care in another area and at a later stage their financial resources reduce to a level where they would qualify for help from a local authority – Annex H paragraph 21–23.

The application of the statutory guidance was straightforward for Ms W and Mrs O. But in situations such as where Mr K goes to live with his daughter for an indefinite period, it would need to be established whether he has the stronger link with the property where he was living or where he is now living with his daughter. Where local authorities cannot agree they must follow the Care and Support (Disputes Between Local Authorities) Regulations 2014.

Agreement by the individual to needs being met

This step is intended to clarify and agree with the individual what eligible needs they want met before proceeding to care and/or support planning. In most cases the individual will want all of their eligible needs met, but there will be some circumstances where they may have eligible needs that they don't want help in meeting, such as Ms W.

Social workers need to be careful to distinguish between an individual not agreeing to have a need met, and being determined to have their need met in accordance with a preference that the local authority will not fund, as with Mr K and Ms O. It may be possible that their preference can be achieved by using a direct payment plus a top-up.

Where the social worker who undertook the assessment and eligibility determination undertakes the care and/or support planning, this step will just be part of the conversation about the care and/or support plan. However, where care and/or support planning is undertaken by a different team or by an external organisation, it is essential to clearly document this step and the conclusion.

Needs being met by a carer

The application of the duty on the local authority to meet any needs being met by a carer would seem to be straightforward to apply. The principle is clear, but there will be many circumstances where the willingness of the carer to continue caring, and in some circumstances their ability to continue doing so, may well depend on how their own support needs are met. Also the extent to which they are able to provide necessary care to the adult may be variable, and its continuation may be precarious, hence the statement in paragraph 10.26 of the statutory guidance which says that the local authority "should consider putting in place plans to respond to any breakdown in the caring relationship".

With Mr K it could make sense to establish what help he would need to order shopping to be delivered, in the event of his daughter not being available. However, any contingencies plan, like any part of a care and support plan, has to be agreed by the adult.

Care and support needs being met by other services

The Care Act is unequivocal that local authorities cannot meet any care and support needs that are the responsibility of the NHS, although the statutory guidance does allow some minor health needs to be met. It is intended that the distinction between social care and healthcare is clear-cut; however there are circumstances where this is not the case and the statutory guidance provides no guidance for these. This is considered in more detail in Chapter 12, including its application to Ms W's circumstances.

If an individual meets the eligibility criteria in part because of inabilities in relation to 'maintaining a habitable home environment', it may be that alternative accommodation would be identified as one of the ways of meeting their needs, as had been the case for Ms W when she was rehoused into her current accommodation. Paragraph 15.51 of the statutory guidance adds to the legal boundary that is clarified in section 23 of the Care Act, by stating: "Where a local authority is required to meet accommodation related needs under housing legislation as set out in the Housing Act 1996 or under any other legislation specified in regulations (and in the case of 2 tier authorities it would include 'another local authority') then the local authority must meet those needs under that housing legislation."

In considering the relationship with other services, it is important to note paragraph 10.25 of the statutory guidance, which states that the "duty to meet eligible needs is not discharged just because a person has another entitlement to a different service which could meet those needs, but of which they are not availing themselves". So if Ms W had refused the offer of her existing flat, the duty to meet her needs to maintain a habitable home environment would remain.

Charging and the duty to meet eligible needs

The charging issues are straightforward for Ms W because she is not a self-funder. In Mrs O's case it is possible that she would not be charged as she is a carer. In both cases there is therefore a duty to meet needs because there is no charge.

If Mr K is a self-funder, the local authority has a duty to meet his needs only if he asks them to. There is no requirement on the local authority to help self-funders to decide whether or not it will be advantageous for arrangements to be made for them by the local authority. There is a general duty to ensure that information and advice is provided by the local authority on "how to access independent financial advice on matters relating to care and support" (paragraph 3.23), and it may be appropriate to suggest that Mr K seek such advice.

Meeting non-eligible needs

Most local authorities have developed a local policy to provide guidance on how they will exercise their power to meet care and support needs that are not eligible. The statutory guidance has little to say about how non-eligible needs should be met, except to specify that the constraints that apply to eligible needs mostly apply to non-eligible needs.

As a minimum, local policies ought to allow for exceptional circumstances on a case-by-case basis. However, some local authorities have developed more comprehensive policies that set out in detail what non-eligible needs will be met. There are others that have redesigned their whole approach to have a strong preventative emphasis, and this informs how they address non-eligible needs.

Requirements that apply when needs are not going to be met

The three case examples demonstrate that there is a wide range of circumstances where a local authority will have to consider whether to exercise its power in meeting non-eligible needs.

With Mr K one of the possible scenarios is that he would not get help with his desired outcome of going to the jazz club. The indications are that he would not go if he has to travel to the jazz club by bus. So if his difficulties with public transport are deemed as a non-eligible need because it is decided that he is able to travel on a bus, the local authority has to either use its power to meet this need or explain in writing to Mr K why it will not do so.

One of the scenarios for Ms W demonstrates a set of circumstances whereby she has a possible non-eligible need (albeit one that she doesn't want met). The consequence of this is that she would not meet the eligibility criteria, because she has only one other need that meets the first two conditions of the eligibility determination. However, the local authority could use its power to meet her single need of not being able to develop social contacts.

For Mr K and Ms W, if the local authority decided not to use its power to meet their non-eligible needs it would have to give reasons and put them in writing. With Mr K this would be included in a statement that says why he meets the eligibility criteria (as he has other needs that meet the criteria), but for Ms W this would be in a statement giving the reasons why she did not meet the eligibility criteria. In both cases tailored information and advice must be provided in relation to the needs that are not eligible. In Mr K's case this statement could be included in his care and support plan.

In the scenario where it is decided that Mrs O is not providing necessary care, the question arises as to whether she can be regarded as having any support needs at all. It might be argued that as she does not have support needs they cannot be deemed as non-eligible, therefore the local authority cannot use its powers to meet her needs.

Nevertheless, she will have received an eligibility determination, so she would be entitled to a written explanation and information and advice.

Many situations where non-eligible needs are being considered can be complex because they require the exercise of professional judgement and expertise in pulling together various strands of the statutory guidance.

The timing of the financial assessment

The relationship between deciding how to apply the duty to meet needs and financial assessment is a bit 'chicken-and-egg'. People with care and support needs may be uncertain about what they want to happen next until they know how much it is going to cost, but the local authority can't confirm whether it has a duty to meet a person's eligible needs until there is agreement from the individual that they want their needs to be met.

To minimise the uncertainties, what usually happens is that the process of financial assessment takes place in parallel with the processes of assessment of needs, eligibility determination and care and support planning. Sometimes it will be necessary to pause the financial assessment because it must not formally be concluded until eligibility has been determined.

Individuals ought to be aware from an early stage in the assessment process that should their needs be met by the local authority, they may have to pay a contribution or possibly the whole cost. However, they won't know exactly how much they will have to pay until a financial assessment is completed (assuming that what is to be provided is chargeable).

Understandably there will be many people who will be reluctant to proceed with care and support planning until they have a better idea about how much it is going to cost them. It may well be that some people will choose not to have their needs met by the local authority once they have this information.

Sections 17 (1–4) of the Care Act make it clear that a financial assessment takes place after eligibility has been determined. Many local authorities have taken this to mean that although the financial assessment cannot be concluded until this decision has been made, it can commence at an earlier stage and often the financial assessment runs concurrently with the needs assessment. This means that the individual can be advised of what they are going to be charged very shortly after eligibility has been determined, and they can then confirm (or otherwise) that they want the local authority to meet their needs. At this point the duty to meet needs is triggered and care and support planning can commence.

This was not an issue for Ms W or Mrs O, but for anyone who is likely to have to pay for some or all of the cost of meeting their needs such as Mr K it is of crucial importance.

Conclusion

For those people whose needs are going to be met by the local authority, they will experience the tasks described in this chapter as an interface between the determination of eligibility and the commencement of care and support planning. For those whose needs are not going to be met, it will be the end-point of their involvement with the local authority – unless there are also safeguarding issues.

Because of the different ways that local authorities manage the processes of eligibility determination and care and support planning, people whose needs are going to be met will experience the interface tasks undertaken between these two processes differently. Some local authorities undertake all of the main processes of assessment, eligibility determination and care and support planning in-house, whereas there are others that contract out care and support planning to independent agencies. Where local authorities do everything, there will be some circumstances where the adult and carer will have the same social worker throughout, and others where there is change of worker at various stages, eg if they start out in hospital or first go through reablement. Also, regardless of how a local authority manages these processes there will be some people who wish to take the lead for themselves with their own care and support planning.

It is essential for all concerned that there is clarity and a good understanding of the decisions that are being made. It is at this stage that commitment is being made to meets needs, and for many people what transpires from this commitment can be life-changing, and it may also represent a significant cost to the local authority and to the adult in some cases.

For some people the decision about what needs are going to be met will closely match the eligible needs that were mapped out through the eligibility determination process. But for many this will not be the case. As we have seen there are some circumstances where there is no duty to meet eligible needs and also there are some eligible needs that individuals don't want met.

Equally important is helping people who are not going to have any of their care and support needs met, to understand why. Saying 'no' can often be a difficult task and requires a high degree of professionalism and good communication skills. However good the local processes are for managing this task, professional skills are required in providing both an explanation that is sensitive to the individual's circumstances and also information and advice about reducing and delaying needs that is personal and specific.

Those people whose needs are going to be met will move on to the next stage of care and support planning. The decision about what care and support needs are to be met is the culmination of what most people will experience as an 'assessment'. They will not necessarily have appreciated all of the intricacies of the needs assessment, eligibility determination and the consideration of the duty and/or power to meet needs. In maintaining a person-centred approach the skilled social worker will have guided the individual, their carer and their families through what can be a complex process, in such a way that it has kept them involved and informed and results in them being satisfied with the decision about what needs are to be met.

Readers will have noted that there is no 'interface stage' described in the statutory guidance. The author hopes that by setting out the content in this way, the case is made for a set of decision-making tasks that focus on enabling adults and carers to better understand if and how their needs might be met.

5 Charging and financial assessment

Introduction

Local authorities are able to charge adults for meeting some care and support needs. They are also able to charge carers for meeting some support needs. Where a charge is going to be made, a financial assessment must be undertaken to determine whether the individual has to pay all of the charge, a proportion of it, or will not have to pay anything.

This chapter considers (1) what local authorities may and may not charge for, and how the charging 'rules' vary according to the different ways that needs can be met and (2) how an individual's financial resources effect how much they will pay, and how financial assessments are to be used to calculate this.

Social workers need to have a good understanding of the principles of charging, in particular what can and cannot be charged for. The essentials of the financial assessment process are relatively straightforward, and social workers need to know enough about how it works to initiate the process and signpost people to sources of specialist information and advice. However, some aspects of financial assessment can be complex, and within local authorities there are specialist staff who have a fuller understanding of the detail set out in the statutory guidance whose role is to work with social workers to resolve these complexities.

This chapter comprises the following sections:

- **Charging and financial assessment prior to April 2015**
- **Key terms and definitions**
- **The essential features of charging and financial assessment**

- **Charging**
- **Financial assessment**
- **Deferred payment agreements**
- **Applying charging and financial assessment using case examples**
- **Conclusion.**

There is a brief window in the care and support journey for reaching a conclusion on if, and how much, an individual will pay. This has to take place between the eligibility determination and the decision about how the local authority is going to apply its duty/power to meet the individual's needs. People should know how much they will have to pay before a care and support plan is put in place, the main exception being where urgent needs are being met.

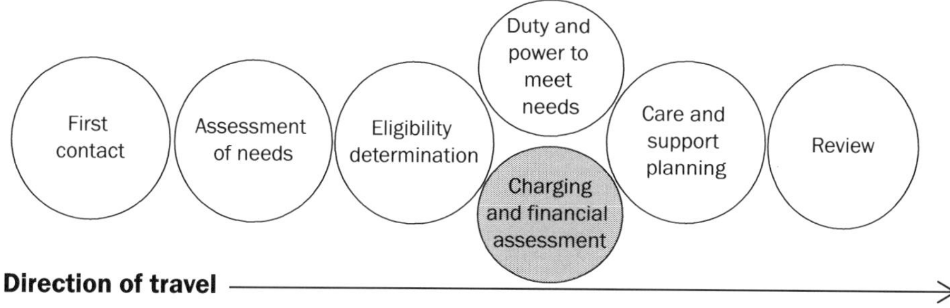

Figure 5.1 *The care and support journey*

Charging and financial assessment prior to April 2015

The Care Act and the Regulations broadly recreate the pre-April 2015 framework for financial assessment and charging – but with some important changes.

The following guidance no longer applies:

- Charging for Residential Accommodation Guidance (CRAG) 2014;
- Fairer Charging Policies for Home Care and other non-residential Social Services (2013).

Key terms and definitions

Key term	Care Act 2014	The Care and Support (Charging and Assessment of Resources) Regulations 2014	The Care and Support Statutory Guidance (revised 2017)
Power to charge	The power to charge both adults and carers is set out in section 14. This section provides for limitations in specific respects to this power, to be made in the Regulations.	Sets out the power of the local authority to charge for care and support, under the following headings in Part 2: • Services to be provided free of charge. • Adults to whom services are to be provided free of charge. • Costs of putting in place arrangements to meet needs. • Personal expenses allowance for residents or temporary residents provided with accommodation in a care home. • Minimum income guaranteed amount for other adults and carers whose needs are being met otherwise than by the provision of accommodation in a care home. • Power of the local authority to financially assess and charge a short-term resident as if the resident is receiving care and support other than the provision of accommodation in a care home.	Paragraph 8.2 summarises the power to charge as follows: "Where a local authority arranges care and support to meet a person's needs, it may charge the adult, except where the local authority is required to arrange care and support free of charge."
Financial assessment	The local authority's duties in this respect are set out in section 17 titled "Assessment of financial resources"	Section 9 specifies that a "local authority must carry out a financial assessment under section 17" in accordance with the following parts of the Regulations: Part 3 – Assessment of financial resources Part 4 – Treatment and calculation of income Part 5 – Treatment and calculation of capital	Paragraph 8.16 states that a local authority "must carry out a financial assessment of what the person can afford to pay and... it must give a written record of that assessment to the person". The exception to this duty is where the local authority is satisfied

Key term	Care Act 2014	The Care and Support (Charging and Assessment of Resources) Regulations 2014	The Care and Support Statutory Guidance (revised 2017)
			that the person can afford the charges, and in these circumstances "a local authority may choose to treat a person as if a financial assessment had been carried out" (paragraph 8.22)

Key term	Care Act 2014	The Care and Support (Deferred Payment) Regulations 2014	The Care and Support Statutory Guidance (revised 2017)
Deferred payment agreement	This provision enables people to defer paying for the cost of a care home, as set out in sections 34 and 35.	These regulations set out the quantification of the deferred amount, the obtaining security for that amount, when the deferred amount is to be paid, and the terms to be included in every deferred payment agreement.	Paragraph 9.7 states: "Deferred payment agreements are designed to prevent people from being forced to sell their home in their lifetime to meet the cost of their care." They must be offered to people who meet the specified criteria.

The essential features of charging and financial assessment

1. The Care Act sets out a single legal framework for charging adults for meeting their care and support needs, and charging carers for meeting their support needs.
2. A local authority can decide what types of care and support it wishes to charge for, and where it does charge it must have a Care Act compliant charging policy.
3. Daily living costs such as rent, food and utilities are usually outside of the scope of charging policies.
4. Where the local authority decides to charge people for meeting care and support needs, or support needs (in the case of a carer), it must have regard to the principles outlined in the statutory guidance.
5. Certain types of care and support must be provided free of charge.
6. Assessment of needs and care and support planning cannot be charged for.

7. The detail of how to charge is different depending on whether someone is receiving care in a care home or at home, although there are common elements.
8. A local authority must not charge more than the cost it incurs in meeting the assessed needs of the person.
9. If a local authority has chosen to charge a person, it must undertake a financial assessment. In some circumstances a 'light-touch' financial assessment will be appropriate, eg where the local authority is satisfied that the person can afford the charges.
10. A financial assessment takes into account both capital and income.
11. People will either pay the full cost, receive some financial support based on a means-test or be entitled to free care.
12. Particular arrangements apply where the individual lacks capacity to give consent to a financial assessment.
13. A written record of the financial assessment must be given to the individual concerned.
14. When a person is receiving care in a care home there are a range of ways of paying for this care, including a deferred payment agreement.

Charging

Although one of the main purposes of charging is to collect income for the local authority, the way that it is done should be in accordance with the overall aims of the Care Act.

Both the charging and financial assessment processes are intended to be clearer and fairer. Paragraph 8.2 of the statutory guidance states that the way the system works should be "clear and transparent" and "reduce the variation in the way people are assessed and charged", and that the "overarching principle is that people should only be required to pay what they can afford".

Other principles included in paragraph 8.2 that apply to the way that charging is undertaken are promoting "wellbeing, social inclusion, and support the vision of personalisation, independence, choice and control", being "person-focused" and supporting people "who wish to stay in or take up employment, education or training or plan for the future costs of meeting their needs to do so".

Charging policy

Section 14 (1) of the Care Act states that a local authority "may make a charge for meeting needs under sections 18 to 20", ie it is a power not a duty. Local authorities are not required to charge for meeting the care and support needs of adults, the support needs of carers or for any other services that might be provided to prevent, reduce or delay needs.

Where a local authority does decide to charge to meet care and/or support needs, paragraph 8.2 of the statutory guidance states that the local authority "must follow the Care and Support (Charging and Assessment of Resources) regulations and have regard to the guidance".

Where there is going to be a charge "a local authority must not charge more than it costs to provide or arrange for the service, facility or resource" (paragraph 2.59, statutory guidance).

For people whose needs are met in a care home the Regulations set out a single model for charging. But for people who have their needs met by any other means, paragraph 8.45 of the statutory guidance states that local authorities "should develop and maintain a policy on how they wish to apply this discretion locally". Many local authorities produce a single document that sets out how charging and financial assessment will be applied, including where they have made local policy decisions.

Services that are to be provided free of charge

Following the Care and Support (Charging and Assessment of Resources) Regulations 2014, paragraph 8.14 of the statutory guidance specifies that the "local authority must not charge for certain types of care and support which must be arranged free", as follows:

- intermediate care including reablement (for up to six weeks);
- community equipment and minor adaptations (a minor adaptation is one costing up to £1,000);
- care and support provided to people with Creuzfeldt Jacob Disease (CJD);
- after care/support provided under section 117of the Mental Health Act 1983;
- services that the NHS has a duty to provide, including continuing healthcare;
- any service that the local authority is under a duty to provide through other legislation;
- assessment of needs and care and support planning.

Exercising discretion to charge

Each local authority will have made policy decisions about what they are and are not going to charge for. These are often set out in a single policy document making it clear that the local authority will be charging for meeting any care and support needs where the local authority incurs a cost. The policy documents will also outline how the local authority has decided to exercise its discretion about charging, especially in relation to preventative services, meeting the support needs of carers, and arranging care and support for self-funders.

Regulation 3 (1) of the Care and Support (Preventing Needs for Care and Support) Regulations 2014 states that local authorities may charge for certain preventative provision. It is recognised in the statutory guidance that it can be necessary to charge for such provision, and in paragraph 2.58 local authorities are advised that they "should take reasonable steps to ensure that any charge is affordable for the person concerned", and goes on to say that in doing so the local authority should not necessarily apply "the method of the financial assessment used for mainstream charging purposes... (because) the use of such a process is likely to be disproportionate".

Local authorities have the power to charge carers when they intend to meet any eligible and non-eligible needs. Many local authorities have made a policy decision not to charge carers, taking heed of paragraph 8.51 of the statutory guidance that states "it is very unlikely to be efficient to systematically charge carers for meeting their eligible needs". However, if a local authority does decide to charge carers, it may not charge the carer for 'respite care'. In paragraph 8.55 it is made clear that where a carer's needs are partly being met by "arranging time away from the person they care for… such services would be provided direct to the cared-for person… the local authority may not charge the carer for these services". In these circumstances the charge applies to the cared-for person who receives the service.

Where an adult is receiving respite care and where this is for a continuous period not exceeding eight weeks, "a local authority may choose to assess and charge them based on the rules for care or support arranged other than in a care home" (paragraph 8.34). This discretion in the application of the charging rules applies to any period of short-term residential care of up to eight weeks, for whatever reason. Also, where the adult is a temporary resident for a period of up to 52 weeks and is expected to return home, "their main or only home is usually disregarded in the assessment of whether and what they can afford to pay" (paragraph 8.34).

Where a self-funder asks the local authority to arrange their care and support, the local authority may charge an arrangement fee that equates to the cost of making this arrangement (see paragraphs 8.57–8). In many local authorities this is a fixed rate, and is not dependent on the nature or the extent of the care and support being arranged. However, the "ability to charge the arrangement fee applies only to circumstances when the authority is required to meet needs" (paragraph 8.59).

Financial assessment

The main tasks for social workers are to initiate the financial assessment process and to help people to understand how it applies to their circumstances.

Deciding when a 'light-touch' assessment is appropriate

Paragraph 8.22 of the statutory guidance states "a local authority may choose to treat a person as if a financial assessment had been carried out".

This can happen where a person can demonstrate that they have significant financial resources such that they would pay the full cost. At the other end of the scale this applies where it is clear that the individual could not contribute anything towards their care and support costs.

A 'light-touch' assessment cannot happen where someone does not agree with the charges being proposed.

Before going ahead with a 'light-touch' assessment, the local authority must have evidence that any such charge can be afforded by the adult or carer. Paragraph 8.24 gives the following examples of evidence that a person can afford to pay the charge:

- property clearly worth more than the upper capital limit, where they are the sole owner or it is clear what their share is;
- savings clearly worth more than the upper capital limit;
- sufficient income left following the charge due.

A 'light-touch' assessment can also take place where the charge for what the individual is going to receive is going to be very low, and it is considered that a full financial assessment would be disproportionate. This may often apply for any charges that are payable by a carer. Certain types of benefit are sufficient evidence that a person would not pay any contribution, eg Jobseeker's Allowance.

If someone owns their own home and has needs that are likely to be best met through being placed in a care home, then it is likely this person will be a self-funder and therefore a 'light-touch' assessment would apply. However, where someone owns their own home and their needs are to be met through non-residential care and support, then they may not be a self-funder because a person's home cannot be included in the determination of their capital in these circumstances.

In any of these circumstances the individual "has the right to request a full financial assessment should they so wish" (paragraph 8.26). This paragraph also specifies that it should be ensured that the individual has "access to sufficient information and advice". The point behind this is that people need to be comfortable about how their financial means are being assessed, and be reassured that they can get advice and information from a range of sources, both through the local authority and from independent organisations.

Assessment of capital and income

In a financial assessment, both capital and income must be assessed, some of which will be disregarded.

The income people get from any employment must be disregarded, but income from savings, pensions and most benefits is taken into account. There are other sources of income that also must be disregarded, and these are set out in Annex B of the statutory guidance. Local authorities have the discretion to add some additional disregards, eg some local authorities have more generous allowances for people over 85.

An important principle is that a person's income must not be below a certain level after charges have been deducted. Where a person is in a care home this level is set by the Personal Expenses Allowance (PEA). For people whose care and support needs are being met in settings other than a care home, the Regulations specify a minimum income guarantee, and this amount must be at least the equivalent of the value of income support or the 'guaranteed credit' element of Pension Credit plus a minimum buffer of 25 per cent.

The main types of capital that are assessed are property and savings. Most other types of capital that a person may have, eg antiques, are disregarded. There is a comprehensive list of capital that must be disregarded that are set out in Annex B of the statutory guidance. The value of a person's own home is disregarded when they are living in it.

Paragraph 8.20 of the statutory guidance specifies that a person may be charged to pay a proportion of their care and support costs where they have "capital at or below the upper capital limit (currently £23,250 in the financial year ending March 2017), but more than the lower capital limit (currently £14,250)". The rate of this contribution is fixed at £1 per week for every £250 in capital between the upper capital limit and the lower capital limit. Sometimes the accountancy term of 'tariff income' is used to describe this rate.

If the person has capital above the upper capital limit of £23,250 they will pay the full cost, and if it is below the lower capital limit of £14,250, they will not have to pay anything from their capital towards the cost of their care.

Paragraph 8.8 of the statutory guidance states that a local authority "has no power to assess couples or civil partners according to their joint resources". Where there are joint assets the financial assessment can take into account the share belonging to the person needing care and support, and it is assumed that their share is 50 per cent unless it is shown otherwise. For example, where two people have a joint savings account, and one of them is financially assessed, then only half of the value of the savings can be considered.

Where a person makes a gift of money or property to family or friends with the intention of deliberately avoided paying for care and support costs, paragraph 8.28 of the statutory guidance states that "the local authority may either charge the person as if they still possessed the asset or, if the asset has been transferred to someone else, seek to recover the lost income from charges from that person". Comprehensive guidance on what is described as 'deprivation of assets' is set out in Annex E of the statutory guidance. In addition to deliberately depriving themselves of capital it is also possible for a person to deliberately deprive themselves of income. An example given in paragraph 13 of Annex E is that "they could give away or sell the right to an income from an occupational pension".

Taking account of the value of a home that is owned by an adult receiving care and support

The value of a home that is owned by an adult receiving care and support is taken into account only when they are permanently placed in a care home. For people who are receiving care and support in any other setting, it is disregarded. This is set out in paragraph 8.43 of the statutory guidance that states "the financial assessment of their capital must exclude the value of the property which they occupy as their main or only home".

There are also some circumstances where the value of a property must be disregarded when an individual is permanently placed in a care home. In paragraph 34.3 (c) of Annex B of the statutory guidance it sets out that this disregard applies when any of the following are living in a home that the person with care and support needs owns:

- a resident's partner, former partner or civil partner, except where they are estranged;
- a lone parent who is the person's estranged or divorced partner;
- a relative who is over 60, under 18 or incapacitated.

The value of a person's home must be disregarded for the first 12 weeks, and also there are other circumstances where longer disregards apply to other sources of capital and income (as set out in Annex B, paragraphs 47 and 48).

Paragraph 42 in Annex B states that there are circumstances where the local authority has discretion to disregard the value of a property, eg where it "is the sole residence of someone who has given up their own home in order to care for the person who is now in a care home or is perhaps the elderly companion of the person".

Arrangements that apply where the individual lacks capacity to give consent to a financial assessment

Paragraph 8.43 of the statutory guidance states that "local authorities should work with someone who has the legal authority to make financial decisions on behalf of a person who lacks capacity", where this is possible. If there is nobody who already has this legal authority then a family member could apply for a property and affairs deputyship to the Court of Protection, which will enable the appointed person to access information about bank accounts and financial affairs. Where there is no family member, the local authority can apply for this.

Information and advice

For many people the financial assessment process will be relatively straightforward. Where it is complex, local authority financial assessment specialists will be able to advise social workers, and often people with care and support needs can contact these specialists directly to get clarification.

Most people will want to know how much they are going to be charged, although not everyone wants to know how it is calculated. Where they do want to know how it is calculated, social workers may need to refer people to other sources of information, such as the local authority website (or in the form of a printout where they do not have internet access). Also, individuals can usually contact financial assessment specialists within the local authority who will provide detailed information and advice.

There will also be circumstances where the complexities of a person's circumstances are such that they ought to be advised to seek independent financial information and advice. For example, the pension flexibilities introduced in 2015 mean that people can choose to take some of their occupational pension fund as a lump sum, and in some circumstances they could unwittingly deprive themselves of an asset.

Putting it in writing

Where a full financial assessment has taken place, the local authority must give a written record of that assessment to the person concerned. This duty does not apply to a 'light-touch' assessment.

Paragraph 8.16 of the statutory guidance states it "should explain how the assessment has been carried out, what the charge will be and how often it will be made, and if there is any fluctuation in charges, the reason". This paragraph allows for this to be done "via online means".

Deferred payment agreements

Deferred payment agreements are designed to prevent people from being forced to sell their home in their lifetime to meet the cost of their care, when they go into a care home. By taking out a deferred payment agreement (DPA), a person can 'defer' or delay paying the costs of their care home until a later date.

A deferral can last until death; however, people may choose to use a deferred payment agreement as a 'bridging loan' to give them the time and flexibility to sell their home when they choose to do so.

'Top-ups' can be included in a DPA to enable individuals to afford a care home that charges more than the standard local authority rate.

A DPA must be offered to people who meet the specified criteria, and the local authority has the discretion to provide a DPA where all of the criteria are not met.

Social workers ought to be able to explain the essentials to people who might qualify, know how to obtain further information and be able to signpost them to further information where appropriate.

Paragraph 9.26 sets out the information and advice people must have. This is summarised as follows:

- the criteria for obtaining a DPA and the requirements;
- interest and admin charges;
- the types of security that the authority is prepared to accept;
- planning how to use, maintain and insure their property;
- implications for income, benefit entitlements and charging;
- termination of the DPA and options for repayment;
- what happens if the person doesn't repay;
- the overall advantages and disadvantages of DPA;
- how to obtain independent financial advice.

Eligibility for a DPA

The Regulations specify that a DPA must be offered to anybody who meets all three of the following criteria:

a) whose needs are to be met by the provision of care in a care home;

b) who has less than the upper capital limit in assets – excluding the value of their home;

c) whose home is not occupied by any of the following:

  - a resident's partner, former partner or civil partner (except where estranged);
  - a lone parent who is the claimant's estranged or divorced partner;
  - a relative over 60, under 18 or incapacitated.

In addition the person has to be able to provide adequate security.

It should be noted that individuals do not have to give an explanation about why they want a DPA.

Local authorities may offer DPAs to others who don't meet the criteria. Paragraph 9.8 of the statutory guidance suggests examples of the circumstances that a local authority may wish to consider, as follows:

- meeting care costs would leave someone with very few accessible assets (this might include assets which cannot quickly/easily be liquidated or converted to cash);
- where someone would like to use wealth tied up in their home to fund more than just their core care costs and to purchase affordable top-ups;
- where someone has any other accessible means to help them meet the cost of their care and support;
- if a person is narrowly not entitled to a deferred payment agreement given the criteria, eg because they have slightly more than the £23,250 asset threshold.

Local authorities have the discretion to offer a DPA to people in supported living accommodation, but paragraph 9.9 of the statutory guidance states that this should not happen "unless the person intends to retain their former home and pay the associated care and accommodation rental costs from their deferred payment".

Circumstances where the local authority may refuse a request for a DPA

To provide local authorities with a reasonable safeguard against default or non-repayment of debt, they can refuse a DPA. Paragraph 9.12 of the statutory guidance allows for this to take place in any of the following circumstances:

- the local authority is unable to secure a first mortgage charge on the property;
- someone wishes to defer a larger amount than they can sustainably afford;
- a person's property is uninsurable and they are unable to provide adequate security.

Determining how much can be deferred

Paragraph 9.34 of the statutory guidance sets out "three elements (that) will dictate how much a person will defer", as follows:

- the amount of equity a person has available in their chosen form of security (usually their property);
- the amount a person is contributing to their care costs from other sources, including income and (where they choose to) any contribution from savings, a financial product or a third party;
- the total care costs a person will face, including any top-ups the person might be seeking.

Each of these is described in more detail in paragraphs 9.36–39 of the statutory guidance.

Applying charging and financial assessment using case examples

This section illustrates and analyses some of the key elements of the processes described in this chapter that are of particular relevance for social workers.

This stage of the care and support journey proceeds in parallel with the consideration of the duty to meet needs, and there is also some overlap with assessment and eligibility determination.

The scenarios for Mr K, Ms W and Mr O are those where they meet the eligibility criteria and there are some non-eligible needs.

The analysis and case examples are set out under the following headings:

- **Charging**
- **Financial assessment**
- **Deferred payment agreements.**

Mr K

Summary of assessment and eligibility determination

Mr K has COPD (Chronic Obstructive Pulmonary Disease) and arthritis. His daughter (Ms K) has been cooking meals for him but is no longer willing to do so, although she is willing to do her father's shopping. Mr K pays a neighbour to help with the cleaning and laundry. He is unable to go to a jazz club that he used to attend regularly, because he cannot use public transport and he cannot use the toilet without someone's help. Ms K has declined to have a carer's assessment so she will not receive a carer's support plan.

Eligible needs	• *The effect of Mr K being unable to cook for himself and do his cleaning and laundry has a significant impact on his physical wellbeing and also control over his day-to-day life.* • *Not being able to go to the jazz club because he cannot use public transport and he cannot use the toilet without someone's help has a significant impact on his wellbeing in relation to participation in recreational activities.*
Desired outcomes	• *He wants someone to come in every day and prepare him a home-cooked meal in the way that his daughter has been doing.* • *Cleaning and laundry – he wants to continue to employ his neighbour to do this.* • *Attending the local jazz club regularly.*
Eligible needs that the carer has agreed to meet	*Shopping (it has not been conclusively determined that Mr K could not do online shopping by himself).*

Charging

To improve Mr K's wellbeing he will require care and support to enable him to have a cooked meal, do his laundry, essential cleaning and facilitate attendance at the jazz club. Local authorities are permitted to charge to provide this type of care and support, and most choose to do so.

To enable him to have a cooked meal the only offer from the local authority may be home meals or frozen meals, for which he would have to pay the non-assessed flat rate.

He has been provided with equipment to help him eat more easily and use the bath safely. This equipment was provided free of charge.

He has also already received reablement, and as part of this he has been receiving some help with meal preparation and doing the laundry. He was not charged for this, as local authorities are not permitted to charge for needs met during the provision of reablement.

If Mr K is a self-funder, the local authority has the power to charge a fee for arranging his care and support.

Alternative scenario

If his needs in relation to attending the local jazz club were considered non-eligible, the local authority could decide to meet them. This may incur a cost, and if so it will probably be chargeable in his particular local authority.

Financial assessment

If Mr K has savings that are between the upper capital limit and lower capital limit he will need to have a full financial assessment, and part of his contribution towards the cost of his care and support will be calculated using the rate of £1 for every £250 in savings. If he has an occupational pension as well as his state pension, he may also pay a proportion of his income towards the cost of his care if his total income exceeds the level of the minimum income guarantee.

If Mr K's needs change and he decides to go into a care home, the new financial assessment would take into consideration the value of the house he lives in if he owns it. He could probably opt for a 'light-touch' assessment, if it is likely that the value of his home would result in him being a self-funder.

It is possible that Mr K could have decided to give his house to his daughter several years ago. His intention may have been to minimise the amount of inheritance tax due upon his death. If he did go into a care home, the local authority would not take the value of his home into account as it seems reasonably clear that he did not act deliberately to deprive himself of this asset. However, if he bought his daughter a car from his savings the week before being admitted to a care home, this is likely to be considered as deliberately depriving himself of assets, and the local authority may wish to recover its loss of income as a result of this from the daughter. In circumstances where individuals own a property they ought to be advised at an early stage to consider seeking independent financial advice and information.

Deferred payment agreements

If Mr K decides to go into a care home, he could be considered for a deferred payment agreement if his savings are below the upper capital limit. For the purposes of determining eligibility for a DPA the value of his home is not taken into account.

It is possible that the value of Mr K's home is such that a DPA would be agreed that enables him to afford a care home where the fee is higher than what the local authority normally pays. This would mean that he could benefit from the additional facilities that this type of care home provides.

If Mr K had given his house to his daughter and she is now the owner, it may be possible to use the home as security if the daughter agrees to enter into a contract as a third-party guarantor.

Alternative scenario

If a DPA was agreed and Mr K's daughter moved into her father's house, when Mr K dies the daughter would no longer have a home as the property would need to be sold.

However, a DPA would be precluded if she was living in the house with him prior to him going into a care home and she was under 18, over 60 or has a condition that falls within the definition of 'incapacitated', as the value of the home cannot be taken into account in Mr K's financial assessment in these circumstances.

Ms W

Summary of assessment and eligibility determination

Ms W (aged 40) has psychotic depression and is socially isolated. The manager of the housing association flat where Ms W lives is concerned that there is a fire risk because of what is believed to be hoarding behaviour.

Desired outcomes	• *She feels regular exercise will improve her mental health and wellbeing.* • *She would like the type of casual social contact with people that she had when she had a job.* • *She does not want help with managing her collection of books and magazines.*
Eligibility	*The cumulative impact on her wellbeing of her social isolation and her hoarding behaviour.*

Charging

At this stage the only element of her possible care package that has been identified that could incur a cost is gym membership and help from a personal trainer. This may be a cost that is met by the NHS if she is eligible for exercise on prescription.

She is no longer subject to a section 117 after-care order, but if she was still subject to this order then the local authority would not be permitted to charge for her care package.

Financial assessment

A 'light-touch' assessment may be appropriate for Ms W because she is on basic benefits (Personal Independence Payment), and says she has no savings. Her father sends her money for birthdays and Christmas and pays for a mobile phone, but this would not be included in the financial assessment.

Alternative scenario

If Ms W was living with her father and he owned his home, and her father then went into a care home, the local authority would have to disregard the value of the property in calculating the parent's contribution to meeting the cost of his care. This disregard applies because Ms W qualifies as someone who is between the age of 18 and 60, and is 'incapacitated' (see paragraph 36 of Annex B).

Mrs O

Summary of assessment and eligibility determination

Mrs O provides necessary care to her husband who is a problem drinker and periodically has episodes where his heavy drinking results in him being incontinent. She is separated from her husband who lives in a neighbouring borough. She also has three children to care for.

Eligible needs	*There are times when Mrs O will have difficulty in caring for her children, and the stress of this has a significant impact on her emotional wellbeing.*
Desired outcomes	*Mrs O wants to continue to help her husband.*

Charging

If it was agreed that Mrs O be provided with support through her preferred option of named social worker, this would not usually be chargeable.

Even if it was deemed to be chargeable in principle, many local authorities have made a local policy decision not to charge carers.

Comment and analysis

Readers should note that what is set out in this section and the previous section is intended to show how the statutory guidance might be applied, and in doing so, what would be complex situations in real life have had to be simplified.

Charging

Local authorities do not have to charge for meeting a person's needs, but where they do so they must follow the Care and Support (Charging and Assessment of Resources) Regulations 2014. As far as the author is aware all local authorities in England have chosen to charge people whose needs are met in a care home. Prior to April 2015 local authorities were required to charge people whose needs were met in this way, and none of them have decided to cease charging.

Where there is discretion within the Regulations, most local authorities charge for meeting a person's care and support needs where they incur a cost in meeting their needs, unless they are prohibited from doing so. There would a charge for some of the care and support that Mr K needs, but he would not be charged for reablement and equipment to help him eat more easily and use the bath safely, as local authorities are not permitted to charge for these services.

In the list of what must not be charged for in paragraph 8.14 of the statutory guidance, it states that "assessment of needs and care and support planning may also not be charged for, since these processes do not constitute 'meeting needs' ".

However, local authorities can charge for arranging care and support for self-funders, as would be the case for Mr K if he went into residential care and is a self-funder. This charge is a one-off fee for brokerage (setting up a care package) and is not usually undertaken by social workers.

As is the case with Mr K many local authorities charge a flat rate for the provision of meals for people who are not in residential care. There is no specific provision for flat-rate charging in the Act, regulations or the statutory guidance. It was done this way prior to the Care Act and has continued.

Financial assessment

The financial assessment will usually be initiated at some point during the needs assessment, although it cannot be finalised until after it has been decided that the local authority is going to meet a person's needs, and that there will be a charge for the way that their needs are going to be met. The previous chapter showed how the amount a person would have to pay can influence their decision about what needs they want the local authority to meet.

Many local authorities have opted to develop 'light-touch' assessment processes, so social workers need to know how to determine whether a 'light-touch' financial assessment would be appropriate, or whether a full financial assessment will be required. This type of assessment might apply to Mr K if he went into residential care, as it is likely that the value of his home would result in him being a self-funder.

When social workers are initiating a financial assessment, there is usually a form (paper or electronic) to guide individuals through the process, and while these forms are self-explanatory many local authorities expect social workers to be able to explain how the process works and also how capital and income is taken into account and what is disregarded.

The extent to which social workers get involved in the detail of the financial assessment process varies. In some local authorities everything will be undertaken by specialist financial assessment staff, whereas in other local authorities social workers are expected to ensure that the necessary information is entered onto the form and to be able to explain the basics. These specialist staff will usually lead on situations where deprivation of assets is suspected, but social workers have a role in helping to identify these circumstances. For example, the social worker may become aware that an adult with care and support needs has given their home to a relative, and in these circumstances the local authority has to decide whether the individual has done so to deliberately avoid paying for care and support costs. However, there will be circumstances that social workers are not always going to be aware of, such as the scenario with Mr K where he sold his car to his daughter.

Deferred payment agreements

The key calculation is whether the local authority will receive the money that it is owed after the death of the person who has taken out a deferred payment agreement. This means that the value of the property has to be such that the eventual sale of the property will realise sufficient funds to cover the cost of the care home fees.

In many parts of the country a house that is in good condition will meet the anticipated costs of care. In low property value areas or where special circumstances apply (eg a house subject to coastal erosion), there may not be sufficient funds available from the future sale of the property. In these circumstances additional sources of security will be necessary for a DPA to be agreed. Examples of other forms of security are a third-party guarantor, a life-insurance policy or a valuable item such as a painting.

Social workers will not be expected to make these calculations. Their role is to alert individuals who are potentially eligible to the availability of this scheme. Most local authorities will expect social workers to know how to access information so that they can explain the basics of eligibility for the scheme.

Conclusion

Social workers have a vital role to play in ensuring that a timely financial assessment takes place, so that people can have their needs met without undue delay. This requires a good knowledge of how to apply charging policies and how to initiate a financial assessment. Social workers need to be able to provide basic advice and information to people and direct them to specialist sources of advice and information. It is also important to know how to link decisions about charging and financial assessment with decisions about the duty to meet needs (as described in Chapter 4).

By making sure that the financial assessment is initiated at the right time, and ensuring that people have the advice and information that they need to help them complete the process, this will contribute to minimising the anxieties that people will have about what they have to pay and it will also help to ensure that payment of financial contributions takes place efficiently.

Ideally the financial assessment should be completed before steps are taken to implement a care and support plan, but it will not always be possible to achieve this. For example, where there are urgent needs the financial assessment may not be completed until after a person's care and support needs have begun to be met. There will also be circumstances where there is a delay in meeting a person's needs because the financial assessment is complex, and in such circumstances the professional judgement may be that the commencement of the care and support plan cannot wait for the financial assessment to be completed, because the person's needs have become urgent. It is important that social workers take the lead in ensuring that any difficulties with the financial assessment are not detrimental to an individual's wellbeing.

There will be circumstances where changes take place at a later stage that affect the financial assessment. During care and support planning (or support planning for carers), additional potential costs may emerge in determining the detail of how a person's needs can be best met. For example, this can sometimes occur where the individual opts for a direct payment to pay for a personal assistant. However, any increase in the cost of the care and support package will only affect what the individual pays if he or she is a self-funder. Where the individual has been assessed to pay a contribution towards the cost of their care, this will not change. Direct payments are considered in the next chapter.

6 Care and support planning

Introduction

Care and/or support planning is the final step before arrangements are made to meet an individual's needs. The process is about giving the individual as much choice and control as possible in deciding how their needs are to be met, so that the plan is closely aligned to their desired outcomes and preferences.

This chapter describes how a plan should be developed in a person-centred way, and how it must be implemented within the constraints of the available funding and what is legal and appropriate. Reference will be made to Chapters 10, 11 and 12 of the statutory guidance.

In reality the elements of the plan are beginning to be developed as soon as first contact is made and the individual starts to explore how the local authority could help them. A plan will have been evolving throughout the needs or carer's assessment, eligibility determination and the process of deciding what needs are going to be met by the local authority. The views, wishes and feelings of the individual and their family will have been explored and taken into account in applying these processes.

The plan itself will summarise what has been decided in the previous stages, as well as setting out arrangements to meet the individual's care and/or support needs.

An essential part of the plan is the personal budget. This sets out the amount of money that the local authority has determined is required to meet the individual's needs. People have a choice about how this personal budget is to be managed, and this includes receiving a direct payment to purchase the services they need.

The chapter comprises the following sections:

- **Care and support planning prior to April 2015**
- **Key terms and definitions**
- **The essential features of care and support planning and personal budgets**
- **Devising the plan**
- **Personal budgets**
- **Signing off the plan**
- **Formats**
- **Applying the statutory guidance using case examples**
- **Conclusion.**

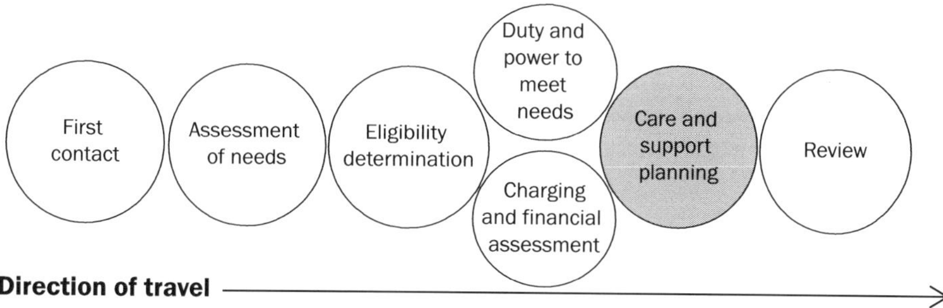

Figure 6.1 *The care and support journey*

Care and support planning prior to April 2015

The duty to provide a care and support plan or a support plan is set out in legislation for the first time in the Care Act 2014. Previously no duties in relation to care and/or support planning had been set out in legislation.

Support planning (applying to both adults and carers) was introduced in the statutory guidance issued in 2010 in *Prioritising Need in the Context of Putting People First: A Whole System Approach to Eligibility for Social Care.* This stated that "if an individual is eligible for help then the council should work with that individual to develop a plan for their care and support" (paragraph 119).

What was described as 'person-centred support planning' had become well established in social work practice for a number of years prior to the implementation of the Care Act, but significantly different models had evolved. The intention of the Care Act and the accompanying statutory guidance is to achieve greater consistency between local authorities in the application of best practice.

Key terms and definitions

The following have been selected because they appear in either the Care Act and/or the Regulations.

Key term	Care Act 2014	The Care and Support Regulations 2014	The Care and Support Statutory Guidance (revised 2017)
Care and support plan	Section 24 (1) specifies that where a local authority is required to meet needs under section 18 or 20 (1), or decides to do so under section 19 (1) or (2) or 20 (6), it must – (a) prepare a care and support plan or a support plan for the adult concerned; (b) tell the adult which (if any) of the needs that it is going to meet may be met by direct payments; and (c) help the adult with deciding how to have the needs met. Section 25 (1) states that a care and support plan or, in the case of a carer, a support plan is a document prepared by a local authority which – (a) specifies the needs identified by the needs assessment or carer's assessment; (b) specifies whether, and if so to what extent, the needs meet the eligibility criteria; (c) specifies the needs that the local authority is going to meet and how it is going to meet them; (d) specifies to which of the matters referred to in section 9(4) the provision of care and support could be relevant or to which of the matters referred to in section 10(5) and (6) the provision of support could be relevant; (e) includes the personal budget for the adult concerned (see section 26); and (f) includes advice and information about – (i) what can be done to meet or reduce the needs in question; (ii) what can be done to prevent or delay the development of needs for care and support or of needs for support in the future.	There are no regulations that pertain to care and support plans	Paragraphs 10.31–48 provide guidance on the application of these sections in relation to care and support plans.

Key term	Care Act 2014	The Care and Support Regulations 2014	The Care and Support Statutory Guidance (revised 2017)
Direct payments	A direct payment must be made where there is a request that the local authority meet some or all of an adult's needs by making payments to, either • the adult or nominated person (where the adult has capacity – section 31 (2)); or • the authorised person (where the adult lacks capacity – section 32 (2)).	The Care and Support (Direct Payments) Regulations 2014 set out constraints on the application of this duty and steps to be taken before and after making a payment.	Paragraphs 12.1–6 provide further definition
Personal budgets	Section 26 (1) states that a personal budget for an adult is a statement which specifies – (a) the cost to the local authority of meeting those of the adult's needs which it is required or decides to meet as mentioned in section 24(1); (b) the amount which, on the basis of the financial assessment, the adult must pay towards that cost; and (c) if on that basis the local authority must itself pay towards that cost, the amount which it must pay.	The Care and Support (Personal Budget Exclusion of Costs) Regulations 2014 set out that certain services, for which the local authority cannot make a charge for, or chooses not to, must be excluded from the personal budget.	Paragraphs 11.7–9 provide further definition

The essential features of care and support planning and personal budgets

1. The ways that needs are met should not rely on a 'menu' of services provided by the local authority. Creativity in meeting needs is encouraged.
2. Developing the plan jointly between the individual and the local authority is the default position. Other people should be involved where appropriate.
3. Plans should not be developed in isolation from other plans, eg the plans for carers or family members such as EHC (Education, Health and Care) plans.
4. The contribution of universal services and community-based and/or unpaid support should be considered, as well as the individual's own strengths.
5. The format of the plan should suit the individual.
6. The personal budget must always be an amount that is sufficient to meet the person's needs.

7. People must be told during the planning process what needs could be met by a direct payment, and if the individual requests a direct payment they are entitled to receive this if the criteria are met.

8. In some cases a panel will make the sign-off decision where there are large or unique personal budget allocations and/or plans.

9. All reasonable steps must be taken to reach agreement with the person for whom the plan is being prepared. In the event that the plan cannot be agreed, people should not be left without support while the dispute is resolved.

Devising the plan

The plan must summarise all that has been decided in the previous stages of the care and support journey, as well as setting out how needs are to be met. The plan is the single key reference document for all people who have their needs met with the assistance of the local authority.

Paragraph 10.2 states that individuals "should be given every opportunity to take joint ownership of the development of the plan ... (and) it should be made clear that the plan 'belongs' to the person it is intended for, with the local authority role being to ensure the production and sign-off of the plan".

Some people may opt to receive tried and tested services provided directly by the local authority, whereas for others their needs will be better met by services and other activities that are tailored to their specific circumstances and preferences.

The components of a plan

Following section 25 (1) of the Care Act, paragraph 10.36 of the statutory guidance specifies that the plan must always comprise of the following:

a) the needs identified by the assessment;

b) whether, and to what extent, the needs meet the eligibility criteria;

c) the needs that the authority is going to meet, and how it intends to do so;

d) for a person needing care, for which the desired outcomes care and support could be relevant;

e) for a carer, the outcomes the carer wishes to achieve, and their wishes around providing care, work, education and recreation where support could be relevant;

f) the personal budget;

g) information and advice on what can be done to reduce the needs in question, and to prevent or delay the development of needs in the future;

h) where needs are being met via a direct payment, the needs to be met via the direct payment and the amount and frequency of the payments.

The planning process has to include other factors in addition to care and/or support needs. Paragraph 10.73 states that plans "should have regard to all of the person's needs and outcomes", and that they should not be developed "in isolation from other plans (such as plans of carers or family members, or EHC (Education, Health and Care) plans)".

Figure 6.2 summarises what social workers must make sure takes place in any care and/or support planning process and how this relates to maintaining and improving wellbeing.

In representing care and/or support planning diagrammatically in Figure 6.2, the process of formulating the plan is represented by the circle at the centre. The decisions that have been made as part of the earlier stages of the care and support journey are the inputs. The outputs of the planning process are shown as arrows out of the central circle.

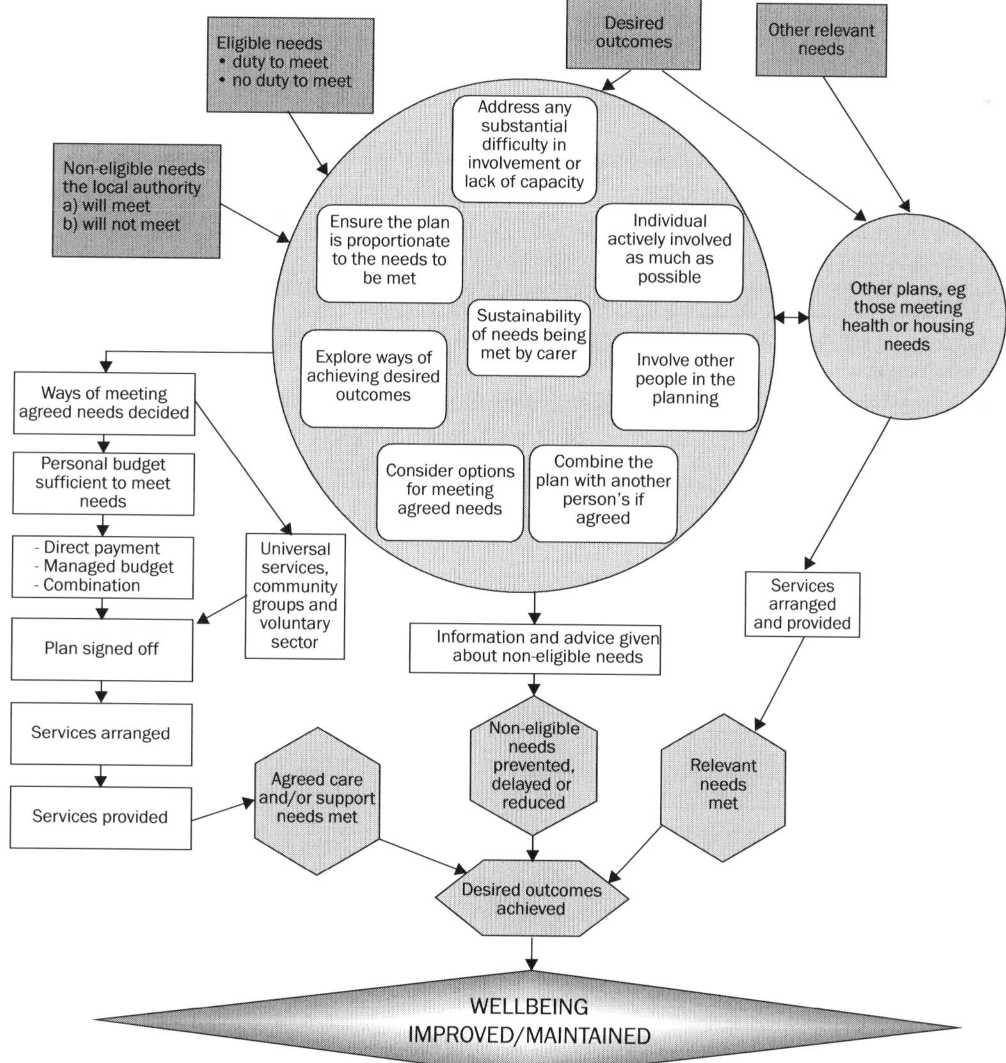

Figure 6.2 *Care and support planning pathway*

Inputs

As previously mentioned, the care and support plan for an adult and the support plan for a carer must address all of the individual's care and/or support needs and identify both those that are eligible and those that are non-eligible. The plan should record the decisions that have been made about the needs that the local authority has previously agreed to meet, and set out the individual's desired outcomes and preferences. The agreed needs will comprise eligible needs that the local authority has a duty to meet, plus any non-eligible needs that the local authority is using its power to meet. In addition the plan should record any eligible needs that the local authority has no duty to meet, eg where a carer has agreed to meet some of the eligible needs.

Other relevant needs should also be recorded. People will often have other needs such as healthcare needs, and the meeting of these needs will have an impact on their care and/or support needs. Also, their desired outcomes may well relate to both types of needs. For example, someone who is in hospital and has completed a period of in-patient treatment may require plans to meet their care and support needs and ongoing healthcare needs, before they can be discharged home.

The planning process

Before decisions can be made about the ways in which needs are going to be met and funded, the following factors have to be considered where relevant:

- any substantial difficulty in involvement and/or lack of capacity;
- the extent to which the individual is going to lead the planning process and be involved;
- who else needs to be involved in the planning process;
- the sustainability of the needs that the carer is meeting;
- the options for meeting agreed needs;
- how these various options can help to achieve desired outcomes;
- the possible combining of the plan with other people's plans.

The way that this planning takes place must be proportionate to the needs to be met.

It is suggested by the author that the social worker's role is as follows:

- *enable an informed choice to be made by the individual, and whoever else needs to be involved, on options for meeting those needs for care and/or support that it has been agreed that the local authority will meet;*
- *put in place arrangements for services to be provided to meet the person's needs;*
- *facilitate and coordinate where the meeting of care and/or support needs is to be undertaken in conjunction with the meeting of other relevant needs;*

- *where there are non-eligible care and/or support needs that the local authority has decided that it will not meet, ensure that information and advice is provided about how these needs can be reduced or delayed.*

Ensuring involvement and putting people in control

In determining how needs are going to be met, social workers must be guided by the principle stated in paragraph 10.32: "that the person be actively involved and is given every opportunity to influence the planning and subsequent content of the plan in conjunction with the local authority, with support if needed".

There will of course be circumstances where the individual will have substantial difficulty in being actively involved in the planning process, and there may also be specific decisions that need to be taken where the individual lacks capacity. In these circumstances steps have to be taken to mitigate against these difficulties by involving family and friends and advocates where necessary. Chapter 10 of this book considers in more detail the involvement of people who lack capacity and/or have substantial difficulty.

The following requirements apply in relation to the involvement of other persons:

- any carer must be involved in the planning process and "any other person the adult requests to be involved" (paragraph 10.49);
- the "level of involvement should be agreed with… any other party they wish to involve" (paragraph 10.50).

Where the individual lacks the capacity to say how they wish to be involved "the local authority must involve any person who appears to the authority to be interested in the welfare of the person and should involve any person who would be able to contribute useful information" (paragraph 10.49). This paragraph clarifies that in deciding who should be involved where the individual lacks capacity it should be a 'best interests decision'.

The skill of the social worker is in working with the individual "to get a sense of their confidence to take a lead in the process and what support they feel they need to be meaningfully involved" (paragraph 10.50).

Regardless of the extent to which the individual is actively involved, the plan must "link back to the outcomes that the adult wishes to achieve in day-to-day life as identified in the assessment process and to the wellbeing principle in the Act" (paragraph 10.31). These desired outcomes will have been mapped out during the needs or carer's assessment, and they will have also been subsequently considered both during the eligibility determination and in deciding what needs the local authority is going to meet. The social worker's task is to find out from the individual and others "which care and support options would best fit into their lifestyle and help them to achieve the day to day outcomes" (paragraph 10.49).

Proportionate planning

Paragraph 10.32 states that the individual "should not be required to go through lengthy processes which limit their ability to be actively involved, unless there are very strong reasons to add in elements of process and decision-making".

However, additional elements to the plan are "encouraged.... where this is proportionate to the needs to be met and agreed with the person the plan is intended for" (paragraph 10.42). The following examples are given:

- "Some people may value having an anticipated review date built into their plan in order for them to be aware of when the review will take place" (paragraph 10.42);
- "[Where a person has fluctuating needs] the plan should make comprehensive provisions to accommodate for this, as well as indicate what contingencies are in place" (paragraph 10.44);
- "Specific consideration should be given to how planning is conducted in end of life care" (paragraph 10.44).

Sustainability of needs being met by a carer

The local authority is not required to meet any of an adult's eligible needs that are being met by a carer, as long as the carer is willing and able to continue to do so. An adult's care and support plan should record "which needs are being met by a carer, and should consider putting in place plans to respond to any breakdown in the caring relationship" (paragraph 10.26).

Options for meeting needs

Section 8 (1) of the Care Act sets out what are described as "examples of what may be provided to meet needs", as follows:

- accommodation in a care home or in premises of some other type;
- care and support at home or in the community;
- counselling and other types of social work;
- goods and facilities;
- information, advice and advocacy.

The statutory guidance emphasises the importance of types of care and support that it contrasts with "more traditional 'service' options, such as care homes or homecare" which are "less intensive or service-focused options" (paragraph 10.12). Examples given are as follows:

- assistive technology in the home (paragraph 10.12);
- equipment/adaptations (paragraph 10.12);
- putting a person in contact with a local community group or voluntary sector organisation (paragraph 10.13);
- support that promotes mental and emotional wellbeing and builds social connections and capital (paragraph 10.41).

Potential ways of meeting needs

Paragraph 10.48 states the importance of people being "allowed to be very flexible to choose innovative forms of care and support, from a diverse range of sources". The local authority has to ensure that whatever is decided is legal, but "there should be no constraint on how the needs are met as long as this is reasonable" (paragraph 10.47). Also this paragraph states that the local authority "should take steps to avoid the decision being made on the assumption that the views of the professional are more valid than those of the person".

Section 8 (2) of the Care Act identifies "examples of ways a local authority may meet needs" as follows:

- by arranging for a person other than it to provide a service;
- by itself providing a service;
- by making direct payments.

Direct payments are expected to be used wherever possible. Paragraph 12.2 states that they are "the Government's preferred mechanism for personalised care and support". A direct payment must be made where this is requested, unless the local authority is prohibited from doing so by the Care and Support (Direct Payments) Regulations 2014, eg where someone is subject to a drug rehabilitation requirement. During the planning process there is a duty to "inform the person which, if any, of their needs may be met by a direct payment" (paragraph 10.46). In addition this paragraph states "the local authority should provide the person… with appropriate information and advice" in relation to the following:

- the usage of direct payments;
- how they differ from traditional services;
- how the local authority will administer the payment (eg, an explanation of the direct payment agreement or contract, and how it will be monitored).

Paragraph 10.11 makes the point that each of the different ways of meeting needs are not mutually exclusive, "and the use of one or more of these will depend on the circumstances", and gives the example of "the local authority arranging a homecare service whilst also providing a direct payment to meet other needs".

Other ways that arrangements can be made for meeting a person's needs that are mentioned in the statutory guidance are as follows:

- arranging an individual service fund, "which is a budget held by a provider... over which the individual has control" (paragraph 10.15);
- 'brokering' a service on behalf of an individual which involves "the local authority supporting an individual to make a choice about the provider of their care, and to enter into a contract with that provider" (paragraph 10.16).

Paragraph 10.48 states the importance of 'non-service' options being available, eg "Information and Communication Technologies (ICT) equipment, club membership, and massage". To encourage diversity, paragraph 10.48 also states that "the range of possibilities should be very wide" and where there are "lists of quality accredited providers to help people choose" these lists "should not be mandated as the only choice (on) offer to people".

Needs can also be met "by putting a person in contact with a local community group or voluntary sector organisation" (paragraph 10.13). This paragraph states that "needs may be met through types of care and support which are available universally, including those which are not directly provided by the local authority".

Plans should be as flexible as possible "to allow adjustment and creativity" (paragraph 10.37). They should also "take a holistic approach that covers aspects such as the person's wishes and aspirations in their daily and community life, rather than a narrow view purely designed to meet personal care needs" (paragraph 10.38). This can mean including "personal elements" into the plan which are important to the individual "but which the local authority is not under a duty to meet" (paragraph 10.37). No examples are given of what this means.

To facilitate flexibility it is proposed that there should be "no restriction or limit on the type of information that the plan contains, as long as this is relevant to the person's needs and/or outcomes" (paragraph 10.45). The plan should be "in a format that makes sense to them, rather than this being dictated by the recording requirements of the local authority" (paragraph 10.45).

Outputs and outcomes

The main output is the implementation of the plan, ie the actions taken to meet needs. In addition information and advice may need to be given about non-eligible needs that the local authority is not going to use its power to meet.

It is also important to identify the extent to which the individual's desired outcomes are intended to be met, as this will be a key element of subsequent reviews of the care and/or support plan.

Implementing the plan

Having considered all of the relevant issues, the following steps can then be taken:

- *agree ways of meeting needs;*
- *decide on ways of meeting needs that do not need to be funded from the personal budget;*
- *agree the personal budget;*
- *decide on the type of personal budget;*
- *set up services and other arrangements to meet needs;*
- *implement these arrangements and commence services.*

Non-eligible needs

An individual may have some care and/or support needs that were identified as non-eligible during the eligibility determination. If the local authority has decided not to use its power to meet any of these needs (or only some) then the care and/or support plan must include "a tailored package of information and advice on how to delay and/or prevent the needs the local authority is not meeting" (paragraph 10.30), and this paragraph goes on to say that this "information should be given to the person in a format accessible to them so they are clear what needs are being met by the local authority".

Relationship with other plans

Paragraph 10.73 states that the general principles that apply are that local authorities

- should not develop plans in isolation from other plans (such as plans of carers or family members, or EHC (Education, Health and Care) plans);
- should have regard to all of the person's needs and outcomes when developing a plan, rather than just their care and support needs.

It is important to find out at an early stage if there are any other relevant plans. Local authorities should "ensure that the package of care and support is developed in a way that fits with what support is already being received or developed" (paragraph 10.74). This can be in relation to other plans that are being developed for the individual, or it could be ensuring that the plans for the individual and for the carer fit together.

Having established that there are other relevant plans, they can only be combined if all parties "agree and understand the implications of sharing data and information" (paragraph 10.74).

Where plans are combined, paragraph 10.80 states that "it is vital to avoid duplicating process or introducing multiple monitoring regimes". This paragraph also states that where other organisations are involved, this may include "appointing a lead professional and detailing this in the plan so the person knows who to contact when plans are combined".

Combining plans where people have healthcare needs is considered further in Chapter 12 of this book.

Outcomes

The intention of the plan is to set out for individuals what needs to happen to "enhance their wellbeing and improve their connections to family, friends and community" (paragraph 10.1), and as the statutory guidance states in the very first paragraph (1.1) the "core purpose of adult care and support is to help people to achieve the outcomes that matter to them in their life".

The two key outputs needed to achieve this are as follows:

a) *services are arranged and provided to meet those needs that the local authority has agreed to meet;*

b) *information and advice is given about how any non-eligible needs that the local authority is not going to meet can be prevented, reduced or delayed.*

There may well be health needs or other types of need that will also have to be met, to ensure that the individual achieves the outcomes that matter to them. The relationship between care and support needs and other needs will be considered further in Chapter 12 of this book.

Personal budgets

Once it has been decided in what way a person's care and/or support needs are going to be met, the next step(s) to be taken are as follows:

a) *determine how the meeting of these needs is to be funded; and/or*

b) *identify what action is required to arrange for the meeting of those needs that do not require funding from the personal budget, eg community-based support.*

A personal budget is the amount of money that the local authority determines is required to meet the needs that it has been agreed that the local authority will meet. This budget can then be used to make arrangements to meet the person's needs.

The three ways that the personal budget can be used are as follows:

a) *a direct payment is made to the individual or their representative to make arrangements;*

b) *the local authority arranges the care and support directly;*

c) *a provider is contracted to provide a range of services that can be used flexibly.*

The social worker's role in relation to the personal budget is to get it agreed and authorised within the local authority, and then work with the adult and/or carer to decide how it will be used to put in place arrangements to meet the individual's needs. Social workers also have a lead role in reviewing the personal budget (see Chapter 7 of this book).

In addition to providing a personal budget there is a requirement "to have regards to how universal services and community-based and/or unpaid support could contribute to factors in the plan" (paragraph 10.41).

Sufficiency of the personal budget to meet needs

A personal budget must be sufficient to meet the needs that it has been agreed will be met.

Every person for whom the local authority is arranging care and/or support to meet agreed needs that have a cost that the local authority can charge for will have a personal budget. For adults this applies to residential care as well as care at home.

It comprises the individual's financial contribution (if any), plus whatever must be paid by the local authority to ensure that the budget is sufficient. Therefore, a financial assessment will have to be completed before the personal budget can be finalised.

Choice and control

It is intended that a personal budget "enables the person, and their advocate if they have one, to exercise greater choice and take control over how their care and support needs are met" (paragraph 11.7). It also "gives the person clear information regarding the money that has been allocated to meet the needs identified in the assessment and recorded in the plan" (paragraph 11.7).

The exact amount of the budget should not be fixed at the outset of the planning. It should be an "indicative (or 'ball-park') allocation at the start of the planning process... (to) help people to develop the plan and make appropriate choices over how their needs are met" (paragraph 11.7). This "indicative amount should be shared with the person, and anybody else involved, with the final amount of the personal budget confirmed through this process" (paragraph 11.7).

This way of doing things is intended to ensure that the wishes and preferences of the individual are considered and respected. Paragraph 11.7 states that the "personal budget should not assume that people are forced to accept specific care options, such as moving into care homes, against their will because this is perceived to be the cheapest option".

Calculating the personal budget

Paragraph 11.23 notes that there "are many variations of systems used to arrive at personal budget amounts, ranging from complex algorithmic-based resource allocation systems (RAS), to more 'ready-reckoner' approaches". But whatever process is used it should achieve the following for each individual as set out in paragraph 11.24:

- they are fully aware of how their budget was calculated;
- they know the amount at a stage which enables them to effectively engage in care and support planning;
- they can have confidence that the amount includes all relevant costs that will be sufficient to meet their identified needs in the way set out in the plan.

At the same time as being sufficient the personal budget also "must be an amount that is the cost to the local authority of meeting the person's needs" (paragraph 11.25). This particularly applies where the individual receives a direct payment (see the next section of this chapter).

The personal budget "must also take into account the reasonable preferences to meet needs as detailed in the care and support plan, or support plan" (paragraph 11.24).

Where the individual wants a type of care and support that costs more than the local authority would pay, eg a place in a particular care home that costs more than what the local authority usually pays, an additional payment can be made to achieve this. In these circumstances "a person or a third party on their behalf is making an additional payment (or a 'top-up') in order to be able to secure the care and support of their choice". This additional payment does not form part of the personal budget.

Carers

In paragraph 11.40 it states that a carer's personal budget must be an amount that does both of the following:

a) enables the carer to meet their needs to continue to fulfil their caring role;

b) takes into account the outcomes that the carer wishes to achieve in their day-to-day life.

Where services such as 'replacement care' are arranged to give the carer a break, it is the adult who is the recipient of the service and therefore "this kind of provision should be incorporated into the plan and personal budget of the person with care needs, as well as being detailed in a care and support plan for the carer" (paragraph 11.38). But "where the adult being cared for does not have eligible needs, so does not have their own personal budget or care plan... the personal budget would be for the costs of meeting the carer's needs" (paragraph 11.42), and thus would include the cost of any replacement care.

In addition to needing a break from caring responsibilities "carers may need support to help them to look after their own wellbeing" (paragraph 11.41). Examples given in this paragraph are as follows:

- a course of relaxation classes;
- training on stress management;
- gym or leisure centre membership;
- adult learning;
- development of new work skills or refreshing existing skills (so they might be able to stay in paid employment alongside caring or take up return to paid work);
- pursuit of hobbies such as the purchase of a garden shed;
- purchase of a laptop so they can stay in touch with family and friends.

Direct payments

Local authorities are expected to promote the use of direct payments, but paragraph 12.9 clearly states "the gateway to receiving a direct payment must always be through the request from the person" and people must not be forced "to take a direct payment against their will, or... be placed in a situation where the direct payment is the only way to receive personalised care and support".

In deciding whether to opt for a direct payment the individual or their representative needs to have good information about the way that this works. Paragraph 12.7 states that the local authority information service should provide information about direct payments that set out the following:

- what direct payments are;
- how to request one including the use of nominated and authorised persons to manage the payment;
- explanation of the direct payment agreement and how the local authority will monitor the use of the direct payment;
- the responsibilities involved in managing a direct payment and being an employer;
- making arrangements with social care providers;
- signposting to local organisations (such as user-led organisations and micro-enterprises) and the local authority's own internal support, who offer support to direct payment holders, and information on local providers;
- case studies and evidence on how direct payments can be used locally to innovatively meet needs.

The social worker's role is as follows:

- *to support the individual and their representatives in making decisions about how a direct payment could be used;*
- *initiate and support the setting up of the direct payment agreement;*
- *lead the review of the implementation of the direct payment.*

The administration of the direct payment and monitoring of its application by the local authority is often undertaken by specialist administrative staff. Where individuals require support with using the direct payment and specialist advice, eg about being an employer, social workers ought to be able to signpost people appropriately.

Meeting the conditions for a direct payment

The steps to follow once a request for a direct payment has been made will depend on whether the person has the capacity to make a decision about having a direct payment or not.

Where the person has capacity to make a request for a direct payment there are four conditions that must all be met before the request is agreed. These conditions are set out in section 31 of the Care Act and paragraph 12.14 of the statutory guidance, as follows:

a) the adult has capacity to make the request, and where there is a nominated person, that person agrees to receive the payments;

b) the local authority is not prohibited by regulations under section 33 from meeting the adult's needs by making direct payments to the adult or nominated person;

c) the local authority is satisfied that the adult or nominated person is capable of managing direct payments either by himself or herself, or with whatever help the authority thinks the adult or nominated person will be able to access;

d) the local authority is satisfied that making direct payments to the adult or nominated person is an appropriate way to meet the needs in question.

A nominated person is defined as "anyone who agrees to manage a direct payment on behalf of the person with care needs" (footnotes to Chapters 10, 11, 12 and 13 of the statutory guidance).

Where the person lacks capacity to make a request for a direct payment there are five conditions, all of which must be met (where applicable) before the request is agreed. These conditions are set out in section 32 of the Care Act and paragraph 12.17 of the statutory guidance, as follows:

a) where the person is not authorised under the Mental Capacity Act 2005 but there is at least one person who is so authorised, and that person who is authorised supports the person's request;

b) the local authority is not prohibited by regulations under section 33 from meeting the adult's needs by making direct payments to the authorised person, and if regulations under that section give the local authority discretion to decide not to meet the adult's needs by making direct payments to the authorised person, it does not exercise that discretion;

c) the local authority is satisfied that the authorised person will act in the adult's best interests in arranging for the provision of the care and support for which the direct payments under this section would be used;

d) the local authority is satisfied that the authorised person is capable of managing direct payment by himself or herself, or with whatever help the authority thinks the authorised person will be able to access;

e) the local authority is satisfied that making direct payments to the authorised person is an appropriate way to meet the needs in question.

An authorised person is defined as "someone who agrees to manage a direct payment for a person who lacks capacity according to the Mental Capacity Act 2005" (this definition appears in the footnotes to Chapter 10 of the statutory guidance and is repeated in the footnotes to Chapters 11, 12 and 13).

Individuals with care and/or support needs cannot receive a direct payment where they are "subject to a court order for a drug or alcohol treatment program or similar schemes" (paragraph 12.20). Also being subject to such a court order prevents people from acting as a nominated person or an authorised person.

Paragraph 12.19 states that "it is expected that in general, direct payments are an appropriate way to meet most care and support needs". This paragraph clarifies that a direct payment can be appropriate in circumstances where "the person is being obliged to receive services", eg "as a condition of mental health legislation (including a community treatment order, guardianship or leave of absence from hospital under the Mental Health Act or provisions in other mental health legislation)".

Before making the decision about whether the individual, authorised person or nominated person can manage the direct payment, local authorities should provide the relevant person with access to support and advice. Paragraph 12.21 states that "many local authorities have contracts with voluntary or user-led organisations that provide support and advice to direct payment holders, or to people interested in receiving direct payments".

Where a request for a direct payment has been declined, the individual, authorised person or nominated person who requested it "should (subject to Data Protection Act requirements) receive the reasons in a format that is accessible to them" (paragraph 12.22). This paragraph specifies that individuals should be told the following:

a) which of the conditions in the Care Act have not been met;

b) the reasons as to why they have not been met;

c) what the person may need to do in the future to obtain a positive decision.

Deciding how much the direct payment will be

The amount derives from the personal budget and therefore "must be an amount which is sufficient to meet the needs the local authority has a duty or power to meet" (paragraph 12.25).

It can be necessary to include the additional costs incurred of recruiting and employing staff, although in some local authorities the individual does not have to meet these costs because local organisations have been commissioned to provide "support services such as brokerage, payroll and employment advice" (paragraph 12.25). The costs of employing staff can include such things as having plans in place to cover redundancy payments and insurance.

The statutory guidance acknowledges that there are circumstances where a direct payment can legitimately exceed the usual 'cost to the local authority'. An example is given following paragraph 11.27 which describes how an hourly rate for a care worker from a particular agency was agreed that is higher than the usual rate, and this was to ensure that the individual had the same care worker on each occasion because it was essential to meet this individual's particular needs.

Paying family members

The Care and Support (Direct Payments) Regulations 2014 exclude relatives from being employed to meet needs except as specified in regulation 3 (2) where "the local authority considers it necessary to do so", as follows:

a) to meet the care needs of the adult; or

b) to provide administrative and management support or services for the purpose of enabling a person to whom the direct payments are made to:

   (i) comply with legal obligations arising from the making of and use of the direct payment; or

   (ii) monitor the receipt and expenditure of the direct payment.

The statutory guidance gives an example of paying a relative to meet care needs where an adult has "severe learning difficulties as well as various physical disabilities... (and) he has serious trust issues and a unique way of communicating that only his family, through years of care as a child, can understand" (paragraph 12.36).

Purchasing care in a care home

Direct payments can be used to purchase short stays in a care home, but not long-term care. Paragraph 12.47 states that "the government intends to extend rights to direct payments (to long term care) from April 2020".

The formula for the maximum amount of short stays that can be purchased through a direct payment is that "each stay is less than 4 weeks and there is an interim period of at least 4 weeks between 2 or more stays which added together exceed 4 weeks" (paragraph 12.36). There has to be at least four weeks between each short stay of a maximum of four weeks.

Becoming an employer

A direct payment will often be used to employ people to meet the individual's needs. In these circumstances the individual should be made aware that being "an employer carries with it certain responsibilities and obligations, in particular to HMRC (HM Revenue & Customs)" (paragraph 12.36).

If there are concerns that "the individual is failing to meet their obligations as an employer generally, the direct payment scheme should be reviewed and consideration given to whether alternative arrangements that result in the direct payment recipient no longer acting as the employer need to be made" (paragraph 12.49). One of the ways in which this situation "should be able to be avoided [is] by effective monitoring where appropriate" (paragraph 12.49).

Monitoring and reviewing

Paragraph 12.24 states that "the local authority must be satisfied that the direct payment is being used to meet the care and support needs set out in the plan, and should therefore have systems in place to proportionally monitor direct payment usage to ensure effective use of public money". But arrangements for monitoring should not "place a disproportionate reporting burden upon the individual" (paragraph 12.24).

Section 7 (1) (a) of the Regulations set out that a direct payment must be reviewed within the first 6 months and then every 12 months.

The first review "is intended to be light-touch to ensure that the person is comfortable with using the direct payment, and experiencing no initial issues" (paragraph 12.62). This paragraph states that it "should ideally be incorporated within the initial review of the care and support plan" and include the following:

- managing and using the direct payment;
- any long-term support arrangements that may be appropriate, eg
  - payroll;
  - insurance cover;
  - third party support.
- where the direct payment recipient is an employer the review should consider checking to ensure the following are being submitted to the HMRC:
  - PAYE returns;
  - tax is being paid;
  - National Insurance deductions are being made.

Because of the need to consider these, staff who undertake reviews need to be "appropriately trained to review direct payments… (and) familiar with financial procedures and employment laws" (paragraph 12.62). Social workers will need to involve staff with this expertise in reviews.

It is suggested that the annual review of the direct payment be aligned with the review of the care and/or support plan to "reduce bureaucracy and allow the local authority to review both at the same time" (paragraph 12.64). This will be considered further in Chapter 7 of this book.

Discontinuing direct payments

The circumstances where direct payments could be discontinued are set out in paragraphs 12.69–75, as follows:

- the person to whom direct payments are made, whether to purchase support for themselves or on behalf of someone else, may decide at any time that they no longer wish to continue receiving direct payments;
- the person no longer appears to be capable of managing the direct payments or of managing them with whatever support is necessary;

- the person no longer needs the support for which the direct payments are made, eg where the direct payments are for short-term packages when leaving a care home or hospital;
- direct payments are discontinued temporarily, eg when an individual does not require assistance for a short period because their condition improves;
- the person fails to comply with a condition imposed under regulations to which the direct payments are subject or if for some reason the local authority no longer believes it is appropriate to make the direct payments, eg if it is apparent that the direct payment has not been used to achieve the outcomes of the care plan;
- direct payments must not be provided under certain conditions, such as where the recipient is placed by the courts under a condition or requirement relating to a drug and/or alcohol dependency.

Where the recipient of the direct payment is an authorised person, the direct payment must be discontinued in the following circumstances as set out in paragraph 12.78:

- the local authority is no longer satisfied for whatever reason that the authorised person is acting in the best interests of the beneficiary;
- the local authority has sufficient reason to believe that the conditions imposed under regulations on the authorised person are not being met.

In these circumstances it may be possible to find someone else to take over as the authorised person, to avoid other arrangements being made.

Before reaching the decision to withdraw direct payments, other options must be explored, eg "the individual should be given an opportunity to demonstrate that they can continue to manage direct payments, albeit with greater support if appropriate" (paragraph 12.80).

Where the local authority decides to withdraw direct payments "it will need to conduct a review of the plan and agree alternative care and support provision with the person, their carer and independent advocate if they have one, unless the withdrawal was following a review after which the local authority concluded that the services were no longer needed" (paragraph 12.81).

Managed accounts

If a direct payment is not possible or appropriate, the two other ways in which the personal budget can be used to arrange and provide services are as follows:

- the local authority arranges the care and support directly;
- a provider is contracted to provide a range of services that can be used flexibly.

Both of these ways of organising services are through what is described as a 'managed account' in paragraph 11.30. There are two types of managed account that provide support in line with the person's wishes, held either by:

- the local authority;
- a third party (often called an individual service fund or ISF).

An example given of an ISF is where an individual has an "arrangement with his provider (that) allows him to save up and then convert the hours of his support into money to purchase personal trainer time at a local gym" (paragraph 11.33).

In some circumstances it may be appropriate to have a 'mixed package' of direct payment and managed accounts. Paragraph 11.31 suggests that this "can be a useful option for people who are moving to direct payments for the first time... (as it) allows a phased introduction of the direct payment, giving the person time to adapt to the direct payment arrangements".

Long-term residential care

Where a person is having their needs met in residential care and paid for through a personal budget, a direct payment cannot be used at present. So the most usual arrangement is for this service to be purchased directly by the local authority.

In these circumstances the Care and Support and Aftercare (Choice of Accommodation) Regulations 2014 apply. Summarising these regulations in the statutory guidance it is stated that the local authority "must provide for the person's preferred choice of accommodation, subject to certain conditions" (paragraph 8.36).

These conditions, all of which have to be met, are set out in section 3 of the Regulations as follows:

a) the care and support plan for the adult specifies that the adult's needs are going to be met by the provision of accommodation of a specified type

b) the preferred accommodation is of the same type as that specified in the adult's care and support plan

c) the preferred accommodation is suitable to the adult's needs

d) the preferred accommodation is available

e) where the preferred accommodation is not provided by the local authority, the provider of the accommodation agrees to provide the accommodation to the adult on the local authority's terms.

The Regulations clarify that preference for particular accommodation can be "by reference to its address or provider" (section 2 (1) (b)).

The requirements on choice apply to care homes, shared lives accommodation and supported living accommodation, as defined in sections 6, 7 and 8 of the Regulations.

Annex A of the statutory guidance provides details on arranging for needs to be met by choosing accommodation in a care home, shared lives or extra care housing. Much of the content is a rephrasing of the Care and Support and Aftercare (Choice of Accommodation)

Regulations 2014 in more straightforward language. Paragraph 5 states that "the person must have the right to choose between different providers of that type of accommodation provided that":

a) the accommodation is suitable in relation to the person's assessed needs;

b) to do so would not cost the local authority more than the amount specified in the adult's personal budget for accommodation of that type;

c) the accommodation is available;

d) the provider of the accommodation is willing to enter into a contract with the local authority to provide the care at the rate identified in the person's personal budget on the local authority's terms and conditions.

Paragraphs 6, 7 and 9 make the following important points about the right to choose:

- choice must not be limited to those settings or individual providers with which the local authority already contracts with or operates;
- if a person chooses to be placed in a setting that is outside the local authority's area, the local authority must still arrange for their preferred care;
- the choice is between different settings, not different types.

Individuals may choose a more expensive setting than is provided for in the personal budget "provided a third party, or in certain circumstances the person in need of care and support, is willing and able to meet the additional cost" (paragraph 20). This is known as a 'top-up' payment.

Universal services, community-based support and unpaid support

Paragraph 10.13 states that "needs may be met through types of care and support which are available universally, including those which are not directly provided by the local authority", and this paragraph gives the example of "putting a person in contact with a local community group or voluntary sector organisation".

This is restated and expanded in paragraph 10.41 as a requirement that local authorities "have regards to" how the following "could contribute to factors in the plan":

- universal services;
- community-based support;
- unpaid support.

This paragraph states that this includes "support that promotes mental and emotional wellbeing and builds social connections and capital".

Signing off the plan

Before services can be arranged, the plan has to be signed off by the local authority. In doing so the "local authority must take all reasonable steps to agree with the person the manner in which the plan details how needs will be met" (paragraph 10.81).

Where the individual is actively involved in the planning or they have a representative supporting them, the main tasks for the social worker are set out in paragraph 10.82 as follows:

- overseeing and providing guidance for the completion of the plan;
- ensuring that the plan:
  - sufficiently meets needs
  - is appropriate
  - represents the best balance between value for money and maximisation of outcomes for the person.

Where the individual is not actively involved, paragraph 10.82 states that "the best interests of the person must be reflected throughout" in the plan that is being prepared on their behalf.

Paragraph 10.83 specifies that the factors that should be agreed wherever possible and recorded in the plan before sign off takes place should include the following:

- how the needs in question will be met;
- the final personal budget amount (which may have been subject to change during the planning process).

It is recognised that where there are "large or unique personal budget allocations and/or plans" that "panels may be an appropriate governance mechanism" (paragraph 10.85).

The plan should be completed in a timely fashion and the "planning process should not unduly delay needs being met" (paragraph 10.84).

Paragraph 10.86 addresses the circumstances where the plan cannot be agreed with the person, or any other person involved. Where this happens "the local authority should state the reasons for this and the steps which must be taken to ensure that the plan is signed-off". But "if a dispute still remains, and the local authority feels that it has taken all reasonable steps to address the situation, it should direct the person to the local complaints procedure". While the dispute is being resolved "people must not be left without support". Disputes are considered in Chapter 11 of this book.

Formats

Some local authorities have developed templates for care and/or support plans, although most wish to avoid being prescriptive so the templates simply list what the plan should contain. These templates and the guides are aimed at informing people with care and/or support needs what to expect and what should be included. To encourage people to write their own plans themselves, some local authorities publish sample plans to demonstrate how the plan can be personal to the individual.

Although there is a degree of variety, many appear to be informed by a guide to care and support planning published by TLAP (Think Local Act Personal) in early 2015 titled 'Delivering Care and Support Planning'.[1] This publication is described as a guide "written for decision makers within councils and their partners (e.g. voluntary and community sector organisations involved in care and support planning) to help them better understand the requirements of the Care Act in relation to Care and Support Planning for adults and carers". It includes "ideas, lessons and practical examples for designing and delivering care and support planning", and also a suggested format for what it describes as a "person-centred care and support plan", which is summarised as follows:

1. PERSONAL DETAILS

   Name, address etc.

2. CARE AND SUPPORT NEEDS AND PERSONAL OUTCOMES

   All of the specified outcomes from the eligibility criteria are listed and for each of these there is a free text box for the following:

   - Personal outcomes/goals;
   - How needs will be met informally through preventative support available from the community or friends and family;
   - Is this particular need considered eligible for Council assistance?
   - How the need will be met by a personal budget (if relevant).

3. BUDGET MANAGEMENT OPTION DECISION

   - Identify option, ie direct payment, direct payment to a nominee or authorised person, or managed account;
   - Reason for chosen budget management option.

4. BUDGET

   - Starter budget amount;
   - Individual's contribution;
   - Direct payment amount (if relevant);
   - Frequency of payments;
   - Planned payment/service start date;
   - Further information, eg one-off payment.

5. SERVICES PROVIDED BY THE COUNCIL

   Details of Council commissioned services.

6. DIRECT PAYMENT PAID TO A NOMINEE OR AUTHORISED PERSON

Name and contact details.

7. INFORMATION AND ADVICE

- What can be done to meet or reduce the needs in question?
- What can be done to prevent or delay the development of needs for care and support or the needs for support in the future?

8. FIRST PLANNED REVIEW DATE

9. SIGNATURES

Includes all relevant parties.

Applying the guidance using case examples

This section illustrates and analyses some of the key elements of the processes described in this chapter that are of particular relevance for social workers.

The care and/or support planning process starts and finishes with the agreed needs and desired outcomes. At the start of the process it ought to be clear what needs the local authority has agreed that it will meet and how this relates to the outcomes that the individual wishes to achieve in their day-to-day life. The plan sets out how agreed needs will be met and how it will contribute to the achievement of desired outcomes.

In many circumstances the only agreed needs will be those that have been determined as eligible, but there can be circumstances where non-eligible needs are included where the local authority has decided to exercise its power to meet them. There will also be some eligible needs that will not be included in the list of needs that it is agreed will be met, because the local authority has no duty to meet them, eg needs that are being met by a carer.

Each case example has a summary of the agreed needs and desired outcomes. This is followed by illustrations of key issues in developing and implementing the plan, including the personal budget pathway. Each example demonstrates different ways that a plan can be written.

In accordance with section 25 (1) of the Care Act this summary of the agreed needs must include the following:

- **desired outcomes;**
- **eligibility;**
- **needs that the local authority has agreed to meet.**

It also ought to include the following where relevant:

- **eligible needs that the local authority has no duty to meet;**
- **non-eligible needs that the local authority has agreed to meet;**
- **non-eligible needs that the local authority has decided not to meet.**

Mr K

Summary of needs and desired outcomes

Mr K has COPD (Chronic Obstructive Pulmonary Disease) and arthritis. His daughter (Ms K) has been cooking meals for him but is no longer willing to do so, although she is willing to do her father's shopping. Mr K pays a neighbour to help with the cleaning and laundry. He is unable to go to the jazz club that he used to attend regularly, because he cannot use public transport and he cannot use the toilet without someone's help. Ms K has declined to have a carer's assessment so she will not receive a carer's support plan.

Eligible needs	• *The effect of Mr K being unable to cook for himself and do his cleaning and laundry has a significant impact on his physical wellbeing and also control over his day-to-day life.* • *Not being able to go to the jazz club because he cannot use public transport and he cannot use the toilet without someone's help has a significant impact on his wellbeing in relation to participation in recreational activities.*
Desired outcomes	• *He wants someone to come in every day and prepare him a home-cooked meal in the way that his daughter has been doing.* • *Cleaning and laundry – he wants to continue to employ his neighbour to do this.* • *Attending the local jazz club regularly.*
Eligible needs that the local authority has agreed to meet	• *Have a daily cooked meal.* • *Cleaning and laundry.* • *Attend the jazz club.*
Eligible needs that the carer has agreed to meet	*Shopping (note: it has not been conclusively determined that Mr K could not do online shopping by himself).*

Alternative scenario

In this scenario Mr K is able to do his laundry and does not have difficulty using the toilet at the jazz club.

Eligible needs	• *The effect of Mr K being unable to cook for himself and do his cleaning has a significant impact on his physical wellbeing and also control over his day-to-day life.* • *Not being able to go to the jazz club because he cannot use public transport has a significant impact on his wellbeing in relation to participation in recreational activities.*
Desired outcomes	• *He wants someone to come in every day and prepare him a home-cooked meal in the way that his daughter has been doing.* • *Cleaning and laundry – he wants to continue to employ his neighbour to do this.* • *Attending the local jazz club regularly.*

Eligible needs that the local authority has agreed to meet	• *Have a daily cooked meal.* • *Cleaning.* • *Attend the jazz club.*
Eligible needs that the carer has agreed to meet	*Shopping*
Non-eligible needs	*Laundry*

The local authority could agree to meet his needs in relation to doing his laundry if this meets local criteria for non-eligible needs.

Developing the plan – involvement, control and proportionate planning

Mr K has been receiving most of the care and support that he needs for some time, and he is used to being in control of managing the services that he receives from his neighbour, so it is likely that he will wish to continue in this way. It is probable that he views the process of assessment and care and support planning as simply a way of getting funding for him to maintain the plan that is already in place, and to add to it in relation to enabling him to attend the jazz club. In light of this, involving him in developing the plan ought to be relatively straightforward.

Ms K must be involved in developing the plan as she is playing an active role as a carer. The extent to which she is involved will need to be negotiated – principally whether Mr K wishes her to be present during discussions about the plan.

Although Mr K may not expressly ask that anyone else be involved, the social worker may wish to suggest that the neighbour who does his cleaning be involved, and also that it may be useful to involve health professionals who help him manage his COPD.

Developing the plan – options for meeting needs and ways of meeting needs

Mr K was prompted to request an assessment because his daughter is no longer willing to cook him a meal every day. His desired outcomes include a preference for someone to cook a meal in his daughter's place. He was made aware during the eligibility determination that this may not be possible, as there are more cost-effective options that enable him to receive a cooked meal. Now is the time to explore how this could be achieved via options such as home delivery of cooked meals and frozen meals.

If the neighbour is being paid above the market rate for doing the cleaning and laundry, then other options may need to be explored. If Mr K is a self-funder this will not be an issue, but if he isn't, the local authority will only fund the market rate for someone to be employed to do the cleaning and laundry. If the latter applies, he could consider employing someone else or find a way of paying a top-up.

For Mr K to attend the jazz club a number of options would need to be explored. Could he get a lift from a friend if he paid a contribution towards the petrol? If a rail could be installed would this solve the problem? If not, could he overcome his embarrassment of asking his friends to help him on and off the toilet?

Purchasing suitable meals, employing someone to do cleaning and laundry and paying for petrol (or a taxi if necessary) could all be done via a direct payment. If Mr K did not want to do it this way it could be done via a managed account.

Developing the plan – relationship with other plans

During the assessment stage it was noted that Mr K may benefit from a pulmonary rehabilitation course, the aim of which is to help people breathe more efficiently and to cope better with feeling out of breath, and it may also have the added benefit of improving Mr K's general fitness and thus his ability to undertake the activities of daily living. If Mr K wants to progress, the care and support plan ought to identify who is going to explore this with his GP. There could also be some value in getting a better understanding of how his GP sees the treatment of his COPD and arthritis going forward.

A key element of the plan is Mr K's daughter's willingness to continue to do his shopping. There are no reasons to indicate that this may not be sustainable, so a contingency plan may not be necessary. However, it may be necessary to explore alternatives for when she is on holiday.

Implementing the plan – personal budget

In circumstances where Mr K has capital below the upper limit and thus is not a self-funder, he will receive a personal budget as a matter of course. If Mr K is a self-funder and the local authority is meeting his needs because he has requested this, he will also receive a personal budget.

Mr K's personal budget will include an amount allocated to paying for cleaning and laundry that may equate to a lower hourly rate than Mr K is currently paying his neighbour. To continue to pay his neighbour her current rate he would have to pay a top-up from his own resources (or his daughter may be willing to pay). Alternatively he would have to employ someone else at the lower rate that is proposed for his personal budget. It would be important that Mr K was informed of any difference in rates at the earliest opportunity, and this could be flagged up as soon as it is known that there is agreement to meet Mr K's needs.

Mr K would most likely be offered a daily delivery of a cooked meal or the provision of frozen meals. Mr K is unlikely to be happy with this, as it doesn't achieve the outcome of him having the home-cooked meal that he desires. This service is often paid for on a flat-rate basis and is not financially assessed. Where this is included in the personal budget it might be listed as a zero-cost item, as the full cost may be reflected in the purchase price. Mr K could choose not to purchase this service and make other arrangements, eg asking the neighbour if he can pay her to cook for him.

Whether the costs in relation to the jazz club are included will depend on local authority policy and practice. Some local authorities may take the view that this need could be met by community resources and family/friends, and therefore would only include this in the personal budget if these resources were not available.

Implementing the plan – direct payment or managed account

Mr K may wish to request a direct payment to continue to pay his neighbour for doing his laundry and cleaning. He would have to formally become an employer and the neighbour would have to be an employee. His daughter could be nominated to receive the direct payment, in which case she would be the employer.

If Mr K is the recipient of the direct payment the local authority may agree that this would include an amount that he could pay his daughter to administer and manage the employment of the neighbour (or whoever else is employed). This administrative task will be relatively straightforward if the local authority has arranged for payroll and other employment-related services to be available, either directly or by commissioning a local organisation.

An alternative to a direct payment would be for Mr K to have a managed account in the form of an individual service fund, if this type of arrangement is available in his locality. It can be attractive where the individual is receiving several services and finds it too complicated to manage them through a direct payment. So if Mr K's neighbour no longer wished to do the laundry and the cleaning, and Mr K wanted help in arranging meals and getting to the jazz club, a provider organisation could take on all of these tasks and would receive payment directly from the local authority. In addition to relieving Mr K of the administrative burden, this type of arrangement could give Mr K more flexibility and control as he could have more jazz club visits and less laundry on occasions if this suited him, and also he wouldn't feel obliged to have the same hours each week from the person cleaning – as he might do if he was employing his neighbour. In practice it would probably make sense for meals to be excluded from this package and to be arranged directly with the provider who has the contract with the local authority.

If Mr K is a self-funder he may prefer to engage the assistance of his neighbour in a more informal way. To achieve this he could decide that he doesn't want the local authority to meet his needs in relation to cleaning and laundry.

Implementing the plan – utilising strengths and community-based support

Mr K wants to maintain his social connections with his jazz club friends. Over the years his involvement with jazz music has been an important source of social capital for Mr K. There is a risk that this could be lost or diminished, and this would have a significant impact on his wellbeing.

Mr K's jazz club friends may be able to help him more than they do at present. Mr K may benefit from talking this through with a social worker, and developing the confidence to ask for help with what he finds embarrassing in relation to accessing the toilet and also getting a lift.

Implementing the plan – residential care

If Mr K decides to go into a care home, he may wish to find a care home close to where his daughter lives in a neighbouring borough. In chapter 5 it was identified that he would probably be a self-funder in these circumstances. So he could decide to make his own arrangements or request that the local authority arranges a care home for him.

Where the local authority makes the arrangements he must be offered the choice of more than one suitable care home in the locality where his daughter lives. But before doing so he ought to be made aware that he could choose a more expensive option and fund this through a top-up.

Alternative scenario

If Mr K's needs change and his daughter decides to provide more help by moving into his home, she could have breaks from her carer role by Mr K going into residential care for short stays. These short stays could be purchased from an amount included in a direct payment. If Ms K wanted regular breaks this could be achieved by Mr K going into a care home one week in every six on a rolling programme, for example. If Ms K preferred to have longer breaks and wants to have more than one per year, the direct payments regulations require that these breaks be for no more than four weeks and that the breaks are at least four weeks apart.

Signing off the plan

There are a number of issues to be resolved with Mr K before the plan can be signed off.

Reaching agreement with Mr K about how many hours are required to do his laundry might be relatively straightforward, but less so for his other needs. Also there is potential for disagreement about the extent to which several of his desired outcomes can be achieved.

The amount of cleaning that is likely to be offered will be the minimum that is sufficient to do the basics that he couldn't do for himself without becoming breathless. Depending on his own personal standards for cleanliness, he may not regard this as acceptable.

He may not be able to continue to employ his neighbour for the number of hours that he requires, because he is paying her at a rate that is higher than the market rate paid to agencies who provide staff to do cleaning and laundry.

He has made it clear that he wants someone to come in every day and prepare him a home-cooked meal in the way that his daughter has been doing. He probably would have been told right from the outset that this was not going to be funded by the local authority, because it is an expensive way of providing him with a cooked meal, but he may maintain that he is dissatisfied with this decision.

The discussions about supporting Mr K to be able go to the jazz club are likely to revolve around ensuring that non-cost options are fully explored.

Requirement to give information and advice when some needs are not going to be met

At some point prior to the development of the care and support plan there will have been a conversation about any needs that are not going to be met. If it was concluded that Mr K's difficulty in getting to the jazz club is not an eligible need and the local authority does not intend to use its power to meet this care and support need, then information and advice about how this need could be prevented, reduced or delayed must be included in his written care and support plan, as well as an explanation of why this need will not be met (see Chapter 4 *for more details).*

The plan

The following care and support plan is for a version of his circumstances where he does not have difficulty using the toilet at the jazz club, and friends have agreed to give him a lift to get there. Mr K has savings below the upper capital limit, so he pays a contribution towards the cost of his care and support. Ms K is to receive the direct payment that she will then use to pay the neighbour to do Mr K's laundry and cleaning. He is unable to do online shopping because he says he finds it painful to use a computer or tablet and would not be able to put the shopping away by himself; therefore his daughter is meeting an eligible need by doing his shopping.

My desired outcomes	***Needs that the local authority has agreed / not agreed it will ensure are met D – duty P – power N – not meeting***	***Needs being met by the carer***	***Needs to be met through friends, family and community resources***	***Personal budget and payment method***	***Evaluation of extent to which my desired outcomes are achieved***
I want someone to come in every day and prepare me a home-cooked meal in the way that my daughter has been doing.	*The effect of me being unable to cook for myself has a significant impact on my physical wellbeing and also control over my day-to-day life (D).*	*My daughter, Ms K, is willing to do my shopping*		*I have opted to purchase meals from the home meals service.*	*Moderately satisfied*

My desired outcomes	Needs that the local authority has agreed / not agreed it will ensure are met D – duty P – power N – not meeting	Needs being met by the carer	Needs to be met through friends, family and community resources	Personal budget and payment method	Evaluation of extent to which my desired outcomes are achieved
Cleaning and laundry – I find this very time consuming and I would rather employ someone to do this.	*The effect of me being unable to do cleaning and laundry has a significant impact on my physical wellbeing and also control over my day-to-day life (D).*			*£ … to pay for … hours of cleaning and laundry Direct payment of £… to Ms K*.*	*I'm satisfied with the time allowed for laundry, but I don't think enough time has been allowed for cleaning.*
Attending the local jazz club.	*Not being able to go to the jazz club has a significant impact on my wellbeing in relation to participation in recreational activities (D).*		*Friends and acquaintances who attend the jazz club will give me a lift.*		*I have agreed to give this plan a try, but I am not comfortable about having to rely on people for a lift.*

* *The administration of the employer requirements will be undertaken via a local third-party organisation. Ms K will also pay a top-up so that the neighbour continues to receive a higher rate of pay than the market rate.*

Information and advice about non-eligible needs – *Not applicable*

Review date – *(six weeks' time)*

Ms W

Summary of agreed needs and desired outcomes

Ms W (aged 40) has psychotic depression and is socially isolated. The manager of the housing association flat where Ms W lives is concerned that there is a fire risk because of what is perceived as hoarding behaviour.

Following the home visit where the social worker undertook an assessment and eligibility determination, the social worker would have consulted with healthcare colleagues. It will be assumed that it is established that Ms W is potentially eligible for exercise on prescription and has agreed to discuss this with her GP.

Her care and support plan will address what is set out in the following summary of her needs assessment and eligibility determination:

Desired outcomes	• *She feels regular exercise will improve her mental health and wellbeing.* • *She would like the type of casual social contact with people that she had when she had a job.* • *She does not want help with managing her collection of books and magazines.*
Eligibility	*The cumulative impact on her wellbeing of her social isolation and hoarding behaviour.*
Needs that the local authority has agreed to meet	*Social interaction.*

The care and support planning will not address the needs associated with her hoarding behaviour, as Ms W is clear that she does not want these needs met. Nevertheless it is recorded as part of the eligibility determination and could be reconsidered at a future date.

Developing the plan – involvement, control and proportionate planning

The indications are that Ms W will want to be actively involved in agreeing the scope and detail of her care and support plan. She is clear about what she does and doesn't want in general terms, but she will need help in constructing a care and support plan that enables her to achieve improvements in social contact and links with the benefits of exercise for her mental health.

At this stage there is nobody else that Ms W would want to be involved. However, if her unwillingness to address the perceived fire risk places her tenancy in jeopardy, she ought to be persuaded of the advantages of involving the housing association.

Developing the plan – options for meeting needs and ways of meeting needs

The option that was discussed during the assessment visit of exercise on prescription has not yet been confirmed as being available to her. In any event this may only be a short-term measure, so longer-term options of improving social interaction ought to be considered.

The social worker may want to try to find a way of positively reframing the perceived dysfunctional behaviour of hoarding by possibly focusing on Ms W's strengths as a collector. This could possibly be achieved by exploring with Ms W getting involved with a local or online group for people with similar interests.

Ms W has said that she enjoyed the social interaction that she had when she was employed, so a possible useful first step might be to support her in obtaining voluntary work. This is not a matter of revisiting her eligibility in relation to "[h] accessing and engaging in work, training, education or volunteering", as it is intended as a means of addressing her social isolation. However, it could be considered in a revised eligibility determination at a later stage.

For any options that require funding, the social worker will need to indicate to Ms W whether they could be arranged by means of a direct payment.

Developing the plan – relationship with other plans

Ms W has a healthcare plan (although it may not be described in this way) insofar as she is taking medication and it is hoped that she will receive exercise on prescription. The social worker may want to keep the option of talking therapy on the table, as this is an option that has positive results with people in similar circumstances to Ms W.

The housing association wants to find a way of reducing the fire risk and they had hoped that this would be achieved by the intervention of mental health services. They may wish to change their approach in the light of developments.

Implementing the plan – personal budget

The options identified in her plan would have little cost to the local authority. If she is able to engage in voluntary work, she may need funding for public transport. She may also need to travel to a local history group meeting.

Implementing the plan – direct payment or managed account

Ms W could receive a direct payment for public transport.

There may be no alternative to receiving a direct payment.

Implementing the plan – utilising strengths and community-based support

Ms W wants to increase her social connections and capital. She doesn't particularly want close friends, but she believes her wellbeing would be improved if she were involved in doing things alongside other people.

She may not be able to undertake voluntary work without some additional help. She would need extra support from within any organisations where she is going to volunteer. She would need to agree to tell them what she wants help with and why.

It might be difficult to help her get support to engage with people who share her interest in history.

Signing off the plan

Ms W would probably agree that this care and support plan is meeting her needs in a way that she finds acceptable, and accords with her preferences.

Requirement to give information and advice when some needs are not going to be met

Ms W has needs that relate to her hoarding behaviour that the local authority is not planning to meet, because Ms W will not agree to this. Giving information and advice on this would have to be handled very carefully, because Ms W doesn't recognise this as an issue and the social worker is hoping to find a way to pursue this with Ms W at a later date, in particular by encouraging her to make use of talking therapies.

The plan

If Ms W agrees to write the care and support plan in her own words, it could be set out in the following way.

My care and support plan

This says what is important to me and what I have agreed with the social worker. The social worker has helped me with making sure that the facts are correct.

Things that are important to me

I live by myself in a flat that my landlord thinks is untidy and might cause a fire, but I'm happy that all of my books and magazines are where I can get them when I want them and they don't need to worry.

I don't do a lot these days except watch TV, and occasionally I go to car boot sales.

A while ago I was diagnosed with depression and I went into a mental hospital. Medication helps me and I'm much better these days.

I did have a job working at the university in the admissions department but I was made redundant when there was a reorganisation. Since then I have been on benefits and I don't have the confidence to try for another job. I liked being at work, because I was able to have conversations with people if I wanted to, although I didn't like my job much.

Although I don't see my dad much he helps me by paying for my phone.

Changes that I would like and things that I don't want to happen

I would like to go to places where there are other people who I might talk to if I felt like it. I think it would be a good idea to go to a gym and work with a personal trainer who would make sure I did the best sort of exercise for me and introduce me to people. I realise that to get help with this I have to ask my GP for exercise on prescription. I agree that the social worker can mention this to the GP before I go to see her.

The social worker wants me to sit down with her and the people from the housing association to talk about what they call a 'fire risk'. I think that they are being unfair to me to call me a fire risk, because nothing has ever caught fire. There is no point in meeting with them because they will just tell me to tidy up and throw stuff out, but I can manage without their help and I don't want them nagging me.

The reasons why social services will help me

I know that I have got into a bit of a rut and it would be good to do something about it. The social worker has told me that I can get help to improve my wellbeing because I have depression and because I am socially isolated. She says that the fact that the housing association people are concerned is also part of the reason why I can get help, even if I don't agree with their concerns and I won't talk to them.

What has been agreed

I think I might like doing some voluntary work, but with people who have different problems from that of mine. The social worker is going to find someone to give me advice and help get me started. It will give me the chance to be with other people and stimulate my brain a bit.

It would be nice to talk to other people who are interested in history and collect things like I do, but when I've looked online the groups are mainly for academics and people who have jobs in museums. I wouldn't want to join these groups. There is a Facebook group so I will try this and see what happens.

I know there are groups for people who are 'hoarders', but I am a collector not a hoarder.

If I have to travel for the voluntary work or to go to a history group the social worker says I will get help with the bus fares. This will be a pre-paid card.

I have been given written information and advice from the housing association about fire risk.

I will let the social worker know what progress has been made and we can meet up if the plan needs changing. I know that the social worker wants to do a review before three months are up.

Signatures

Ms W……

Social worker…….

Mrs O

Summary of agreed needs and desired outcomes

Mrs O provides necessary care to her husband who is a problem drinker and periodically has episodes where his heavy drinking results in him being incontinent. She is separated from her husband who lives in a neighbouring borough. She also has three children aged 11, 15 and 19. The youngest child has Down's syndrome.

Eligible needs	*There are times when Mrs O will have difficulty in caring for her children, and the stress of this has a significant impact on her emotional wellbeing.*
Desired outcomes	*Mrs O wants to continue to help her husband.*
Needs that the local authority has agreed to meet	*Emotional support.*
Non-eligible needs	*None.*

Developing the plan – involvement, control and proportionate planning

During the assessment and eligibility determination Mrs O expressed a strong preference that the support she wants should be provided by a named social worker. The feasibility of this option is likely to be the focus of the planning.

In many situations where a support plan is being formulated the carer will want the cared-for person to be involved. However, in this case Mr O may not wish her husband to be involved.

Consideration ought to be given to the involvement of Mrs O's children, particularly the 19 year old.

Developing the plan – options for meeting needs and ways of meeting needs

Other ways of providing Mrs O with the support she wants would need to be suggested at this stage. This could be individual sessions provided by specialist organisations such as Addaction.

If a named social worker is provided this would be a local authority employee and thus it would not be appropriate to make a direct payment.

Developing the plan – relationship with other plans

The most likely scenario is that Mr O continues to refuse the offer of an assessment of his care and support needs, so there is no formal plan for the cared-for person to coordinate with. But given that his condition fluctuates and may well deteriorate, contingency planning ought to feature in Mrs O's support plan.

Implementing the plan – personal budget

Mrs O's personal budget could be based on the cost of an agreed amount of time from a named social worker, or alternatively the cost of purchasing support from a trained counsellor. Alternatively the view might be taken that as the required service is available from a voluntary organisation (ie Addaction), a personal budget is not required.

Implementing the plan – direct payment or managed account

If Ms O's needs are to be met by purchasing a service from a trained counsellor, she could receive a direct payment.

Implementing the plan – utilising strengths and community-based support

The loss of social connections and capital, or the need to develop them, is not an issue for Mrs O. She makes good use of the voluntary organisation Al-Anon, and doing so has partly met her needs by providing an opportunity to share her anxieties. It will also have provided her with the opportunity to develop social connections with people who have similar experiences.

Signing off the plan

Mrs O had expressed a preference early on for support from a named social worker. If one-to-one specialist counseling is available from Addaction in a way that is suitably responsive, this might prove to be a suitable solution for Mrs O and would have the added advantage of support being provided from someone who has expertise in supporting the relatives of problem drinkers.

The plan

In this version of Mrs O's support plan, she agrees to obtain support from Addaction. She has completed it using the local authority's recommended template.

Personal details

My name is Mrs O and I am 47 years old. I live with my three children (aged 11, 17 and 19). I am separated from my husband who lives in... [an area of a neighbouring local authority].

Support needs and personal outcomes

Eligibility

I meet the eligibility criteria because I am providing necessary care for my husband who is a problem drinker (which includes helping him clean himself up when he overdoes it), and I am worried that there will be times when the stress of helping my husband and looking after my children will mean that I can't cope. My two older children can look after themselves when there is a crisis, but my youngest child has Down's syndrome and she needs a lot of attention.

I understand that on the records held by Adult Social Care it says the relevant 'inability' category is "carrying out any caring responsibilities for a child", and the stress I have described is recorded as something that is likely to have a significant impact on my emotional wellbeing.

Personal outcomes/goals

I want to have access to a professional person to talk through my problems with on a regular basis. Ideally I would like this to be a named social worker.

How needs will be met informally through preventative support available from the community or friends and family

I get support from attending meetings of Al-Anon and the friends I have made there. My husband's father used to help him but he has now died. There is nobody else in the family he will accept help from, and he has refused to have an assessment of his care and support needs.

Is this particular need considered eligible for council assistance?

I understand that the local authority has a duty to ensure that my need is met.

Personal budget

Because my needs can be met by services provided by Addaction I will not have a personal budget.

Information and advice

I do not have any non-eligible support needs so this does not apply to me.

First planned review date

I have agreed that this should take place in about 12 weeks' time. It could be sooner or later but it all depends on whether I have had a successful session with Addaction.

Signatures

Mrs O…

Social worker…

Comment and analysis

Readers should note that what is set out in this section and the previous section is intended to show how the statutory guidance might be applied, and in doing so, what would be complex situations in real life have had to be simplified.

Developing the plan – involvement, control and proportionate planning

Many people will have a good idea about what they want in their plan. Mr K, Ms W and Mrs O all know broadly what they want and what they don't want. However, there will also be many people who will require assistance in devising their plan. But even where they require this assistance they may nevertheless wish to play an active role or delegate this active role to others.

Although the statutory guidance only requires that local authorities take the initiative in involving others where the individual lacks capacity, it could be considered good practice for social workers to make suggestions about who could usefully be involved. The individual may not have considered the relevance of involving other parties in the planning process, and may well appreciate the social worker's expertise on this as in the case of Mr K, where it was suggested that the neighbour be involved.

There will also be situations such as with Ms W, where the decision about who not to involve ought to be respected. In her case she did not want the involvement of the housing association.

Developing the plan – options for meeting needs and ways of meeting needs

There will be circumstances where right from first contact, individuals and/or their family members will express a preference about the most suitable way of meeting needs. In other circumstances individuals may not have formed a view about how best to have their needs met, and indeed may not have a clear view about what their needs are.

But whatever the circumstances, individuals are likely to be forming a view about what options would best meet their needs during the process of assessment, eligibility determination and deciding what needs are going to be met, so the focus of this final stage is about making decisions on options that will have already been explored to some extent. The main point is that care and/or support planning doesn't start with a blank sheet.

People will have ideas about the best ways of meeting their needs that may need to be unpacked before alternatives can be considered, as is the case with Mr K's preference for a home-cooked meal and Mrs O's preference for a named social worker.

For each of Mr K's needs there are options that require exploring in relation to finance, maintaining an existing way of meeting needs and considering community resources – all of which emerged early on in the assessment. With Ms W the idea of going to a gym emerged early on, but the options of doing voluntary work and building on her strengths as a collector didn't emerge until the care and support planning got underway.

While there may have been some discussion of options at an earlier stage, there may not have been much discussion about the different ways that a personal budget can be deployed. This exploratory stage of care and/or support planning is probably the best time to implement the requirement that people be informed of which of their needs can be met by a direct payment, so that they can decide if they wish to request one. It also might be considered advisable to mention whether the local authority provides the services being considered to meet individuals' needs, or makes arrangements for other organisations to provide such services.

There will often be some needs that can be met from services that are available in the community or through help provided by friends and family, without expenditure needing to be incurred. This may have been discussed during the assessment stage as a way of preventing, reducing or delaying needs, but such resources can also provide the means of meeting eligible needs that the local authority has a duty to meet, and thus ought to be revisited as part of the care and/or support planning process.

Developing the plan – relationship with other plans

Linking up with other plans is important because the meeting of other relevant needs such as health and/or housing can have an impact on care and/or support needs, and vice versa. Also it may be the case that an individual's desired outcomes can be achieved only by meeting both health needs and care and/or support needs.

For Ms W there is a potential interdependency, in that meeting her health needs via exercise on prescription may also help to address the social isolation that has been identified as a care and support need.

Mr K's health needs are stable at present and while his poor health is significant in determining his care and support needs, there are no plans currently in place that need to be taken into account. The relationship works both ways because if his care and support needs are not met this could lead to deterioration in his health.

Implementing the plan – personal budgets

The key factor in setting up the personal budget is reaching agreement about it being sufficient to meet the individual's care and/or support needs. The bottom line is that the personal budget must be sufficient to meet the needs that the local authority has agreed to meet. In determining the usual cost to the local authority, account must be taken of the particularities of the individual's needs. For example, if the usual rate for home care is not sufficient to secure a specialist care worker for someone who is autistic, a higher rate may be required and the personal budget ought to reflect this.

Mr K might take the view that the amount allowed in his personal budget for cleaning and laundry is insufficient, for two reasons:

a) because not enough time has been allowed to clean his house to a satisfactory standard; and

b) he wants to retain the services of his neighbour who is currently being paid more than the usual rate.

Responding to (2) is relatively straightforward because the usual cost to the local authority will be established by the market rate for this type of service, and no special circumstances have been identified that would justify a higher rate being paid. But agreeing the number of hours allocated to cleaning could develop into a dispute, unless there is an acceptable methodology for this determination. In such circumstances there is particular value in producing an indicative budget at an early stage so that the matter can be resolved sooner rather than later. Also the fact that a budget is described as indicative signals that further discussion is encouraged.

Implementing the plan – direct payments and managed accounts

Putting control of making payments for services in the hands of people with care and/or support needs can result in more flexible and responsive services. Having a direct payment enables the individual to vary the level of the service that they need and to organise services directly, without having to go through cumbersome administrative procedures. However, in the case of Mr K he may not be able to achieve this flexibility with the current arrangements with his neighbour, but he could do so if he has a managed account and he no longer employs his neighbour.

Being an employer is an additional task for individuals to take on, but for many people this is worth it for the control it gives them and it can often be a valuable learning experience. The local authority has to be satisfied that the individual or their nominee is capable of managing all aspects of the direct payment (with help if necessary). Taking on the role of employer can be challenging, so particular attention may need to be given to this. For many people it can be too much responsibility, and a managed account can be a better option. Alternatively some people may want to receive the direct payment, but use a local umbrella organisation to process wages and undertake other employer responsibilities.

Implementing the plan – utilising strengths and community-based support

In addition to arranging for a personal budget to meet the individual's care and/or support needs, it can be just as important to include ways that people can get their needs met by utilising their strengths and the resources available in the community, and also getting help from friends and family.

The case examples demonstrated that this applied where there was significant impact on an individual's wellbeing as a consequence of inability to participate in recreational activities. It also applied where someone is socially isolated as a result of his or her needs. The aim was to provide the opportunity for individuals to develop meaningful interaction with others where this is lacking, so that 'social connections and capital' are developed and/or maintained.

With Mr K the emphasis is on maintaining his social connections so that the social capital that he has developed through his involvement with the local jazz community is not lost or diminished.

Ms W has almost no social capital so the emphasis with her is to develop this through volunteering, and encouraging her to see herself as a collector.

Mrs O has already developed particular social connections through being a carer of someone who is a problem drinker.

Implementing the plan – residential care

Some admissions to a care home will be on a planned basis, but many admissions of older people are as a result of a sudden change in a person's health and can often follow a hospital admission. There will also be circumstances where an older person goes into a care home for short periods on a planned basis to provide their carer with a break.

But whatever the circumstances the regulations on choice apply. These regulations are phrased in a slightly unusual way in that there is a requirement that an individual's preference must be adhered to (subject to certain conditions). Whereas elsewhere preferences are something that the local authority only has a duty to 'consider' or 'have regard to'.

Where people own their own home, this life-changing decision will include making complex financial arrangements, particularly if there is someone else who will remain living in their home after they have gone into residential care. See Chapter 5 for more details of how this applies.

Signing off the plan

Social workers have a key role in ensuring that the individual's desired outcomes are achieved wherever this is possible. But they are also expected to represent the interests of the local authority in ensuring that ways of meeting needs at no cost to the local authority are fully utilised, as well as helping people to understand that the local authority can only pay what is the 'cost to the local authority' to meet agreed needs.

The professional skill is in being able to achieve a balanced approach where there is tension between these requirements. Sometimes this will involve advocating for the individual where the indicative budget is not sufficient to meet their needs, but it can also mean helping individuals to understand and accept a plan that is less (both in scope and funding) than they had hoped for.

There were several aspects of Mr K's plan that he was not completely satisfied with and this dissatisfaction is expressed in the written record of the plan. But these dissatisfactions did not lead to a dispute and the plan was signed off, although some issues would need to be reconsidered when the plan is reviewed.

In Ms W's case it was clear from the outset that she would not sign off a plan that required her to talk to the housing association about the perceived fire risk. Nevertheless the concerns of the housing association are recorded and this would allow the issue to be revisited at the review stage.

The plan for Mrs O is to have her needs met in a way that does not accord with her preference to have access to a named social worker, so again there is an issue being flagged up for the review.

Requirement to give information and advice when some needs are not going to be met

Where an assessment identifies any non-eligible care and/or support needs it has been decided that the local authority will not meet, there is a requirement to provide information and advice about how these needs can be prevented, reduced or delayed. This information and advice must be "personal and specific advice based on the person's needs assessment" (paragraph 10.29). Furthermore this paragraph makes it clear that this information and advice should not be "a generalised reference to prevention services or signpost to a general web-site".

There is a general duty to provide information and advice on prevention throughout the care and support journey, and this will have taken place particularly during the assessment stage. In addition there is a specific requirement to include in the care and/or support plan "a tailored package of information and advice" (paragraph 10.30), in relation to needs that are not going to be met by the local authority.

Mostly the needs that are not going to be met are those that are not eligible. But there are some eligible needs that are not going to be met because there is no duty to meet the need, eg it is being met by a carer. However, it is not clear in the statutory guidance whether this requirement to provide information and advice applies to such needs.

As demonstrated with Mr K, the giving of this information and advice is something that would normally happen as part of the ongoing assessment and planning conversation, but it has to be summarised in writing in the care and support plan.

Ms W has an eligible need that the local authority will not meet because she does not wish the need to be met. Nevertheless the duty to provide information and advice in writing would appear to remain.

The plan

For each of the three case examples, the plan has been written up in a different way to reflect the "default assumption that the person, with support if necessary, will play a strong pro-active role in planning if they choose to" (paragraph 10.2).

Mr K's plan is a version of a standardised format completed by the social worker on his behalf, although he could have completed it himself if he wished to.

Ms W has written her plan herself, using headings provided by the social worker. The social worker has to ensure that it is written in such a way that both she and Ms W are in agreement, as it has to be signed off by both the social worker and the individual.

In Ms W's case she has only used headings that are relevant to her circumstances. Mrs O is an example of where the individual has also written the support plan in her own words, but where standardised headings and sub-headings are included.

Where an individual lacks capacity to make relevant decisions or has substantial difficulty in involvement, the plan may need to be written and signed off with their representative. But the plan would usually still be completed in the first person format.

Conclusion

There are a lot of factors for a social worker to ensure are considered and pulled together in the planning process, and inevitably the setting up of the plan can often require the individual to be guided through a significant amount of administrative requirements. Local procedures will need to be followed to determine the amount of the personal budget, how the budget is to be managed and the process of arranging services, as well as helping the individual to get help in ways that do not require funding. But in addition to using their administrative skills, an important task for social workers is to guide individuals in using the available funding creatively, so that desired outcomes are achieved and preferences adhered to as much as possible.

Complex though the process might be, the plan itself ought to be straightforward and concise. A robust care and support plan will be underpinned by the social worker using their skill in bringing issues to a conclusion, as well as applying their knowledge and experience of what is required by the Care Act.

The care and/or support plan is the point at which things start to happen for the individual – the talking stops and the doing starts. Much of the plan will be about specifying what is to be arranged to meet the agreed care and/or support needs, so it is essential that the individual or their representative fully understands and owns the plan. This ownership is particularly important where the individual's preferences cannot be adhered to and/or their desired outcomes will only be partially achieved.

Clarity, conciseness and ownership of the plan can be enhanced if it is set out in the individual's own words as far as this is possible. The social worker's role is to make sure that the plan includes the essential elements, as well as ensuring that there is a 'paper trail' to evidence how decisions were arrived at.

When the care and/or support plan is signed off, the involvement of the social worker mostly ceases until it is time to review the plan. The arranging of services is usually undertaken by specialist brokerage or commissioning staff in the local authority, or by the individual or their representative where they are in receipt of a direct payment.

A social worker is often involved later on when the plan is reviewed, particularly if the plan requires revising, and a reassessment of needs takes place. The review process is the subject of the next chapter.

Reference

1. www.thinklocalactpersonal.org.uk/Latest/Delivering-Care-and-Support-Planning/

7 Review

Introduction

Once a person has a care and support plan, or a support plan, their ongoing experience of the requirements of the Care Act will be via the review process. Everyone ought to be receiving a review at least once a year.

The majority of people in the care and support system are those who already have a care and/or support plan, so much of the activity of social workers is with people who need help with their ongoing care and/or support plans. For those people with long-term care and/or support needs whose first assessment was prior to April 2015, they will have experienced changes brought about by the Care Act only through reviews.

Although the planning of periodic reviews is important, the Care Act also emphasises the importance of keeping plans 'under review'. This means having systems in place that encourage the reporting of changes in circumstances and identifying when the plan is not working well.

The key skill that social workers bring to the process is in determining the extent to which the care and support journey requires revisiting. For example, there could be some needs that require reassessing, or it could be that matters can be addressed by amending the plan without the need for a reassessment.

This chapter describes when a plan should be reviewed and how the stages of the care and support journey can be re-engaged to revise the plan. It comprises the following sections:

- **Reviews prior to April 2015**
- **Key terms and definitions**
- **The essential features of reviews**
- **Deciding when a review is required**
- **The review and revision process**

- **Formats**
- **Applying the statutory guidance using case examples**
- **Conclusion.**

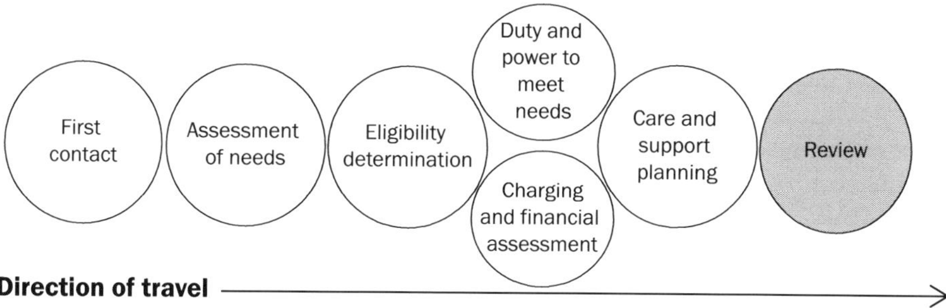

Figure 7.1 *The care and support journey*

Reviews prior to April 2015

The duty to review a care and support plan, or a support plan, appears in legislation for the first time in the Care Act 2014. Previously no duties in relation to care and/or support planning had been set out in legislation.

The requirement to undertake reviews was first introduced in the statutory guidance issued in 2010 in *Prioritising Need in the Context of Putting People First: A Whole System Approach to Eligibility for Social Care.* This stated that "councils should therefore ensure that arrangements are put in place for regular reviews of support plans" (paragraph 141).

Key terms and definitions

The following have been selected because they appear in the Care Act. There are no Regulations that add to these terms.

Key term	Care Act 2014	The Care and Support Statutory Guidance (revised 2017)
Review	Section 27 (1) states that a local authority must – (a) keep under review generally care and support plans, and support plans, that it has prepared; and (b) on a reasonable request by or on behalf of the adult to whom a care and support plan relates or the carer to whom a support plan relates, review the plan.	The aim of a review of a care and support plan, or a support plan, is so that people who have a plan "have the opportunity to reflect on what is working, what is not working and what might need to change" (paragraph 13.1). Paragraph 13.23 states that in response to a request "the local authority must consider this and judge the merits of conducting a review".

Key term	Care Act 2014	The Care and Support Statutory Guidance (revised 2017)
Circumstances have changed	Where a local authority is satisfied that circumstances have changed in a way that affects the plan, it must repeat any aspect of the assessment, eligibility determination, financial assessment and planning it considers appropriate (see section 27 (4)).	Paragraph 13.19 states that these changes are such that they could affect the plan in terms of the following: • efficacy; • appropriateness; • content.
Revise	Sections 27 (2 and 3) provide local authorities with the power to revise a care and support plan, or support plan, and sets out that in making this decision it must have regard to the matters referred to in section 9 (4) and specified in section 25 (1) (d), ie whether needs are being met and desired outcomes are being achieved, and if there is a carer, whether they can continue caring for the adult.	Paragraph 13.27 states that the process "should wherever possible follow the process used in the assessment and care planning stages... (and) should not start from the beginning of the process but pick up from what is already known about the person". Paragraph 13.28 clarifies that the revision to the plan may sometimes only require "minor adjustments", as well as cases where "a complete change of the plan may be required".

The essential features of reviews

1. Reviews are expected to take place no later than every 12 months, regardless of whether there has been a change in circumstances.
2. The first review is recommended 6–8 weeks after the plan has been signed off.
3. The planned review of the care and/or support plan should be combined with the review of direct payments where possible. The review of direct payments must take place in the first eight weeks.
4. Where the review concludes that there has been a change of circumstances, because the plan is not working well or could be improved, then the plan will need to be revised and this may involve a reassessment of needs.
5. Where there has been little or no change, the process of the review should be proportionate.
6. In addition to planned reviews, an unplanned review may be required where there has been a significant change.
7. Anyone supporting an individual or is interested in his or her wellbeing can request a review, and this should take place unless there is a good reason not to do so.

Deciding when a review is required

Paragraph 13.1 of the statutory guidance specifies that it is important that "plans are kept up to date and relevant to the person's needs and aspirations", to achieve the following:

- provide confidence in the system;
- mitigate the risks of people entering a crisis situation.

To comply with the duty to keep plans under review as specified in section 27 (1) (a) of the Care Act, paragraph 13.11 of the statutory guidance states that "local authorities should establish systems that allow the proportionate monitoring of both care and support plans and support plans". This can include making this part of the contract with a provider organisation. An example is given of when a service is being commissioned from a provider organisation; the contract could include a 'duty to request a review'. This means "that employees are required to inform the local authority if they think that there is a need for a review" (paragraph 13.18).

The types of review are set out in paragraph 13.13 as follows:

- a planned review – the date for which was set with the individual during care and support or support planning, or through general monitoring;
- an unplanned review – which results from a change in needs or circumstance that the local authority becomes aware of, eg a fall or hospital admission;
- a requested review – where the person with the care and support or support plan, or their carer, family member, advocate or other interested party makes a request that a review is conducted.

Keeping under review on a planned basis

Paragraph 13.14 states that there is value for individuals in the review being planned "so that they can anticipate when the review will take place, rather than the review being an unexpected experience".

Important considerations for a planned review are as follows:

- "proportionate to the circumstances, the value of the personal budget and any risks identified" (paragraph 13.16);
- "where plans are combined with other plans (for example the plan of a carer, or education, housing, and health and care plans which may be reviewed annually) the local authority should be aware of the review arrangements with these other plans and seek to align reviews together" (paragraph 13.15);

- "the method of review should, wherever reasonably possible, be agreed with the person and must involve the adult to whom the plan relates, any carer the adult has and any person the adult asks the authority to involve" (paragraph 13.17).

Paragraph 13.18 identifies circumstances where the risks are higher and consequently reviews may need to be more frequent, as follows:

- conditions are progressive and the person's health is deteriorating;
- a person has few or no family members or friends involved in supporting them.

Considering a request for a review

To fulfill the duty to conduct a review when an appropriate request is received as specified in section 27 (1) (b) of the Care Act, it is stated in paragraph 13.20 of the statutory guidance that local authorities should undertake the following:

a) provide information and advice to people at the planning stage about how to make a request for a review;

b) devise a process that is "accessible and include multiple routes to make a request – phone, email, or text for example";

c) set out what happens after a request is made, and the timescales involved in the process.

Paragraph 13.22 clarifies that the "right to request a review applies not just to the person receiving the care, but to others supporting them or interested in their wellbeing". The example is given of "a person with advanced dementia (who) may not be able to request a review, but a relative or a neighbour may want to draw the attention of the local authority to a deterioration in the person's condition".

Paragraph 13.23 states that a request to review a plan should take place unless any of the following apply:

- the local authority is reasonably satisfied that the plan remains sufficient;
- the request is frivolous;
- it is made on the basis of inaccurate information;
- it is a complaint.

Where the local authority decides not to conduct a review it "should set out the reasons for not accepting the request in a format accessible to the person, along with details of how to pursue the matter if the person remains unsatisfied" (paragraph 13.25).

The review and revision process

Where a review determines that the individual is receiving the care and support required to meet their needs and the plan remains relevant to their goals and aspirations, then no further steps need be taken. Where this is not the case the plan will need to be revised.

There will be circumstances where "the review and revision of the plan should be intrinsically linked" and that "it should not be possible to decide whether to revise a plan without a thorough review to ascertain if a revision is necessary" (paragraph 13.5). However, paragraph 13.6 and 13.7 refer to circumstances where "it may not be appropriate for the person to go through a full review and revision of the plan", eg, "there are occasions when a change to a plan is required but there has been no change in the levels of need (for example, a carer may change the times when they are available to support)".

The review

The purpose of a review is "to take stock and consider if the plan is enabling the person to meet their needs and achieve their aspirations" (paragraph 13.12).

Paragraph 13.12 specifies that the review process "should not be overly-complex or bureaucratic" and that the purpose of the review "should be communicated to the person before the review process begins".

Paragraph 13.12 also sets out the following questions that the review should consider:

a) Have the person's circumstances and/or care and support or support needs changed?

b) What is working in the plan, what is not working, and what might need to change?

c) Have the outcomes identified in the plan been achieved or not?

d) Does the person have new outcomes they want to meet?

e) Could improvements be made to achieve better outcomes?

f) Is the person's personal budget enabling them to meet their needs and the outcomes identified in their plan?

g) Is the current method of managing it still the best one for what they want to achieve, eg should direct payments be considered?

h) Is the personal budget still meeting the sufficiency test?

i) Are there any changes in the person's informal and community support networks which might impact negatively or positively on the plan?

j) Have there been any changes to the person's needs or circumstances which might mean they are at risk of abuse or neglect?

k) Is the person, carer, independent advocate satisfied with the plan?

There should be "an initial 'light touch' review of the planning arrangements 6–8 weeks after sign-off of the plan" (paragraph 13.15). The aim of this is to "provide reassurance to all parties that the plan is working as intended, and will help to identify any teething problems" (paragraph 13.15).

Paragraph 13.16 outlines options to be considered to ensure that the review is proportionate, as follows:

- peer-led review;
- reviews conducted remotely;
- face-to-face reviews with a social worker or other relevant professional.

This paragraph describes an example of "where the person has a stable, longstanding support package with fixed or long-term outcomes", and in these circumstances one option would be for the person "to complete a self-review at the planned time which is then submitted to the local authority to sign-off, rather than have a face to face review with their social worker".

An important caveat is set out in paragraph 13.33 stating that "reviews in general must not be used to arbitrarily reduce a care and support package" and that "any reduction to a personal budget should be the result of a change in need or circumstance".

Revising the plan

The guiding principles for revising the plan derive from those already established within other stages of the care and support journey. They are set out in paragraph 13.28 as follows:

- the person's wishes and feelings should be identified as far as possible and they should be supported to be involved;
- the revision should be proportionate to the needs to be met;
- where the plan was produced in combination with other plans, this should be considered at the revision stage;
- the person, carer or person acting on their behalf should be allowed to self-plan in conjunction with the local authority where appropriate;
- the development of the revised plan must be made with the involvement of the adult/carer, and any person the adult asks the authority to involve;
- any additional elements that were incorporated into the original plan should be replicated in the revised plan where appropriate and agreed by all parties;
- there needs to be clarity on the sign-off process, especially where the revised plan is prepared by the person and the local authority.

Paragraph 13.27 specifies that the revision "should wherever possible follow the process used in the assessment and care planning stages". This paragraph goes on to state that where the local authority is "satisfied that the circumstances have changed in a way that affects a care and support or support plan" it must "carry out a needs or carer's assessment and financial assessment, and then revise the plan and personal budget accordingly".

The review and revision process

The review process will vary depending on whether the review is planned or unplanned, and also the nature of the review. An unplanned review may have been prompted by an event such as a hospital admission, or something less specific such as a neighbour reporting concerns about possible self-neglect.

Initial reviews are recommended after six to eight weeks to make sure that the plan is working as intended. Also there can often be something in the plan about which there is uncertainty, eg whether a carer can cope.

The outcome sought from the review and revision process is that the plan continues to enhance the individual's wellbeing and is in accordance with their aspirations as much as possible. Where it is concluded that there has been a change of circumstances that may have an impact on wellbeing and aspirations, the plan may need to be revised in some way.

The nature of the revision will depend on at what stage of the care and support journey that the change of circumstances has an impact. For example:

- where a person's needs have changed, then a reassessment of needs would take place – and this may or may not lead to changes in the eligibility determination;
- if there is a carer who is no longer willing and able to meet certain needs, then the local authority would now have a duty to meet those needs;
- the amount that a person is assessed to pay would change to zero if their capital falls below the lower capital limit, and this could result in them being willing to receive services that they had previously not agreed to;
- if the individual decides to change from the local authority arranging their care and support for them to a direct payment, the care and support plan would need to be organised in a different way.

The eligibility determination can never be the starting point because any change to eligibility has to be preceded by a reassessment of needs.

The conclusion of the review process will be either a revised plan, or no further action other than to set the date of the next review. In some circumstances a review could result in a safeguarding enquiry being initiated.

Figure 7.2 summarises what social workers should consider in reviewing and revising an individual's care and/or support plan.

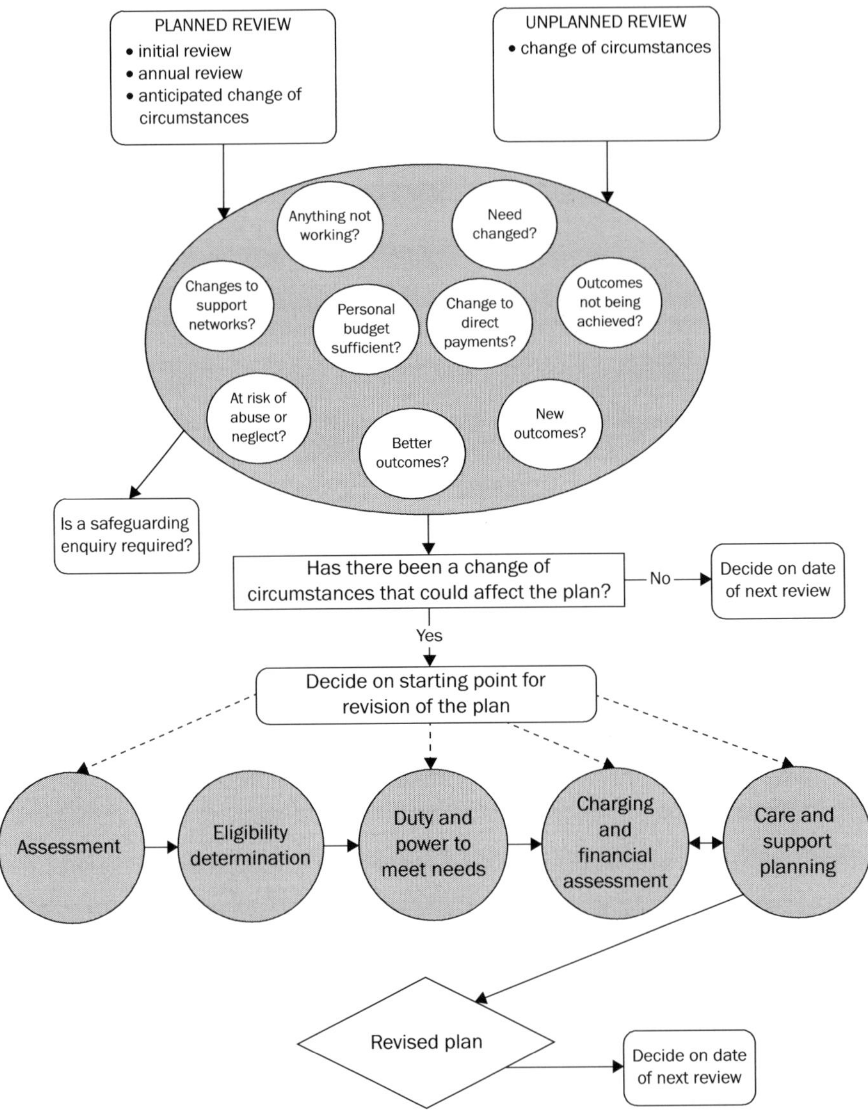

Figure 7.2 *Review pathway*

Formats

The questions that individuals are asked to consider when reviewing their plan are usually based on paragraph 13.2 (see page 173). Individuals are encouraged to record reviews in their own words.

As with care and/or support plans there is usually the opportunity for individuals to write the review themselves, and some local authorities encourage individuals to undertake their own reviews.

Given that there are a significant number of annual reviews where there are no changes of circumstances, local authorities have developed ways of streamlining the process and some take place through a telephone call. These are sometimes described as 'desktop' or 'light-touch' reviews.

Where the care and/or support plan needs to be revised, some or all of the care and support journey will be revisited, so the relevant forms and formats for each stage of the journey would usually be applied. To ensure that the revision process is proportionate and not 'overly-bureaucratic', local procedures often encourage going straight to the relevant part of the care and support journey, eg it could be that the only change that is required can be accommodated within the existing personal budget.

Where the review is unplanned the same format can be used as for a planned review, although there will be circumstances where the review is not only unplanned but is unanticipated, ie a conversation turns into a review.

Sometimes a safeguarding enquiry will prompt a revision of the plan. The safeguarding enquiry may have considered issues that are normally part of a review, and made recommendations about how the care and support journey should be revisited.

Whatever route is followed the output of the process will be either an amended care and/or support plan for the individual, or no change to the plan.

Applying the statutory guidance using case examples

This section illustrates and analyses some of the key elements of the processes described in this chapter that are of particular relevance for social workers.

As with the previous chapters the same three examples of Mr K, Ms W and Mrs O are used to illustrate the review and revision processes. In addition the example of Mr Y is used to illustrate the review and revision of a care and support plan for someone who has had a plan for a lengthy period.

The examples that follow use a variety of different formats for recording the review. They are set out under the following headings:

- **Summary;**
- **Review;**
- **Revision.**

Mr K

Summary

Mr K has COPD (Chronic Obstructive Pulmonary Disease) and arthritis. His daughter (Ms K) has been cooking meals for him but is no longer willing to do so, although she is willing to do her father's shopping. Mr K pays a neighbour to help with the cleaning and laundry. He is unable to go to a jazz club that he used to attend regularly, because he cannot use public transport. Ms K has declined to have a carer's assessment so she does not have a carer's support plan.

Mr K has savings between the upper and lower capital limits, so he pays a contribution towards the cost of his care and support. Ms K receives a direct payment that she uses to pay a neighbour to do Mr K's laundry and cleaning.

His care and support plan is as follows:

My desired outcomes	**Needs that the local authority has agreed / not agreed it will ensure are met D – duty P – power N – not meeting**	**Needs being met by the carer**	**Needs to be met through friends, family and community resources**	**Personal budget and payment method**	**Evaluation of extent to which my desired outcomes are achieved**
I want someone to come in every day and prepare me a home-cooked meal in the way that my daughter has been doing.	*The effect of me being unable to cook for myself has a significant impact on my physical wellbeing and also control over my day-to-day life (D).*	*My daughter, Ms K, is willing to do my shopping*		*I have opted to purchase meals from the home meals service.*	*Moderately satisfied*

My desired outcomes	**Needs that the local authority has agreed / not agreed it will ensure are met D – duty P – power N – not meeting**	**Needs being met by the carer**	**Needs to be met through friends, family and community resources**	**Personal budget and payment method**	**Evaluation of extent to which my desired outcomes are achieved**
Cleaning and laundry – I find this very time consuming and I would rather employ someone to do this.	*The effect of me being unable to do cleaning and laundry has a significant impact on my physical wellbeing and also control over my day-to-day life (D).*			*£ … to pay for … hours of cleaning and laundry Direct payment of £ … to Ms K**	*I'm satisfied with the time allowed for laundry, but I don't think enough time has been allowed for cleaning.*
Attending the local jazz club.	*Not being able to go to the jazz club has a significant impact on my wellbeing in relation to participation in recreational activities (D).*		*Friends and acquaintances who attend the jazz club will give me a lift.*		*I have agreed to give this plan a try, but I am not comfortable about having to rely on people for a lift.*

* *The administration of the employer requirements is undertaken via a local third-party organisation. Ms K also pays a top-up so that the neighbour continues to receive a higher rate of pay than the market rate.*

Review

The review takes place eight weeks after the plan was signed off. The main issues anticipated to be explored would be those where Mr K had said he was not completely satisfied. Also the review of the care and support plan is combined with a review of the direct payment.

Review summary (completed by social worker using Mr K's words):

Have your circumstances and/or care or support needs changed, including any changes to your informal support networks?	*No.*
What is working in the plan, and what is not working and what might need to change?	*I was worried about having to rely on people to go to the jazz club, but this is working out OK so far and my daughter says she will take me if nobody else can do it. Unfortunately my neighbour has decided that she doesn't want to continue to be an 'employee', so I will need to find an alternative.*
How satisfied are you with the extent to which your desired outcomes are being achieved? Are there any changes to your desired outcomes?	*The meals from the home meals service are not as good as my daughter's cooking, but I can put up with them especially as my daughter has agreed to cook me a Sunday dinner. I still don't think enough time has been allowed for cleaning.*
Is the personal budget sufficient?	*I knew I was not going to get enough money to pay my neighbour, so my daughter has been paying a top-up. I understand that the money I get is based on the going rate.*
Is the current method of managing the personal budget working well?	*It was working OK and hopefully it will continue to do so when I find someone else to do my cleaning and laundry.*
Is there anything else that you think is important?	*My daughter wants to have a carer's assessment. She is doing more than she planned to, so she might need some help.*

Revision

The care and support plan requires a minor amendment to rectify what is not working, ie his neighbour will no longer be doing his cleaning and laundry. The plan is also updated to acknowledge what is working well.

My desired outcomes	Needs that the local authority has agreed / not agreed it will ensure are met D – duty P – power N – not meeting	Needs being met by the carer	Needs to be met through friends, family and community resources	Personal budget and payment method	Evaluation of extent to which my desired outcomes are achieved
I want someone to come in every day and prepare me a home-cooked meal in the way that my daughter has been doing.	*The effect of me being unable to cook for myself has a significant impact on my physical wellbeing and also control over my day-to-day life (D).*	*My daughter, Ms K, is willing to do my shopping cook me a Sunday dinner.*		*I have opted to purchase meals from the home meals service.*	*Moderately satisfied.*
Cleaning and laundry – I find this very time consuming and I would rather employ someone to do this.	*The effect of me being unable to do cleaning and laundry has a significant impact on my physical wellbeing and also control over my day-to-day life (D).*			*£ … to pay for … hours of cleaning and laundry Direct payment of £ … to Ms K.*	*My neighbour has decided that she doesn't want to continue to be an 'employee', so I will need to find an alternative.**
Attending the local jazz club.	*Not being able to go to the jazz club has a significant impact on my wellbeing in relation to participation in recreational activities (D)*		*Friends and acquaintances who attend the jazz club give me a lift and my daughter says she will take me if nobody can do it.*		*I was worried about having to rely on people to go to the jazz club, but that is working out OK so far.*

* *The local authority brokerage team will help Mr K find someone who can be employed to do the cleaning and laundry.*

Ms K was present at the review and arrangements have been made for her to receive a carer's assessment.

Review date – *(date to be set for an annual review).*

Ms W

Summary

Ms W (aged 40) has psychotic depression and is socially isolated. The manager of the housing association flat where Ms W lives is concerned that there is a fire risk because of her hoarding behaviour. Ms W wrote the care and support plan in her own words, as follows:

My care and support plan

This says what is important to me and what I have agreed with the social worker. The social worker has helped me with making sure that the facts are correct.

Things that are important to me

I live by myself in a flat that my landlord thinks is untidy and might cause a fire, but I'm happy that all of my books and magazines are where I can get them when I want them and they don't need to worry.

I don't do a lot these days except watch TV, and occasionally I go to car boot sales.

A while ago I was diagnosed with depression and I went into a mental hospital. Medication helps me and I'm much better these days.

I did have a job working at the university in the admissions department but I was made redundant when there was a reorganisation. Since then I have been on benefits and I don't have the confidence to try for another job. I liked being at work most of the time because I was able to have conversations with people if I wanted to, although I didn't like my job much.

Although I don't see my dad much he helps me by paying for my phone.

Changes that I would like and things that I don't want to happen

I would like to go to places where there are other people who I might talk to if I felt like it. I thought it would be a good idea to go to a gym and work with a personal trainer who would make sure I did the best sort of exercise for me and introduce me to people. I realise that to get help with this I have to ask my GP for exercise on prescription. I agree that the social worker can mention this to the GP before I go to see her.

The social worker wants me to sit down with her and the people from the housing association to talk about what they call a 'fire risk'. I think that they are being unfair to me to call me a fire risk, because nothing has ever caught fire. There is no point in meeting with them because they will just tell me to tidy up and throw stuff out, but I can manage without their help and don't want them nagging me.

The reasons why social services will help me

I know that I have got into a bit of a rut and it would be good to do something about it. The social worker has told me that I can get help to improve my wellbeing because I have depression and because I am socially isolated. She says that the fact that the housing association people are concerned is also part of the reason why I can get help, even if I don't agree with their concerns and I won't talk to them.

What has been agreed

I think I might like doing some voluntary work, but with people who have different problems to me. The social worker is going to find someone to give me advice and help get me started. It will give me the chance to be with other people and stimulate my brain a bit.

It would be nice to talk to other people who are interested in history and collect things like I do, but when I've looked online the groups are mainly for academics and people who have jobs in museums. I wouldn't want to join these groups. There is a Facebook group so I will try this and see what happens.

I know there are groups for people who are 'hoarders', but I am a collector, not a hoarder.

If I have to travel for the voluntary work or to go a history group, the social worker says I will get help with the bus fares. This will be a pre-paid card.

I will let the social worker know what progress has been made and we can meet up if the plan needs changing. I know that the social worker wants to do a review before three months are up.

Signatures

Ms W…

Social worker…

Review

A review takes place six months after the plan was signed off. This was to allow enough time for Ms W to evaluate her 'exercise on prescription' and voluntary work. She did not receive a direct payment so a review was not required in the first eight weeks. Prior to meeting with the social worker, Ms W completed the following self-review.

What is working, and what is not working

I had my exercise on prescription for 12 weeks and the exercise itself was good, but I didn't really get to meet anybody. Even with the classes for yoga and spinning, people just keep to themselves. I was hoping that I could carry on going to the gym, but the NHS only pays for 12 weeks.

I'm pleased with my volunteering. I do two days a week for a charity that redistributes surplus food to charities and community groups. They pay my fares and I get lunch. We are quite busy but I do get the chance to chat to people.

I am now on loads of Facebook groups, but most of the stuff is not of great interest to me. I have found out about books that would be interesting, but of course they cost money. I go to Oxfam regularly and I have bought a couple of books, as they don't cost much.

I didn't bother with the local history group that meets in the library. They are only interested in things that happen locally, and it's all about recent history.

Changes that I would like and things that I don't want to happen

I would like to keep going to the gym – will social services pay?

I have put most of my magazines and pamphlets in boxes, and I think this makes my landlord happier. I showed them what I had done and I haven't heard any more about it.

Signature

Ms W…

Following receipt of this self-review the social worker arranges to meet with Ms W to discuss how her care and support plan will need to be revised in light of developments with 'exercise on prescription'. A reassessment is not necessary, as her needs have not changed.

Revision

The main issue to consider is Ms W's desire to continue to go to a gym. In addition the elements of the plan that are not working will need to be considered.

The main purpose of the 'exercise on prescription' was to meet a health need, but it had the additional benefit of potentially improving her social networks and thus reducing her social isolation – however, it has not succeeded in achieving this. If there was no other means of reducing her social isolation then other ways of making use of gym attendance to achieve this could be considered, but as the volunteering is achieving this objective, the local authority could reasonably conclude that it is discharging its duty to meet this need in a way that accords with her desired outcome, ie having the type of casual social contact with people that she had when she had a job.

Ms W has taken steps to reduce the fire risk, and it may be that the emphasis on her being a collector rather than a hoarder has helped her to take some responsibility. Nevertheless, the social worker concludes that Ms W remains unable to maintain a "habitable home environment" from her observations of the way that her collection is laid out in her flat, so her eligibility in this respect has not changed.

There are indications that Ms W's needs could be shifting. It could be argued that she is now able to maintain social interaction without any help. Also she might now need help with moving from volunteering to paid work, so the specified outcome of "accessing and engaging in work, training, education or volunteering" might apply.

Ms W's care and support plan is revised as follows (the changes are underlined for the benefit of the reader):

My care and support plan

This says what is important to me and what I have agreed with the social worker. The social worker has helped me with making sure that the facts are correct.

Things that are important to me

I live by myself in a flat that my landlord thinks is untidy and might cause a fire, but I'm happy that all of my books and magazines are where I can get them when I want them and they don't need to worry. The magazines have now been put in boxes and the social worker confirms that my landlord is pleased with this progress.

I've started getting books from the Oxfam shop, although when the summer comes I might start going to a few car-boot sales. I would like to talk to other collectors but I haven't found the right Facebook group yet.

A while ago I was diagnosed with depression and I went into a mental hospital. Medication helps me and I'm much better these days. I had my exercise on prescription for 12 weeks and the exercise made me feel good. I would like to carry on going to the gym, but the NHS is no longer paying for this service.

I'm pleased with my volunteering. I do two days a week for a charity that redistributes surplus food to charities and community groups. They pay my fares and I get lunch. We are quite busy but I do get the chance to chat to people if I want to. The social worker says I might want to start thinking about whether I want to do more volunteering to maybe help me get a job one day, but I'm not ready for that yet.

Although I don't see my dad much he helps me by paying for my phone. I sent him a text to tell him what I was doing, and he says he is pleased.

Changes that I would like and things that I don't want to happen

I am disappointed that the NHS won't pay for me to keep going to the gym. I was hoping that social services might pay, but I'm told that they can't pay for activities that improve my health and it wasn't helping increase my social contacts.

The reasons why social services will help me

I get help to improve my wellbeing because I have depression and because I am socially isolated, although not as much as I used to be. Also because the housing association people are still concerned about 'fire-risk' this is part of the reason why I can get help, even if I don't agree with their concerns.

What has been agreed

Continue with volunteering.

I will look into ways of joining in with other people doing exercise that doesn't cost anything.

I will think about sorting out my books and maybe getting more boxes and bookshelves.

At my next review in six months' time we will decide if I still need help from a social worker.

Signatures

Ms W…

Social worker…

Mrs O

Summary

Mrs O is due for the first review of her support plan:

Personal details

My name is Mrs O and I am 47 years old. I live with my three children (aged 11, 17 and 19). I am separated from my husband who lives in… [an area of a neighbouring local authority].

Support needs and personal outcomes

Eligibility

I meet the eligibility criteria because I am providing necessary care for my husband who is a problem drinker (which includes helping him clean himself up when he overdoes it), and I am worried that there will be times when the stress of helping my husband and looking after my children will mean that I can't cope. My two older children can look after themselves when there is a crisis, but my youngest child has Down's syndrome and she needs a lot of attention.

I understand that on the records held by Adult Social Care it says that the relevant 'inability' category is "carrying out any caring responsibilities for a child", and the stress I have described is recorded as something that is likely to have a "significant impact on my emotional wellbeing".

Personal outcomes/goals

I want to have access to a professional person to talk through my problems with on a regular basis. Ideally I would like this to be a named social worker.

How needs will be met informally through preventative support available from the community or friends and family

I get support from attending meetings of Al-Anon and the friends I have made there. My husband's father used to help him but he has now died. There is nobody else in the family he will accept help from and he has refused to have an assessment of his care and support needs.

Is this particular need considered eligible for council assistance?

I understand that the local authority has a duty to ensure that my need to talk to someone is met.

Personal budget

Because my needs can be met by services provided by Addaction I will not have a personal budget.

Information and advice

I do not have any non-eligible support needs so this does not apply to me.

First planned review date

I have agreed that this should take place in about 12 weeks' time. It could be sooner or later but it all depends on whether I have had a successful session with Addaction.

Signatures

Mrs O…

Social worker…

Review

Before the review is due Mrs O contacts the social worker who worked on the support plan with Mrs O. Her husband had turned up at their daughter's school in a drunken state and wanted to take her out of school for the day. The school had dealt with the matter satisfactorily, but Mrs O needed to talk and her next Addaction counselling session was two weeks away.

The social worker concluded that enough was known about Mrs O's circumstances to proceed directly to a revision of the support plan. It may have been necessary for the social worker to record her discussion with Mrs O as an unplanned review, to comply with the recording system used by the local authority.

Revision

This revision allows for Mrs O to contact the social worker if she needs support in between Addaction counselling sessions. Her revised support plan is as follows (the changes are underlined).

Personal details

My name is Mrs O and I am 47 years old. I live with my three children (aged 11, 17 and 19). I am separated from my husband who lives in … [an area of a neighbouring local authority].

Support needs and personal outcomes

Eligibility

I meet the eligibility criteria because I am providing necessary care for my husband who is a problem drinker (which includes helping him clean himself up when he overdoes it), and I am worried that there will be times when the stress of helping my husband and looking after my children will mean that I can't cope. My two older children can look after themselves when there is a crisis, but my youngest child has Down's syndrome and she needs a lot of attention.

I understand that on the records held by Adult Social Care it says that the relevant 'inability' category is "carrying out any caring responsibilities for a child", and the stress I have described is recorded as something that is likely to have a "significant impact on my emotional wellbeing".

Personal outcomes/goals

I want to have access to a professional person to talk through my problems with on a regular basis. Ideally I would like this to be a named social worker.

How needs will be met informally through preventative support available from the community or friends and family

I get support from attending meetings of Al-Anon and the friends I have made there. I am also receiving counselling once every two months from Addaction. My husband's father used to help him but he has now died. There is nobody else in the family he will accept help from and he has refused to have an assessment of his care and support needs.

Is this particular need considered eligible for council assistance?

I understand that the local authority has a duty to ensure that my need to talk to someone is met.

Personal budget

£... has been allocated as representing the cost of me talking to the social worker on an average of once a month. I do not want to have a direct payment because I want to have a social worker who is employed by the local authority.

I do not need a personal budget for services provided by Addaction.

Information and advice

I do not have any non-eligible support needs so this does not apply to me.

Next planned review date

I have agreed that this should take place in about six months' time.

Signatures

Mrs O...

Social worker...

Mr Y

Summary

Mr Y is a young adult with a learning disability who lives in supported living accommodation. He has a PA (personal assistant; funded through a direct payment) who comes to his flat twice a week to help him to plan his activities, organise his shopping and ensure that he adheres to the conditions of his tenancy. His parents live in a town 20 miles away but they are in close contact. His father is the nominated person for the direct payment, and he has also been appointed as the appropriate person to help Mr Y to be involved in the review process as much as possible. Mr Y's receives a PIP (Personal Independence Payment) that is paid directly to him. He also receives a small payment for working in a social enterprise. He pays his bills via direct debits. Mr Y only usually sees a social worker at the annual review of his care and support plan.

A recent safeguarding enquiry concluded that his needs should be reassessed, as set out in the following enquiry summary (for more details see Chapter 8).

Heading	***Summary***
Allegation	*Mr Y's PA (personal assistant) has reported his concern on 20 May that Mr Y is becoming unkempt and his flat is becoming untidy and dirty. This change coincided with Mr Y acquiring some new friends who he sees regularly. The PA also believes that he spends less money on food than he used to, and is worried that he is giving money to these new friends.*

Heading	***Summary***
Consent by the adult, or capacity assessment	*Mr Y initially indicated that he would not consent to an enquiry, but subsequently agreed after an independent advocate was appointed. Mr Y has substantial difficulty in involvement, but does not lack the capacity to make the decision to consent or to make the decisions that are the subject of the enquiry.*
Chronology of the abuse or neglect	*20 May – PA reports his concerns to the social worker who undertook the last review of his care and support plan.*
Category of abuse/ neglect	*Financial abuse and self neglect*
Decision-making prior to enquiry	*22–28 May – social worker explores the situation with Mr Y's father who acts as the appropriate person at Mr Y's annual review. Mr Y's father talks to the PA. Agreed that Mr Y senior will visit his son and talk to him.* *30 May – visit takes place and Mr Y senior reports that his son says that there is no problem and he doesn't need any help. Mr Y senior was shocked about how unkempt his son is and annoyed that his son refused to show him his bank statements.* *1 June – Team Manager authorises a section 42 enquiry because of financial abuse and specifies that the enquiry also investigates the deterioration in Mr Y's wellbeing that appears to be linked to alleged self-neglect. Enquiry to be led by the social worker who knows Mr Y.* *25 June – Mr Y visited by an independent advocate and Mr Y agrees to participate in the enquiry.*
Account given by the person at risk or their representative	*1 July – Independent advocate and social worker visit Mr Y. Mr Y admits that he has been under pressure from his friends to withdraw money from his account and wants advice about this.*
Views and wishes of the adult (and family) including risk and desired outcomes	• *Mr Y wants to maintain contact with his new friends* • *Family want to have more control over Mr Y's bank account as they are not convinced that he will resist pressure to withdraw money.*
Enquiry findings and analysis	*Financial abuse is taking place insofar as there is pressure on Mr Y to withdraw money from his bank account that he is uncomfortable with. There is also concern from Mr Y's family that the changes to his lifestyle that are linked with the association with his new friends is having a negative impact on Mr Y's wellbeing, although Mr Y has not expressed any concern.*
Conclusion about whether abuse/ neglect has occurred	*Mr Y is at risk of financial abuse. There are some indicators of self-neglect and psychological abuse (linked to the financial abuse).*

Heading	**Summary**
Determination of extent to which the adult has achieved their desired outcome	*Mr Y's desired outcomes have shifted in the course of the investigation, although he has consistently maintained that he wants to remain in contact with these new friends.*
Determination of extent to which the adult feels safer	*Mr Y is reassured that he will get some help to address his concern about being under pressure from his friends to withdraw money from his account.*
Recommendations for the next step or safeguarding plan	• *Mr Y to be offered a reassessment of his care and support needs to consider whether the way that he has developed personal relationships is having a significant impact on his wellbeing. Whether or not his eligible needs have changed, consideration is to be given to revising his care and support plan to better meet needs that are already agreed.* • *Independent advocate to be retained for this reassessment.* • *Family to be advised of this plan, if Mr Y agrees.*

His current care and support plan is as follows:

I want to ...	• *Live independently but I need help with planning things like shopping and paying my bills* • *Have a job* • *Make friends of my own age* • *I only want my parents to help me when I ask them to*
Help I need to make my everyday life better	• *Choosing and buying the right food, and cooking meals* • *Wearing the right type of clothes when I go out* • *Keeping my job* • *Making friends*
How social services help	*Pay John (PA) to visit twice a week to help me plan activities and shopping, and remind me what I need to do when I go out to work*
Help I get from my family	• *My dad* – *gets money from social services to pay John* – *makes sure the bills are paid by the bank that has my money* – *helps me to understand things like reviews and to say what I want* • *Sometimes I stay with my family and go on holiday with them*
My circle of support	• *I go to clubs with people who live in the same place as me* • *I like to go into town by myself sometimes*
My flat	*I have a supported living tenancy. There are staff who can help if there are problems like blocked sinks.*

My job	*I help in the kitchen of a café two mornings every week*
My hobbies	*I like football and I support Manchester United and a local team*
Things that are difficult that I have had advice about	• *Keeping the flat clean* • *Cooking* • *Making friends*
Next review	• *[a date in one year's time]*

Signatures

Mr Y…

Social worker…

Revision

A meeting is held with Mr Y and the social worker who knows him to reassess his needs and revise his care and support plan. Mr Y is supported by an independent advocate and his PA participates at Mr Y's request. Mr Y says he doesn't want his dad there.

When his eligibility was determined previously, the decision was as follows:

1. *He experiences distress and anxiety in*
    - *choosing and buying the right food;*
    - *choosing the right clothes to wear when going out and this has a significant impact on his wellbeing in relation to 'control over day-to-day life';*
2. *He is unable to access and engage in work, and this has a significant impact on his wellbeing in relation to 'participation in work'.*

The social worker concludes that recent events show that he is unable to safely develop and maintain personal relationships, and as a result there is a risk of this having a significant impact on his wellbeing because of the risk of financial abuse. His difficulties in making friends had been considered previously, but at the time there was no risk factor. A more detailed plan to address this need is to be worked out to minimise his vulnerability, comprising the following elements:

- *Mr Y agreeing to temporary restrictions on the use of his debit card;*
- *an offer to his new friends to involve them in Mr Y's circle of support;*
- *more support for Mr Y in attending football matches – recognising that there might be a need to revise the personal budget to pay for this.*

The specified outcome of 'maintaining personal hygiene' was considered but as there is no identifiable inability or risk factor, it was concluded that his unkempt appearance is not an eligible need. The duty to give advice on this will be part of the overall advice about the relationship with his new friends. Likewise his untidy and dirty flat does not trigger the 'maintaining a habitable home environment' specified outcome, because there is no safety risk. He already receives reminders from his PA about the importance of keeping his flat clean as a condition of his tenancy.

Subsequently a revised care and support plan was agreed as follows (additions are underlined):

<table>
<tr><td>I want to …</td><td>• Live independently but I need help with planning things like shopping and paying my bills.
• Have a job
• Make friends of my own age
• I only want my parents to help me when I ask them to</td></tr>
<tr><td>Help I need to make my everyday life better</td><td>• Choosing and buying the right food, and cooking meals
• Wearing the right type of clothes when I go out
• Keeping my job
• Making friends</td></tr>
<tr><td>How social services help</td><td>• Pay John (PA) to visit twice a week to help me plan activities and shopping, and remind me what I need to do when I go out to work
• <u>The social worker will help me make sure I don't spend money on things that I don't need</u>
• <u>The social worker will find a way of me going to local football matches with people that I know</u></td></tr>
<tr><td>Help I get from my family</td><td>• My dad
– gets money from social services to pay John;
– makes sure the bills are paid by the bank that has my money;
– helps me to understand things like reviews and to say what I want;
• Sometimes I stay with my family and go on holiday with them</td></tr>
<tr><td>My circle of support</td><td>• I go to clubs with people who live in the same place as me
• I like to go into town by myself sometimes</td></tr>
<tr><td>My flat</td><td>I have a supported living tenancy. There are staff who can help if there are problems like blocked sinks.</td></tr>
<tr><td>My job</td><td>I help in the kitchen of a café two mornings every week</td></tr>
<tr><td>My hobbies</td><td>I like football and I support Manchester United and Shrewsbury Town</td></tr>
</table>

Things that are difficult that I have had advice about	• _Keeping the flat clean_ • _Keeping myself clean_ • _Cooking_ • _Making friends_
Next review	• _[a date in one year's time]_

Signatures

Mr Y...

Social worker...

Comment and analysis

Readers should note that what is set out in this section and the previous section is intended to show how the statutory guidance might be applied, and in doing so, what would be complex situations in real life have had to be simplified.

Each of the four case examples demonstrate different pathways from review to revision of the plan, which can be summarised as follows:

- planned review records minor revision to the plan – Mr K;
- planned self-review identifies a request for a revision because of developments with the healthcare plan – Ms W;
- events precipitate informal review and these events demonstrate that the plan needs revising – Mrs O;
- safeguarding enquiry identifies changes in needs – Mr Y.

With Ms W, Mrs O and Mr Y there is a gap between the review and the revision. For Mrs O and Mr Y this is because the review is unplanned in both cases. Ms W's review takes place in advance of the revision because she undertakes a self-review. However, in many cases the review and revision take place in the same meeting, as it did with Mr K. Social workers ought to be prepared to undertake a review and revision in the same meeting, unless it is otherwise indicated.

It is only in Mr Y's case that new needs have emerged. In each of the other cases the change of circumstances is as a result of aspects of the plan not working. This can often be the case where the plan is being reviewed for the first time, as it is not always possible to get everything right – hence the recommendation in the statutory guidance that the first review should take place six to eight weeks after the plan is signed off.

Ms W's first review did not take place until six months had elapsed. This illustrates that the statutory guidance need not be followed to the letter, if there is a good reason for doing otherwise.

The review took place for Mrs O and Mr Y earlier than the planned review date because of events. In Mrs O's case it became clear that her needs could not be fully met by the counselling available from Addaction, and in Mr Y's case there had been a change of circumstances uncovered by a safeguarding enquiry.

In all of the case examples it was decided that there should be a revision of the plan following the review. However, there will be situations where no revision is required. With Mr K, for example, if his neighbour had continued working for him there would have been no need for a revision of the plan.

The starting point for revisiting the care and support journey was the plan itself in every case except for Mr Y, where the change in his needs meant that a reassessment of needs was required. This reassessment led to the decision that he is unable to safely develop and maintain personal relationships, and as a result there is a risk of this having a significant impact on his wellbeing because of financial abuse, ie an additional eligible need was identified.

It should be noted that there can be circumstances where although the starting point is the plan, it is also necessary to revisit the 'charging and financial assessment' stage. Mrs O previously did not have a personal budget, but now that she is going to receive support from a social worker, this is something that her local authority normally makes a charge for. However, because it is the policy of this local authority not to charge carers, there is no need for a financial assessment.

The format used to evaluate Mr K's plan asks the individual to evaluate the extent to which their desired outcomes are being met, and this highlighted that his neighbour didn't want to continue being an employee. In his case the review process is captured in the evaluation column of the review format and is then followed by revised plan, whereas in other local authorities the review element may take place verbally and the outcome is recorded only in the revised plan, as is the case with Mrs O.

The change to Mr K's plan is relatively minor, and is simply because the person being employed to provide the cleaning and laundry is no longer willing to do this. Having said this it is likely that this change will be very anxiety-provoking for Mr K, and it may take time and effort to organise a replacement.

Quite a lot has changed for Ms W, most of it for the better. The review is an opportunity to reflect on what is working well and to build on successes where possible. In fact with Ms W there are indications that her needs could be shifting. She appears to be able to maintain social interaction without any help, and she might now need help with moving from volunteering to paid work, so the specified outcome of "accessing and engaging in work, training, education or volunteering" could apply in the near future. What's more there has been an unanticipated positive development, in that she has taken some small steps towards better organising her books and magazines. Very little has actually changed in Ms W's revised plan this time round, although at the next review the positive developments that are emerging may come to fruition.

In these examples all of the potential stages of the care and/or support journey were revisited except for the 'duty and power to meet needs'. This could have applied to Mr K if Ms K was no longer willing and able to do his shopping for him, and in which case consideration would have to be given as to whether the local authority has a duty to include the meeting of this need in the care and support plan.

Conclusion

The review process can often be relatively straightforward, and indeed it needs to be so to facilitate it being led by the individual. There will be many situations where a revision is not required, and thus the review can proceed in a streamlined way that is proportionate to the circumstances. However, there will be circumstances where even the most experienced of social workers will encounter situations in a review where they will want to have time to reflect and consult before deciding how to proceed with revising the care and/or support plan. There are so many variables that can occur when applying the review and revision processes together, that unique situations will frequently occur.

In some ways the undertaking of a review and revision of a care and/or support plan is the part of the care and support journey that can require the most knowledge, skills and experience. In all circumstances the reviewing social worker will want to be alert to what's working and what's not working, and evaluate the impact of the plan on the individual's wellbeing. Revising the plan requires having a sufficient understanding of the care and support journey to be able to know where to start, and then to complete all of the stages without unnecessary bureaucracy and delay – making sure that the individual's strengths and community resources are fully utilised, and that the individual is involved as much as they can and want to be.

This part of the book has concentrated on the essentials of the care and/or support journey, and in doing so has put to one side some important elements of the Care Act and the statutory guidance. Subsequent chapters of the book explore safeguarding and the special provisions for helping people with substantial difficulty in being involved.

Part II Safeguarding

The statutory guidance sets out the safeguarding duties of local authorities (and other organisations) and how these should be applied. In addition it consolidates current thinking by providing a description of the principal types of abuse and neglect.

Chapter 8 of this book focuses on those parts of the statutory guidance that are of particular relevance to the day-to-day practice of social workers, ie safeguarding enquiries and safeguarding plans.

Other useful information is set out in Chapter 9 by providing summaries of the following:

- a list and description of the types of abuse and neglect that have been brought together in the statutory guidance;
- the new powers and duties in relation to Safeguarding Adults Boards;
- the new powers and duties in relation to Safeguarding Adults Reviews.

The Care Act and its accompanying statutory guidance provides the basic framework for safeguarding, and because safeguarding is such a complex activity the statutory guidance encourages each local Safeguarding Adults Board to develop their own policies and procedures. Paragraph 14.53 recommends that procedures "be updated to incorporate learning from published research, peer reviews, case law and lessons from recent cases and Safeguarding Adults Reviews". In addition it states "procedures should also include the provisions of the law – criminal, civil and statutory – relevant to adult safeguarding". The scope of some of these local policies and procedures can be very broad, eg some include sections on radicalisation.

Many Safeguarding Adults Boards have also developed additions to the statutory guidance where there is thought to be insufficient definition, eg non-statutory enquiries.

Even though these local policies and procedures go into more detail than the statutory guidance, they are not social work manuals. They reflect the framework set out in the statutory guidance, so they expand on what should be included in a safeguarding plan but do not give guidance on how the content of the plan might be applied.

8 Safeguarding enquiries

Introduction

A major provision of the Care Act 2014 is the duty of local authorities to undertake safeguarding enquiries. This duty applies to people who, it is thought, have care and support needs, are experiencing (or at risk of) abuse or neglect and are unable to protect themselves because of their care and support needs. Local authorities must decide whether any action should be taken to help and protect them.

Although a safeguarding enquiry is a distinct and separate process from a needs assessment there are many similarities. Safeguarding enquiries must be driven by the outcomes that the individual wants to achieve, and the individual's strengths are to be taken into account and use made of community resources and support networks. There is also a prevention element, but with safeguarding the focus is on prevention of harm and reducing the risk or the impact of abuse or neglect.

Safeguarding can often be complex and challenging, and in many cases a social worker will be the most appropriate professional to take the lead in coordinating a safeguarding enquiry and developing a safeguarding plan. The professional skill and judgement of a social worker is often essential in helping to achieve an acceptable balance between a person's safety and their wellbeing.

The statutory guidance provides a description of different types of abuse and neglect and the different circumstances in which they may take place. In addition to being applied in safeguarding enquiries, this typology is usually included in the adult safeguarding policies and procedures that all relevant organisations should have.

This chapter comprises the following sections:

- **Summary of the system prior to April 2015**
- **Key terms and definitions**

- **The scope of safeguarding duties**
- **The role of social workers**
- **Aims, principles and definitions**
- **Safeguarding enquiries and safeguarding plans**
- **Record-keeping**
- **Sharing information and confidentiality**
- **Applying the guidance using case examples**
- **Conclusion.**

Summary of the system prior to April 2015

Prior to April 2015 the previous statutory guidance *No Secrets: Guidance on Developing and Implementing Multi-agency Policies and Procedures to Protect Vulnerable Adults from Abuse* was issued in 2000. This guidance placed responsibilities only on local authorities, and it did not require any co-operation from other agencies.

Guidance was provided on determining "how serious or extensive abuse must be to justify intervention" (paragraph 2.18 of 'No secrets').

Key terms and definitions

The following have been selected because they appear in the Care Act as well as the statutory guidance (note that there are no regulations for safeguarding).

Key term	Care Act 2014	The Care and Support Statutory Guidance (revised 2017)
Abuse and neglect	It is included in section 1 (2) which defines 'wellbeing' as including "protection from abuse and neglect".	Paragraph 14.17 lists the following types of abuse and neglect, but with the caveat that local authorities "should not limit their view of what constitutes abuse or neglect": • Physical abuse; • Domestic violence; • Sexual abuse; • Psychological abuse; • Financial or material abuse; • Modern slavery; • Discriminatory abuse; • Organisational abuse; • Neglect and acts of omission; • Self-neglect.

Key term	Care Act 2014	The Care and Support Statutory Guidance (revised 2017)
Safeguarding	The introductory paragraph states that the Care Act makes "provision about safeguarding adults from abuse or neglect".	Paragraph 14.7 identifies the following key features: • it "means protecting an adult's right to live in safety, free from abuse and neglect"; • preventing and stopping "both the risks and experience of abuse or neglect"; • "making sure that the adult's wellbeing is promoted including, where appropriate, having regard to their views, wishes, feelings and beliefs in deciding on any action".
Safeguarding enquiry	Section 42 states the local authority's duties. 1. It applies where a local authority has reasonable cause to suspect that an adult in its area (whether or not ordinarily resident there) – (a) has needs for care and support (whether or not the authority is meeting any of those needs), (b) is experiencing, or is at risk of, abuse or neglect, and (c) as a result of those needs is unable to protect himself or herself against the abuse or neglect or the risk of it. 2. The local authority must make (or cause to be made) whatever enquiries it thinks necessary to enable it to decide whether any action should be taken in the adult's case (whether under this part or otherwise) and, if so, what and by whom.	**Definition and Purpose** Paragraph 14.77 states that a safeguarding "enquiry is the action taken or instigated by the local authority in response to a concern that abuse or neglect may be taking place", and clarifies that the enquiry "could range from a conversation with the adult… or their representative or advocate… to a much more formal multi-agency plan or course of action". Paragraph 14.78 states: "The purpose of the enquiry is to decide whether or not the local authority or another organisation, or person, should do something to help and protect the adult." **Causing the enquiry to be made** Although local authorities may 'cause others' to make enquiries, paragraph 14.81 states that it "is likely that many enquiries will require the input and supervision of a social worker, particularly the more complex situations". **Action** Paragraph 14.93 clarifies that the action to be taken is "to help and protect the adult", and the "local authority must determine what further action is necessary" (paragraph 14.107). This process is described as "safeguarding planning" in paragraph 14.106 and its purpose is "to enable the adult to achieve resolution or recovery, or fuller assessments by health and social care agencies".

The scope of safeguarding enquiries

1. Safeguarding enquiries apply to adults with care and support needs regardless of whether the local authority is meeting their needs.
2. The duties apply in any setting, other than prisons and 'approved premises'.
3. In some circumstances it will be appropriate for the police to instigate a criminal investigation.
4. The consent of the adult concerned should be sought before a section 42 enquiry is undertaken. This consent can be set aside in specified circumstances.
5. A local authority can choose to undertake a safeguarding enquiry for an individual where they do not have a duty to undertake a section 42 enquiry, in circumstances where this would promote the person's wellbeing and have a preventive impact.
6. Where the individual is subject to an enquiry and has care and support needs, an assessment of their care and support needs must also take place.
7. A safeguarding enquiry that identifies that an adult is experiencing or at risk of abuse will conclude with a safeguarding plan to set out what further action is necessary to help and protect the adult.

Aims, principles and definitions

This section describes the following:

- **the aims of adult safeguarding;**
- **principles;**
- **making safeguarding personal;**
- **what constitutes abuse and neglect;**
- **criminal investigation;**
- **carers and safeguarding.**

The aims of adult safeguarding

Paragraph 14.11 sets out the following aims:

- prevent harm and reduce the risk of abuse or neglect to adults with care and support needs;
- stop abuse or neglect wherever possible;
- safeguard adults in a way that supports them in making choices and having control about how they want to live;
- promote an approach that concentrates on improving life for the adults concerned;

- raise public awareness so that communities as a whole, alongside professionals, play their part in preventing, identifying and responding to abuse and neglect;
- provide information and support in accessible ways to help people understand the different types of abuse;
- how to stay safe and what to do to raise a concern about the safety or wellbeing of an adult.

Paragraph 14.12 sets out that to achieve these aims it is necessary to:

- ensure that everyone, both individuals and organisations, is clear about their roles and responsibilities;
- create strong multi-agency partnerships that provide timely and effective prevention of and responses to abuse or neglect;
- support the development of a positive learning environment across these partnerships and at all levels within them to help break down cultures that are risk-averse and seek to scapegoat or blame practitioners;
- enable access to mainstream community resources such as accessible leisure facilities, safe town centres and community groups that can reduce the social and physical isolation which in itself may increase the risk of abuse or neglect;
- clarify how responses to safeguarding concerns deriving from the poor quality and inadequacy of service provision, including patient safety in the health sector, should be responded to.

The six key principles

These are set out in paragraph 14.13, which states: "The principles should inform the ways in which professionals and other staff work with adults." It is intended that these principles "apply to all sectors and settings including care and support services".

They are as follows:

- Empowerment – people being supported and encouraged to make their own decisions and give informed consent;
- Prevention – it is better to take action before harm occurs;
- Proportionality – the least intrusive response appropriate to the risk presented;
- Protection – support and representation for those in greatest need;
- Partnership – local solutions through services working with their communities; communities have a part to play in preventing, detecting and reporting neglect and abuse;
- Accountability – accountability and transparency in delivering safeguarding.

Making safeguarding personal

The Care and Support Statutory Guidance 2015 states in paragraph 1.31 that it "endorses the: 'Making Safeguarding Personal' approach". This was set out in a guide published in 2014 by the Local Government Association and ADASS (the Association of Directors of Adults Social Services).[1] Paragraph 1.31 describes this approach as representing "a fundamental shift in social work practice in relation to safeguarding, with a focus on the person not the process".

Paragraph 14.15 states that "making safeguarding personal means it should be person-led and outcome-focused". This means:

- engaging the person in a conversation about how best to respond to their safeguarding situation;
- doing this in such a way that it enhances involvement, choice and control as well as improving quality of life, wellbeing and safety.

Paragraph 14.14 also makes the point that in protecting individuals who have "different preferences, histories, circumstances and life-styles... it is unhelpful to prescribe a process that must be followed whenever a concern is raised".

What constitutes abuse and neglect

The categories of abuse and neglect listed in the Care Act 2014 are as follows:

- physical abuse;
- domestic violence;
- sexual abuse;
- psychological abuse;
- financial or material abuse;
- modern slavery;
- discriminatory abuse;
- organisational abuse;
- neglect and acts of omission;
- self-neglect.

Paragraph 14.16 clarifies that this list is not intended to be exhaustive "but an illustrative guide as to the sort of behaviour which could give rise to a safeguarding concern".

The list is set out with additional description in paragraphs 14.17–25 and this is reproduced in full in Chapter 9.

Options for protecting the adult

The first decision to be made by a local authority when a safeguarding concern is raised is whether there should be a safeguarding enquiry, and then whether the local authority will undertake the enquiry directly or 'cause' it to be undertaken by another organisation.

In many circumstances where there has been what paragraph 14.42 describes as "poor, neglectful care or practice" by staff employed in health or social care, "then an employer-led disciplinary response may be more appropriate".

In many cases it will be necessary to refer "the matter to the police to consider whether a criminal investigation would be required or appropriate" (paragraph 14.41). Where there is uncertainty about how to proceed in this respect those concerned "should contact the police for advice" (paragraph 14.41). Paragraph 14.83 adds "the early involvement of the police is likely to have benefits in many cases".

Carers and safeguarding

The circumstances in which a carer could be involved in a situation requiring a safeguarding response are set out in paragraph 14.45, as follows:

- a carer may witness or speak up about abuse or neglect;
- a carer may experience intentional or unintentional harm from the adult they are trying to support or from professionals and organisations they are in contact with;
- a carer may unintentionally or intentionally harm or neglect the adult they support on their own or with others.

Safeguarding enquiries and safeguarding plans

Enquiries are often described as 'section 42 enquiries' because this duty is set out in section 42 of the Care Act. Section 42 (1) states:

> This section applies where a local authority has reasonable cause to suspect that an adult in its area (whether or not ordinarily resident there) –
>
> a) has needs for care and support (whether or not the authority is meeting any of those needs),
>
> b) is experiencing, or is at risk of, abuse or neglect, and
>
> c) as a result of those needs is unable to protect himself or herself against the abuse or neglect or the risk of it.

The local authority is responsible for undertaking the enquiry, but may "cause others to do so" (paragraph 14.76).

Paragraph 14.6 states that "adult safeguarding duties apply equally to those adults with care and support needs regardless of whether those needs are being met, i.e. the care and support needs are not required to have met the eligibility criteria".

It should be noted that paragraph 14.17 adds a caveat "that self-neglect may not prompt a section 42 enquiry". Self-neglect is defined as "neglecting to care for one's personal hygiene, health or surroundings and includes behaviour such as hoarding". The key issue is whether individuals can "protect themselves by controlling their own behaviour", and the section 42 criteria would only be met when "they are no longer able to do this, without external support".

A local authority may choose to undertake a safeguarding enquiry where the criteria are not met and thus there is not a section 42 enquiry duty, where this "will enable the local authority to promote the person's wellbeing and support a preventative agenda" (paragraph 14.44).

Paragraph 6.57 states: "Where the adult has care and support needs, local authorities must continue to carry out a needs assessment and determine whether they have eligible needs, and if so, how these will be met." This will always apply where a section 42 enquiry takes place (because the criteria requires the individual to appear to have needs for care and support), but may not necessarily apply where the local authority chooses to undertake a non-statutory enquiry.

Inputs, process and outputs

An enquiry proceeds following a safeguarding concern being raised, if either the section 42 criteria are met or the local authority chooses to use its power to undertake a non-statutory enquiry.

The major process is the safeguarding enquiry itself, but the statutory guidance describes an 'initial enquiry' stage for "deciding when intervention is appropriate" (paragraph 14.52).

Once the local authority has taken the decision about which organisation will provide the lead professional, then the enquiry can be planned.

The enquiry itself will establish whether abuse or neglect has taken place and what the adult wants to happen. What happens next will then be set out in a safeguarding plan.

Figure 8.1 sets this out in a diagrammatic form.

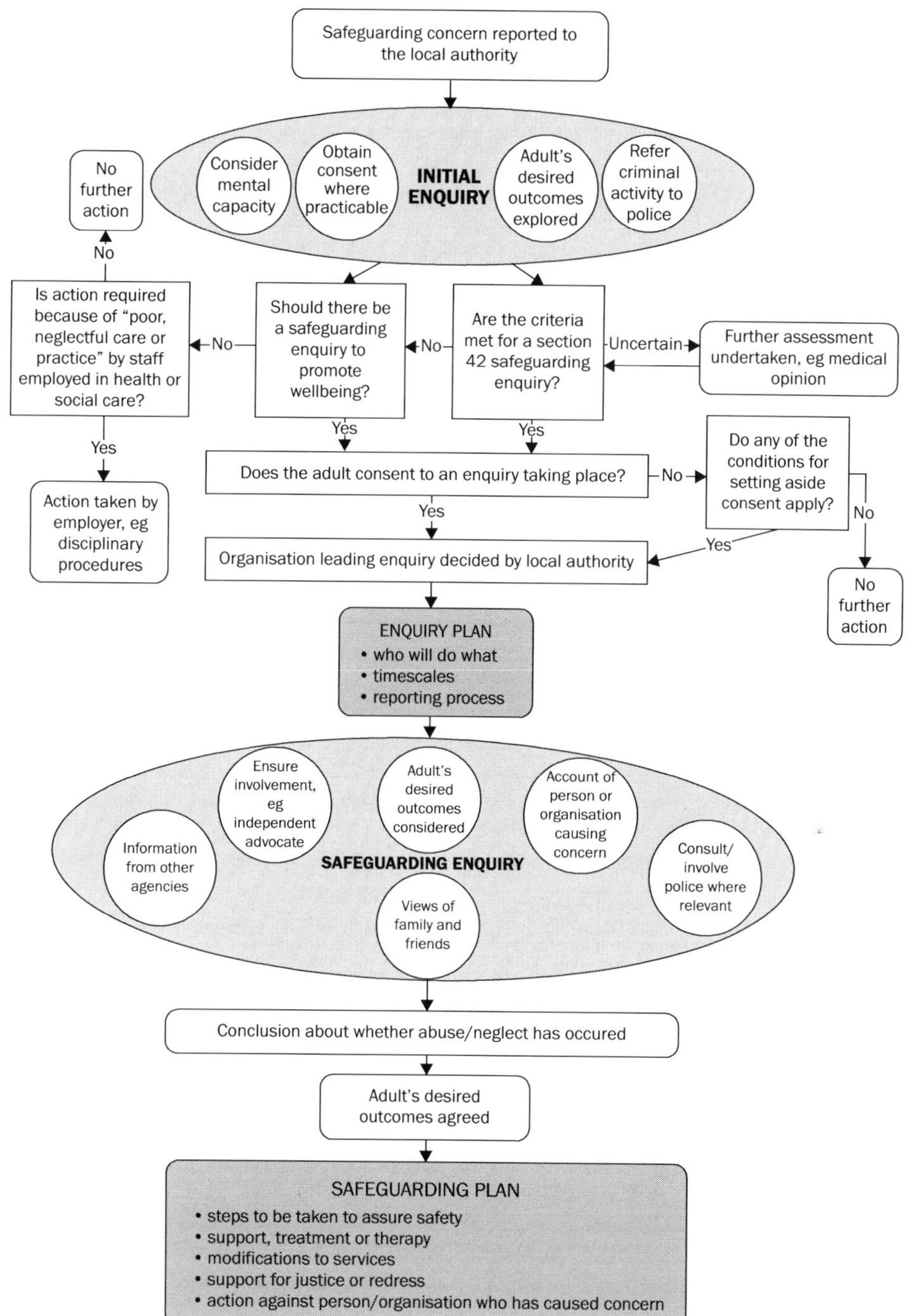

Figure 8.1 *Safeguarding enquiry pathway*

Purpose and objectives

The purpose of an enquiry "is to decide whether or not the local authority or another organisation, or person, should do something to help and protect the adult" (paragraph 14.78).

The objectives of an enquiry are summarised in paragraph 14.94, as follows:

a) establish facts;

b) ascertain the adult's views and wishes;

c) assess the needs of the adult for protection, support and redress and how they might be met;

d) protect from the abuse and neglect, in accordance with the wishes of the adult;

e) make decisions as to what follow-up action should be taken with regard to the person or organisation responsible for the abuse or neglect;

f) enable the adult to achieve resolution and recovery.

The factors to be considered are summarised in paragraph 14.99, as follows:

- the adult's needs for care and support;
- the adult's risk of abuse or neglect;
- the adult's ability to protect themselves or the ability of their networks to increase the support they offer;
- the impact on the adult, their wishes;
- the possible impact on important relationships;
- potential of action and increasing risk to the adult;
- the risk of repeated or increasingly serious acts involving children, or another adult at risk of abuse or neglect;
- the responsibility of the person or organisation that has caused the abuse or neglect.

Involvement, empowerment and consent

Paragraph 14.80 states that the "adult should always be involved from the beginning of the enquiry unless there are exceptional circumstances that would increase the risk of abuse", and also the outcome of an enquiry "should reflect the adult's wishes wherever possible" (paragraph 14.79).

To ensure that the adult experiences the enquiry as empowering, social workers and other practitioners "should wherever practicable seek the consent of the adult before taking action" (paragraph 14.95). Circumstances identified in this paragraph where the need for consent can be set aside are as follows:

- the adult lacks the capacity to give it, but it is in their best interests to undertake an enquiry;
- action may need to be taken if others are or will be put at risk if nothing is done;
- it is in the public interest to take action because a criminal offence has occurred.

As is made clear in paragraph 14.95 "the first priority should always be to ensure the safety and wellbeing of the adult".

In circumstances where the adult does not want any action taken, "this does not preclude the sharing of information with relevant professional colleagues" (paragraph 14.92). This means that the police can be informed and they can consider whether the adult is a 'vulnerable adult witness' who is being intimidated. This paragraph identifies that in these circumstances the adult need not be told of this sharing of information if it "would increase the risk of harm."

A needs assessment must take place and run in parallel with the safeguarding enquiry, and the adult may not decline to be assessed. Following section 11 (2) of the Care Act, paragraph 6.20 of the statutory guidance states that "where the adult who is [*sic*] or is at risk of abuse or neglect has capacity and is still refusing an assessment, local authorities must undertake an assessment so far as possible and document this".

The Care Act 2014 does not confer any additional powers in respect of gaining access to an adult who is the subject of an enquiry and a social worker is prevented from seeing them.

Proportionality

As with the assessment of needs and carers' assessments, the enquiry has to be appropriate and proportionate and "could range from a conversation with the adult... right through to a much more formal multi-agency plan or course of action" (paragraph 14.77).

It is most important that any intervention in family and personal relationships is carefully considered and proportionate. Paragraph 14.98 states: "Safeguarding needs to recognise that the right to safety needs to be balanced with other rights, such as rights to liberty and autonomy, and rights to family life." This paragraph also states that "interventions which remove all contact with family members may also be experienced as abusive interventions and risk breaching the adult's right to family life if not justified or proportionate".

Partners

There will be circumstances where aspects of an enquiry "may be best undertaken by others with more appropriate skills and knowledge" (paragraph 14.82). An example is given where "health professionals should undertake enquiries and treatment plans relating to medicines management or pressure sores" (paragraph 14.82).

Other organisations can undertake an enquiry, eg where a particular professional knows the adult concerned, but in these circumstances paragraph 14.100 specifies that the following conditions apply:

- the local authority retains the responsibility for ensuring that the enquiry is referred to the right place and is acted upon;
- the local authority should assure itself that the enquiry satisfies its duty under section 42 to decide what action (if any) is necessary to help and protect the adult and by whom and to ensure that such action is taken when necessary.

Where the abuse or neglect constitutes a criminal offence the police must undertake a criminal investigation and a "criminal investigation by the police takes priority over all other enquiries" (paragraph 14.91), but in these circumstances the "local authority has an ongoing duty to promote the wellbeing of the adult in these circumstances" (paragraph 14.101). Paragraph 14.84 states that established good practice is that "police investigations should be coordinated with health and social care enquiries".

Safeguarding plans

Paragraph 14.106 states: "Once the facts have been established, a further discussion of the needs and wishes of the adult is likely to take place. This could be focused safeguarding planning to enable the adult to achieve resolution or recovery, or fuller assessments by health and social care agencies (e.g. a needs assessment under the Care Act)."

Safeguarding planning must take place regardless of whether "it is concluded that the allegation is true or otherwise, as many enquiries may be inconclusive" (paragraph 14.106).

It is the responsibility of the local authority to determine "what further action is necessary" (paragraph 14.107), and "the appropriateness of the outcome of the enquiry" (paragraph 14.110). However, the adult should be involved and once the enquiry is completed the local authority "should then determine with the adult what, if any, further action is necessary and acceptable" (paragraph 14.110).

Paragraph 14.107 clarifies that "where the local authority determines that it should itself take further action (e.g. a protection plan), then the authority would be under a duty to do so".

An outcome from the enquiry may be a "formulation of agreed action for the adult... (which) will be the responsibility of the relevant agencies to implement" (paragraph 14.110). This paragraph also states that it "should be recorded on their care plan". Paragraph 14.111 states that in relation to the adult, this should set out:

a) what steps are to be taken to assure their safety in future;

b) the provision of any support, treatment or therapy including on-going advocacy;

c) any modifications needed in the way services are provided (eg same gender care or placement; appointment of an OPG* deputy)

d) how best to support the adult through any action they take to seek justice or redress;

e) any on-going risk management strategy as appropriate;

f) any action to be taken in relation to the person or organisation that has caused the concern.

Paragraph 14.93 provides two diagrams to illustrate "the different routes and actions that might be taken" with safeguarding enquiries and safeguarding planning. In the first of these, one of the steps is "Review Plan", but there is no further guidance on what a review should involve.

The role of social workers

The statutory guidance is clear in paragraph 14.81 that social workers will often have a role in safeguarding enquiries, as follows:

- it is likely that many enquiries will require the input and supervision of a social worker, particularly the more complex situations;
- where abuse or neglect is suspected within a family or informal relationship it is likely that a social worker will be the most appropriate lead.

Social workers are identified in this paragraph as having the skills to handle "enquiries in a sensitive and skilled way to ensure distress to the adult is minimised" and an example given of this is where "an adult may make a choice to be in a relationship that causes them emotional distress which outweighs, for them, the unhappiness of not maintaining the relationship".

Following the initial stages of an enquiry, social workers have an important role to play in discussing with the adult what action could be taken (including whether further enquiry is needed), in terms of the options available and how these can best reflect their wishes. Paragraph 14.105 states: "Social workers must be able to set out both the civil and criminal justice approaches that are open and other approaches that might help to promote their wellbeing, such as therapeutic or family work, mediation and conflict resolution, peer or circles of support."

In addition social workers may have a role to play in implementing a safeguarding plan, especially where the decision is taken to undertake a needs assessment to identify how the adult can be helped with planning "for their future safety and wellbeing" (paragraph 14.106).

* [Office of the Public Guardian]

In circumstances where the local authority is 'causing others' to make enquiries, paragraph 14.68 highlights that social workers "may need to be involved in order to support the adult to recover".

Paragraph 14.66 highlights "the need for preventing abuse and neglect wherever possible... (and) making early, positive interventions with individuals and families can make a huge difference to their lives preventing the deterioration of a situation or breakdown of a support network". Paragraph 14.67 gives an example of how a social worker coordinated a plan to help someone safely maintain their independence by working with the family and police, and putting the individual in touch with a specialist to help her build her resilience.

Record-keeping

The importance of good record-keeping is highlighted in paragraph 14.180 which specifies that "whenever a complaint or allegation of abuse is made, all agencies should keep clear and accurate records" and it goes on to say that "each agency should identify procedures for incorporating... all relevant records into a file to record all action taken".

Paragraph 14.181 states: "Staff should be given clear direction as to what information should be recorded and in what format." The statutory guidance itself provided no specific guidance on this, and it is the responsibility of organisations to decide how to achieve this. In paragraph 14.139, which lists the duties of the Safeguarding Adults Board (SAB), one of these is "formulate guidance about the arrangements for managing adult safeguarding, and dealing with complaints, grievances and professional and administrative malpractice in relation to safeguarding adults" – the implication is that this 'clear direction' will include written guidance. In some areas there are jointly agreed procedures between a number of local authorities, eg the London Multi-Agency Safeguarding Policy and Procedures.

The Social Care Institute of Excellence (SCIE) publication *Adult Safeguarding – practice questions*[2] provides some guidance about what a section 42 enquiry ought to record, as follows:

- details of the safeguarding concern and who raised it;
- the views and wishes of the adult affected, at the beginning and over time, and where appropriate the views of their family;
- any immediate action agreed with the adult or their representative;
- the reasons for all actions and decisions;
- details of who else is consulted or the concern is discussed with;
- any timescales agreed for actions;
- sign-off from a line manager and/or the local safeguarding lead.

As noted in previous chapters SCIE are providing an interpretation, which social workers should only apply where they believe it accords with the statutory guidance.

Where the local authority has a recording format, typical headings are as follows:

- consent by the adult, or capacity assessment where appropriate;
- chronology of the abuse or neglect;
- categories of abuse/neglect;
- account given by the person at risk or their representative;
- decision-making prior to enquiry;
- views and wishes of the adult (and family) including risk and desired outcomes;
- enquiry findings and analysis;
- conclusion about whether abuse/neglect has occurred;
- determination of the extent to which the adult has achieved their desired outcome;
- determination of extent to which the adult feels safer;
- recommendations for the next step or safeguarding plan.

The statutory guidance does not specify any duties with regard to how and in what form records are to be made available to those adults subject to an enquiry, as is the case with needs assessment and eligibility determination. The guidance states in paragraph 14.183 that "all agencies should identify arrangements, consistent with principles and rules of fairness, confidentiality and data protection for making records available to those adults affected by, and subject to, an enquiry".

Paragraph 14.183 specifies the following in relation to recording information about the alleged abuser:

- If the alleged abuser is using care and support themselves, then information about their involvement in an adult safeguarding enquiry, including the outcome, should be included in their case record.
- If it is assessed that the individual continues to pose a threat to other people then this should be included in any information that is passed on to service providers or other people who need to know.

Sharing information and confidentiality

Paragraph 14.187 states that the principles governing the sharing of information and confidentiality should follow those of the Caldicott Review 2013,[3] as follows:

- information will only be shared on a 'need-to-know' basis when it is in the interests of the adult;
- confidentiality must not be confused with secrecy;
- informed consent should be obtained but, if this is not possible and other adults are at risk of abuse or neglect, it may be necessary to override the requirement;

- it is inappropriate for agencies to give assurances of absolute confidentiality in cases where there are concerns about abuse, particularly in those situations when other adults may be at risk.

The statutory guidance identifies two sets of circumstances where there is a duty to share information, and reference is made to instances in the past "where the withholding of information has prevented organisations being fully able to understand what 'went wrong' and so has hindered them identifying, to the best of their ability, the lessons to be applied to prevent or reduce the risks of such cases reoccurring" (paragraph 14.185). This paragraph states: "If someone knows that abuse or neglect is happening they must act upon that knowledge, not wait to be asked for information." Added to this is the duty set out in paragraph 14.186 on any person to supply information to a Safeguarding Adults Board (SAB) where they are requested to do so, and this includes where "the request is made in order to enable or assist the SAB to do its job".

Paragraph 14.190 clarifies that the application of these principles "must never be allowed to conflict with the welfare of an adult", and goes on to identify that employees have a duty to disclose where it appears to them "that such confidentiality rules may be operating against the interests of the adult".

Applying the guidance using case examples

The statutory guidance contains case studies that are based on cases that occurred prior to the introduction of the Care Act. They are not focused on the social work role and they do not demonstrate the application of section 42, but they do illustrate the following:

- person-led and outcome-focused (see paragraph 14.14);
- impact of financial abuse on health and wellbeing (see paragraph 14.26);
- vulnerability because of loneliness (see paragraph 14.36);
- abused carer (see paragraph 14.50);
- prevention of exploitation (see paragraph 14.67);
- sexual abuse (see paragraph 14.83);
- abuse and neglect from a relative in the same household (see paragraph 14.92);
- at risk of abuse and neglect (see paragraph 14.102);
- self-neglect (see paragraph 14.141);
- a Serious Case Review – what is now called a Serious Adult Review (see paragraph 14.164);
- poor practice in a care home (see paragraph 14.201).

What follows in this section are four examples that have been constructed to illustrate some of the typical aspects of section 42 enquiries. It should be noted that these are not the same examples as used in Part I of this book, except for a case that was used in chapter 7. Each case, and the subsequent analysis, is set out using the following headings:

- **Details of the safeguarding concern;**
- **Decision to undertake a safeguarding enquiry;**
- **Views and wishes of the adult and their family;**
- **Assess the needs of the adult for protection, support and redress and how they might be met, in accordance with the wishes of the adult;**
- **Make decisions as to what follow-up action should be taken with regard to the person or organisation responsible for the abuse or neglect;**
- **Enable the adult to achieve resolution and recovery;**
- **Section 42 enquiry record.**

Mr P

Details of the safeguarding concern

Bruising has been seen on the arms of Mr P by staff from a home care agency who provide help twice a day.

Mr P lives at home with his wife. They have a private arrangement with a home care agency to provide staff to go in morning and night to help Mr P get up, get dressed and washed and to go to bed. They also help him take a bath several times a week.

Over the previous six days Mr P has completed the task of dressing and undressing himself with Mrs P's assistance before the home care staff have arrived, so they did not see his arms until he had a bath.

The home care staff think that the bruising on both of Mr P's upper arms is as a result of him being grabbed, although they have not discussed the bruising with either Mr or Mrs P. They reported this to their manager who raised a Safeguarding Concern with the local authority.

Mr and Mrs P have had no previous contact with the local authority. The home care manager says that when Mrs P first made contact with them two months ago, she said that Mr P recently had a 'dense stroke' that reduced his mobility and his speech. It was arranged that assistance would be provided for Mr P to help him prepare for the day and going to bed, by helping him get dressed/undressed and washed. In addition he is helped to have a bath twice a week, and more frequently if required. Mrs P had said that she is not strong enough to manage the dressing and undressing and does not wish to help with washing and bathing. As far as the home care agency knows, Mrs P has no significant physical or mental impairment or illness.

Decision to undertake a safeguarding enquiry

The information received is sufficient to conclude that Mr P meets all three of the criteria for an enquiry to take place.

It seems clear that Mr P has care and support needs and it is reasonable to suspect that he could be experiencing physical abuse. Given his physical condition it is also reasonable to suspect that as a result of his care and support needs, he is unable to protect himself against the abuse.

It is decided that a social worker will undertake the section 42 enquiry. The home care agency manager will inform Mr and Mrs P that the information brought to her attention by the home care staff has been reported to the local authority, and seek Mr P's agreement to an enquiry taking place.

Views and wishes of the adult and their family

In these circumstances the plan would be for the social worker to make contact with Mr and Mrs P to explain that in light of information received, he/she will be undertaking an enquiry to establish the facts, whether and to what extent Mr P is at risk of physical abuse and what help can be offered. It would also be explained that in addition there will be an assessment of Mr P's care and support needs, and that an assessment of Mrs P's support needs can be provided as well.

At the initial contact if either Mr or Mrs P said that they did not want any help, the social worker would explain that he/she has a duty (on behalf of the local authority) to undertake this enquiry but can only do so with their consent. However, he/she must assess Mr P's care and support needs – even if Mr P does not agree to participate. There is no duty to undertake an assessment of Mrs P's support needs – only to offer it.

Assuming consent is given, the essential next step is to get an account of how this bruising took place from Mr P. Also to ascertain his view about whether there might be any future incidents, and if so what steps might need to be taken to protect him.

It would be necessary to establish whether there might be any difficulties with communication as it has been reported that Mr P's stroke has affected his speech. There is no indication that he lacks capacity to make decisions, but difficulties with his speech may result in him having substantial difficulty in communicating his views, wishes and feelings. If it was established that he did have substantial difficulty, there would be a requirement to ensure that there is a friend or relative who is an appropriate person to represent and support him, and failing that, there is a duty to appoint an independent advocate. In these circumstances the local authority is unlikely to agree that Mrs P could undertake the role of appropriate person, because at this stage she is the alleged perpetrator and there would be a conflict of interest.

If it transpires that Mrs P was the person who caused the bruising, it will be necessary to establish whether this was intentional or unintentional. But whatever the explanation, a key determinant in what subsequently happens will be what outcomes Mr P wants. However, it may not be possible to fully establish what his desired outcomes are until an assessment of his care and support needs has been undertaken.

It would be necessary to obtain Mrs P's account of how the bruising took place, and in doing so it could be considered good practice to take note of her desired outcomes. However, there is no requirement that her views be considered as part of the section 42 enquiry.

Assess the needs of the adult for protection, support and redress and how they might be met, in accordance with the wishes of the adult

If both Mr and Mrs P agree that bruising has taken place as a result of something that Mrs P did, either intentionally or unintentionally – then it can be concluded that abuse has taken place. If there is any doubt about the cause of the bruising, it may be necessary for the bruising to be assessed by a suitably qualified health practitioner, eg he may have a skin condition that causes him to bruise easily.

It is possible that Mrs P grabbed Mr P to stop him from falling or she may have shaken him while they were having an argument. Whatever the explanation, the social worker will want to assess the likelihood of the circumstances reoccurring and how these circumstances might be linked to Mr P's care and support needs and Mrs P's support needs.

If Mrs P did grab Mr P to stop him from falling, then the emphasis on protection would be on making suggestions about how his care and support needs could be better met to minimise the risk of him falling. This could involve the provision of equipment and adaptations such as a walking frame, rails and so on, and additional tasks that could be undertaken by the home care staff.

In circumstances where the bruising took place in the context of an argument between Mr and Mrs P, any steps taken to protect Mr P would depend on what he wants and secondarily, what Mrs P wants. Mr P may take the view that getting additional help with his care and support needs would be sufficient, because it would reduce the frustration that his wife experiences as a result of his circumstances. Mrs P may meet the carer eligibility criteria, and thus it may be possible to arrange for her to have more time for herself, and this may improve their relationship.

Whatever the circumstances, it would be up to Mr and Mrs P to decide whether they wanted this help. Should they refuse any of the help that is on offer, it is unlikely that any alternative steps would be taken to protect Mr P from abuse and neglect.

Make decisions as to what follow-up action should be taken with regard to the person or organisation responsible for the abuse or neglect

In these circumstances, it is unlikely there would be a referral to the police for them to consider a criminal investigation. This would certainly not take place where the bruising was as a result of unintentional harm by Mrs P. Where the bruising was done in the heat of an argument this would also be unlikely to result in a criminal investigation.

The most appropriate response to Mrs P is to offer her a carer's assessment, and provide her with information about support available from local groups for carers.

Enable the adult to achieve resolution and recovery

The combination of the experience of the section 42 enquiry and subsequent plans to better meet the care and support needs of Mr P and the support needs of Mrs P is likely to be sufficient to achieve resolution for Mr P.

Section 42 enquiry record

This is a version of this case where the bruising is concluded to be unintentional.

Heading	***Summary***
Allegation	*Unexplained bruising on both of Mr P's upper arms observed by home care staff on 12 January. No explanation sought at the time.*
Consent by the adult, or capacity assessment	*On 19 January the Home Care Manager explained that this information from her staff has been referred to social services and that a social worker will make contact. Mr P reluctantly agreed to this. He didn't think that it was necessary as he says that Mrs P grabbed him to stop him falling. There is no evidence of lack of capacity or substantial difficulty with involvement.*
Chronology of the abuse or neglect	*12 January – bruising observed by home care staff* *12 January – bruising reported by home care staff to manager* *13 January – home care manager sends email to local authority* *14 January – telephone discussion between home care manager and duty social worker* *19 January – home care manager visits Mr and Mrs P* *19 January – home care manager emails outcome of visit*
Category of abuse/ neglect	*Physical abuse*
Decision making prior to enquiry	*17 January – senior practitioner decides that a section 42 enquiry should take place as soon as possible after the Home Care Manager's planned visit.*
Account given by the person at risk or their representative	*21 January – Mr P confirms to the social worker that Mrs P grabbed him to stop him falling. They were having an argument at the time about his intention to make himself a cup of tea, and he stood up abruptly and toppled over. They both agree that it would be best to try and avoid such situations where Mr P might fall over, but Mrs P says that if she has to grab him to prevent this in the future that she will do so.*

Heading	Summary
Views and wishes of the adult (and family) including risk and desired outcomes	• Both Mr and Mrs P would value expert opinion on what is safe for Mr P to attempt to do for himself, and to get additional help where it is thought necessary to minimise the risk of Mr P endangering himself. • Mrs P would value being able to go out by herself and not have to worry about her husband having an accident or be alone if he had another stroke.
Enquiry findings and analysis	• Mr and Mrs P have provided an account of the bruising that is consistent with the observations made by the home care staff and their circumstances. • Both Mr and Mrs P are pleased that the enquiry is likely to result in them both getting more help and support.
Conclusion about whether abuse/neglect has occurred	No abuse or neglect took place. The bruising was as a result of unintentional harm.
Determination of extent to which the adult has achieved their desired outcome	Initially Mr P was reluctant to accept any involvement from social services, but he subsequently agreed that both he and Mrs P would like more help.
Determination of extent to which the adult feels safer	Mr P says he will feel safer once he has received advice about what is reasonable for him to aim to do for himself, and has a care and support plan.
Recommendations for the next step or safeguarding plan	Referral of Mr P to the reablement team, followed by an assessment of Mr P's care and support needs and Mrs P's support needs.

Mrs J

Details of the safeguarding concern

During a routine visit to Mrs J from a CPN (Community Psychiatric Nurse), she discloses to the CPN that her husband has been telling her she cannot attend any community activities, has not been allowing her to have any money of her own, requires receipts for any money she spends and shouts at her and threatens her if she doesn't behave as he wants and expects her to do. Her mother-in-law lives with her and reports all of her movements to Mr J when he returns from work.

Mrs J says she wants to leave her husband as she feels his behaviour is becoming more extreme and he is starting to be controlling of their children, particularly their daughter.

Mrs J is married with two young children, aged nine years and seven years old. Since the birth of her youngest child, she has had a history of psychotic illness, including periods of voluntary admission to hospital. Following the first of these periods of hospitalisation, her mother-in-law, who doesn't speak much English, moved into the family home to help look after the children.

Mrs J is supported at home by a CPN who visits her fortnightly and administers her depot injections, which she has always complied with. Her CPA (Care Programme Approach) plan includes community activities but she has taken these up only sporadically.

The CPN said she would consult with colleagues about how best to help Mrs J and visit on the following day, but before she could do so she was left a message from Mr J to say that she should only visit when he is able to be present.

Decision to undertake a safeguarding enquiry

There is reasonable cause to suspect that Mrs J is experiencing, or is at risk of, abuse or neglect. Her description of a pattern of incidents of controlling, coercive and threatening behaviour falls within the scope of the definition of domestic abuse.

It has been previously established that Mrs J has care and support needs as part of her CPA assessment, although none of her needs were determined as meeting the eligibility criteria.

It could be concluded that she is not able to take steps to protect herself, and that her inability to do this is in part as a result of the impact of her psychotic illness on her confidence.

Following consultation with the relevant manager in the local authority it is decided that the criteria for a section 42 enquiry are met, and that the Mental Health Trust will undertake the enquiry with the CPN being the lead professional.

A referral could also be made to Children's Services for them to consider whether there should be a section 47 enquiry under the Children Act 1989.

Views and wishes of the adult and their family

At the CPN's last visit Mrs J was clear that she wanted to leave her husband and the CPN concluded that she had the capacity to make this decision. The CPN will want to find out if she still wants to give this serious consideration, but the CPN would not want to do this in the presence of Mr J. The CPN could meet with Mr J to try and persuade him of the importance of her being able to discuss things in confidence with her patient. Failing that she could see them both together and assess the situation further.

As Mrs J has a mental illness the CPN could request that an approved mental health practitioner use their power to enter premises under section 115 of the Mental Health Act to interview Mrs J. In extreme circumstances an approved mental health practitioner could apply for a section 135 warrant (under the Mental Health Act) to allow the police to take

Mrs J to a place of safety. This would ensure that Mrs J's desired outcomes could be clarified without undue interference from Mr J and then acted upon, if appropriate.

There are no indications that Mrs J lacks the capacity to make the decision about whether or not to leave Mr J, but it is possible that because of her psychotic illness that she experiences substantial difficulty in weighing up information. In these circumstances an independent advocate would need to be appointed unless there is someone who can act as the appropriate person.

Until the CPN meets with Mrs J she will not be able to find out if Mrs J agrees to the section 42 enquiry; also Children's Services will want her to be consulted about them acting on the referral. However, it is possible to initiate the safeguarding procedures in relation to herself and her children, without her expressed consent if it is thought that the children are at risk or because a criminal offence has been committed.

Assess the needs of the adult for protection, support and redress and how they might be met, in accordance with the wishes of the adult

There is no direct evidence of abuse or neglect so a decision would need to be taken about whether to accept Mrs J's description of her circumstances as a basis for further action. In light of the stance taken by Mr J, it might be considered necessary to interview Mrs J to determine whether she is in any immediate danger. However, even if she is not in immediate danger, it ought to be recognised that the time of the greatest danger to any victim of domestic abuse is when they are perceived as trying to leave the abusive relationship. There may also be ethnic and cultural factors to take into account.

If possible the enquiry ought to identify whether or not Mrs J wants to take any immediate action to leave her husband, although it may be the case that Mrs J has not yet reached a decisive conclusion.

If Mrs J confirms that she wants help with leaving her husband, the objective of the safeguarding plan would be to explore options and support her in achieving them. If she decides to go to a women's refuge she could get benefits to pay for this, but if she needs to move away from the local area she may need help from social services with the travel costs. Any financial help could be given only if this is meeting an eligible need, or the local authority uses its power to meet a non-eligible need.

If she decides against leaving him, then ways of increasing support for her could be considered, and the situation kept under review via her CPA plan.

Mrs J may wish to consider whether she wants Mr J investigated for having possibly committed a criminal offence.

Make decisions as to what follow-up action should be taken with regard to the person or organisation responsible for the abuse or neglect

Consideration should be given as to when to inform the police of the concerns about Mr J, as his behaviour could be seen to constitute a crime as a result of his coercive or controlling behaviour. Mrs J would be advised to consider the impact of this on her desired outcomes before agreeing to this course of action.

Enable the adult to achieve resolution and recovery

Mrs J initially thought that the only way to stop the domestic abuse is if she leaves her husband. However, there may be other ways of dealing with the problem that prove to be acceptable, that a local specialist domestic abuse service could help her with.

Section 42 enquiry record

This is a version where Mr J withdraws his objection to Mrs J being seen alone by the CPN, and where Mrs J decides not to leave her husband.

Heading	***Summary***
Allegation	*On 4 June Mrs J reported that her husband has been telling her she cannot attend any community activities, has not been allowing her to have any money of her own, requires receipts for any money she spends and shouts at her and threatens her if she doesn't behave as he wants and expects her to do.*
Consent by the adult, or capacity assessment	*Mrs J agreed to the section 42 enquiry and understands that no action will be taken without her agreement. Mrs J is showing no signs of psychotic behaviour and there is no evidence of lack of capacity or substantial difficulty with involvement.*
Chronology of the abuse or neglect	*4 June – Routine visit by CPN where allegation was made and Mrs J expressed a desire to leave her husband. She said that it had been taking place for many years.*
Category of abuse/ neglect	*Domestic abuse*
Decision making prior to enquiry	*5 June – Mr J telephones and leaves a message for the CPN to say that he does not want her to visit his wife unless he is present.* *5 June – following consultation with the Safeguarding Team Manager it is agreed that the CPN will lead a section 42 enquiry.* *10 June – CPN meets with Mr J who reluctantly agrees that CPN can talk to Mrs J without him being present. He had been against this because his mother had told him that Mrs J was very upset during the last visit from the CPN. He made no reference to Mrs J having plans to leave him.*
Account given by the person at risk or their representative	*12 June – CPN interviewed Mrs J alone. She reiterated the allegations made on 4 June. She said that he has been like this for a long time and she has decided to do something about it because he has started to be very controlling towards their seven-year-old daughter.*

Heading	Summary
Views and wishes of the adult (and family) including risk and desired outcomes	*Mrs J wants to have more freedom and responsibility, and when the children are older she would like to go back to work. She can't see her husband changing his controlling behaviour, so the only way she can see of achieving her desired outcomes is to leave him and start a new life. But she doesn't think she can go through with it, because she is worried that the stress of it would mean that she would end up back in hospital. She doesn't want a referral made to Children's Services because this would mean confronting Mr J and this would cause too much trouble.*
Enquiry findings and analysis	*There is no reason to doubt Mrs J's account of her husband's behaviour towards her and her children. She is uncertain about what she wants to do and may benefit from specialist help to enable her to explore the options.*
Conclusion about whether abuse/ neglect has occurred	*Mrs J is experiencing domestic abuse from her husband. There have been incidents of controlling, coercive and threatening behaviour over a long period.*
Determination of extent to which the adult has achieved their desired outcome	*There has been no resolution for Mrs J. Further exploration of ways that Mrs J can achieve her desired outcomes is required.*
Determination of extent to which the adult feels safer	*Mrs J feels safer now that she is able to talk about her difficulties*
Recommendations for the next step or safeguarding plan	• *The CPN will refer Mrs J to the local domestic abuse voluntary organisation. This will provide the opportunity for Mrs J to discuss options with someone who has specialist knowledge and expertise.* • *The CPN will meet with Mrs P more frequently for the next six months.*

Mrs B

Details of the safeguarding concern

Shortly after Mrs B is admitted to hospital for treatment for a UTI (Urinary Tract Infection) and a chest infection, it is noticed that she has a pressure ulcer that was not mentioned in the GP referral letter.

Mrs B (aged 95) has Alzheimer's disease and is physically frail. She was admitted from a care home by ambulance. She has been receiving antibiotics for the chest infection. The hospital admission has been prompted by a suspected UTI because Mrs B has rapidly become lethargic and sometimes she is agitated, and she is already being treated with antibiotics.

The senior nurse on duty on the ward has raised a Safeguarding Concern with the hospital social work team because Mrs B has a previously unreported grade 3 pressure ulcer on her sacrum.

Decision to undertake a safeguarding enquiry

At this stage, more information is required about the background to Mrs B's admission to hospital, and what may have led to the pressure ulcer developing. For example, if preventive measures were not being taken in the care home a pressure ulcer could quickly develop. Equally, if she has been waiting in an ambulance to be admitted to hospital or been waiting in hospital for the admission process to be completed, a pressure ulcer could have developed.

At this stage it is not possible to conclude whether there has been organisational abuse, and if so, whether Mrs B needs protection from further such abuse. The key issue is whether this pressure ulcer could have been avoided or managed better, or whether it is an unavoidable consequence of her current condition. The cause of the pressure ulcer will require an opinion from a suitably qualified healthcare professional.

Views and wishes of the adult and their family

If it is decided that there should be a section 42 enquiry Mrs B may not have the capacity to consent, in which case a decision will need to be taken as to whether an enquiry is in her best interests. In these circumstances the local authority has to decide whether there is anyone willing and able to support Mrs B in this decision, and if not the local authority is likely to appoint an Independent Mental Capacity Advocate. There may be other decisions that have to be taken that do not relate directly to the safeguarding enquiry, where Mrs B lacks capacity, eg returning to the care home.

Because of her dementia it is likely that it has already been determined that she has substantial difficulty in involvement. A relative may have been identified who can act as the appropriate person, but if this is not the case an independent advocate will need to be appointed. Any relative being considered for the appropriate person role will have to be able to distinguish between what are Mrs B's desired outcomes and what they think is best for her.

The same family member could assist with both the best interests decision and Mrs B's substantial difficulty in involvement. If an Independent Mental Capacity Advocate is appointed this person could also take on the role of the independent advocate.

Assess the needs of the adult for protection, support and redress and how they might be met, in accordance with the wishes of the adult

It will be important to ensure that the risk of future pressure ulcers is minimised, although this will be a safeguarding issue only if there has been organisational abuse.

Whatever steps are taken, if Mrs B does not have the capacity to agree to decisions that directly affect her then it would need to be a best interests decision.

Make decisions as to what follow-up action should be taken with regard to the person or organisation responsible for the abuse or neglect

It is possible that the structure, policies, processes and practices within an organisation have contributed to the pressure ulcer developing. If this was judged to be a case of serious neglect, the local Safeguarding Adults Board may initiate a Safeguarding Adults Review. If it was decided that a SAR was not required, this concern could be raised through informal channels and action taken as deemed appropriate within the hospital.

Enable the adult to achieve resolution and recovery

If the pressure ulcer occurred due to poor professional practice, the appropriate redress may be through the employer undertaking disciplinary procedures with the relevant employees.

Section 42 enquiry record

This is a version of the scenario where the GP states that Mrs B did not have a pressure ulcer when he examined her before calling for an ambulance, and it is concluded that a safeguarding enquiry is not required as there is no evidence of abuse or neglect. Even though a section 42 enquiry did not take place, the enquiry record format has been used.

Heading	***Summary***
Allegation	*On the day that Mrs B is admitted to hospital for treatment for a urinary tract infection and a chest infection, it is noticed that she has a pressure ulcer that was not mentioned in the GP referral letter. Date of admission – 10 September.*
Consent by the adult, or capacity assessment	*In the initial stages while an enquiry was being considered, it was decided to see how she responded to treatment before assessing capacity to consent to an enquiry. But it turned out not to be required, as no enquiry took place.*
Chronology of the abuse or neglect	*Shortly after Mrs B was admitted to hospital for treatment for a UTI (Urinary Tract Infection) and a chest infection, it was noticed that she had a pressure ulcer that was not mentioned in the GP referral letter. The senior nurse on duty on the ward raised a Safeguarding Concern with the hospital social work team because Mrs B had a previously unreported grade 3 pressure ulcer on her sacrum.*
Category of abuse/ neglect	*Not applicable as no abuse or neglect has been identified and therefore there was no enquiry.*

Heading	***Summary***
Decision making prior to enquiry	*10 September– Senior nurse on duty on the ward raised a Safeguarding Concern with the hospital social work team because Mrs B has a previously unreported grade 3 pressure ulcer on her sacrum.* *11 September – GP states that Mrs B did not have a pressure ulcer when he examined her before calling for an ambulance.* *11 September – Ambulance Service state that she was in the ambulance for 15 minutes; she was not undressed. They weren't advised of any pressure ulcers but were aware that she had urinary incontinence and had received a fresh pad shortly before she left the care home.* *11 September – A&E records show that she was in an examination bay for one hour. No relatives were present. There is no record of pressure ulcers being observed.* *12 September – Medical examination concludes that pressure ulcer is likely to have developed in the previous two days. It stated that she would have been at greater risk of developing a pressure ulcer because she had not been eating and drinking properly prior to her admission.* *14 September– Mrs B was given a provisional discharge date of 19 September.*
Account given by the person at risk or their representative	*Mrs B was interviewed by a hospital social worker, with Mrs B's son. Mrs B has substantial difficulty in involvement because of Alzheimer's Disease. Her son is acting as the appropriate adult. Mrs B was not able give an account of the cause of the pressure ulcer, but she was able to acknowledge the location of her discomfort.*
Views and wishes of the adult (and family) including risk and desired outcomes	*Mrs B's son believes that Mrs B wants to return to the care home as soon as possible. The family believe that the pressure ulcer occurred in A&E and they intend to make a complaint.*
Enquiry findings and analysis	*Not applicable as no abuse or neglect has been identified and therefore there was no enquiry.*
Conclusion about whether abuse/ neglect has occurred	*The decision not to undertake a section 42 enquiry was based on medical examination and there being no other indications that abuse may have occurred.*
Determination of extent to which the adult has achieved their desired outcome	*It was not possible to ascertain Mrs B's views.*
Determination of extent to which the adult feels safer	*It was not possible to ascertain Mrs B's views.*

Heading	Summary
Recommendations for the next step or safeguarding plan	*Concerns about the pressure ulcer developing at some point during the admission to be reported through appropriate channels.*

Mr Y

Details of the safeguarding concern

Mr Y's PA (personal assistant) has reported his concern that Mr Y is becoming unkempt and his flat is becoming untidy and dirty. This change coincided with Mr Y acquiring some new friends whom he sees regularly. The PA also believes that he spends less money on food than he used to, and is worried that he is giving money to these new friends.

Mr Y is a young adult with a learning disability who lives in supported living accommodation. He has a PA (funded through a direct payment) who comes to his flat twice a week to help him to plan his activities, organise his shopping and ensure that he adheres to the conditions of his tenancy. His parents live in a town 20 miles away and his father is the nominated person for the direct payment. Mr Y receives a PIP (Personal Independence Payment) that is paid directly to him. He also receives a small payment for working in a social enterprise. He pays his bills via direct debits.

Mr Y usually sees a social worker only at the annual review of his care and support plan.

The PA reported his concern to the social worker who undertook the last annual review. He has not told Mr Y.

Decision to undertake a safeguarding enquiry

Two of the three criteria can definitely be considered as met, as follows:

- *Mr Y is a person with eligible care and support needs;*
- *there is reasonable cause to suspect:*
  - *he might be the subject of financial abuse*
  - *there is self-neglect.*

From what is previously known of Mr Y's care and support needs, it is not clear whether he is able to protect himself from financial abuse, or that there is a risk of this as a result of his needs. It is also not clear if the self-neglect is a matter for protection.

However, as Mr Y is receiving care and support because he is not able to live independently, and given the evidence presented by the PA, it is reasonable to suspect that he is unable to protect himself against the risk of financial abuse. He is potentially subject to what is described in the statutory guidance as "coercion in relation to an adult's financial affairs or arrangements" (paragraph 14.17). This overlaps with psychological abuse and the enquiry may reveal that the financial abuse is part of a pattern of control and intimidation, as well as wider coercion.

There is not much evidence that self-neglect is taking place, although the changes to his living conditions could be an indicator of financial abuse.

If it was thought that it was not reasonable to suspect that he is unable to protect himself from financial abuse and/or care for himself, an alternative approach could be for the local authority to use its power to undertake a non-statutory enquiry and devise a plan to prevent potential deterioration.

Views and wishes of the adult and their family

Assuming that the PA hasn't discussed his concern with Mr Y and established what his desired outcomes are, a decision will need to be made as to who is best placed to have that discussion with him. It might be the PA, a member of staff in the supported living accommodation, a member of his family or a social worker allocated specifically for that task.

As he has a learning disability it is possible that he has substantial difficulty in involvement. This could be because of difficulties that he has in understanding relevant information. This would mean that at his annual reviews a member of his family might act as the appropriate person, or if there is nobody suitable to take on this role an independent advocate would be appointed to help him to be more involved. If this were the case, the appropriate person or the independent advocate would need to be involved in the enquiry. Where a member of the family has been acting as the appropriate person for the annual review, Mr Y may not agree that this person should continue with this role for the purpose of this enquiry. But even if he had no objections, the local authority may decide that this member of the family is not able to be sufficiently objective and therefore decide to appoint an independent advocate. An independent advocate would have a duty to assist My Y in understanding that the behaviour of his friends is potentially abusive, as well as assisting him to communicate his views, wishes and feelings.

The professional skill is in achieving a balance between involving the family in any way that has been previously agreed, maintaining Mr Y's right to privacy and ensuring the relevant information is available to the enquiry.

Given that there are no indications that Mr Y lacks capacity to make decisions about who his friends are, he has every right to insist that he maintains his relationship with his new friends (however unwise this may be). At this stage there is no evidence that he has, or is going to, give significant sums of money to his friends – but if this was the case this should be reported to the police (see paragraph 14.29).

Even though he has substantial difficulty in involvement, he would still have the right to refuse to consent to a safeguarding enquiry.

Assess the needs of the adult for protection, support and redress and how they might be met, in accordance with the wishes of the adult

A worst case scenario would be that Mr Y has been targeted and groomed by these new friends, and their intention is to use his flat for their own purposes and to take as much of his money as they can. It is already known that he is spending less on food and his living conditions have changed, and these are two of the indicators of financial abuse. Further assessment may establish that there are more areas of concern.

If there is no evidence that he has given significant sums of money to his friends and that his flat is just very untidy, it could still be concluded that there is a risk of financial abuse and self-neglect taking place. In these circumstances the most appropriate way of helping Mr Y may be through a revision of his care and support plan. This could consider changes to the level and timing of the support he receives from his PA, to better manage the level of risk he is currently exposed to. Also it may be possible to adjust the way his finances are managed to reduce the opportunity for his money to be misappropriated. In addition, his needs could be reassessed to consider the relationship between the opportunities he has for social interaction and the level of risk of a similar situation arising again in the future.

Make decisions as to what follow-up action should be taken with regard to the person or organisation responsible for the abuse or neglect

If it is believed that no crime has been committed, depending on what Mr Y's desired outcomes are, it could be appropriate to check with the police to see if these friends are known to them and if so whether they think he is at risk.

Enable the adult to achieve resolution and recovery

The enquiry into the allegation of financial abuse may prove to be inconclusive in this case. It may be that no further evidence is obtained other than what the PA reported, and Mr Y may not accept that financial abuse has taken place.

Alternatively Mr Y may be appreciative and accepting of the help that is being offered, whether or not there is more evidence of financial abuse.

Section 42 enquiry record

This is a version of the scenario of a section 42 enquiry where there is no evidence of financial abuse having taken place, but where Mr Y is considered to be at risk of financial abuse.

Heading	***Summary***
Allegation	*Mr Y's PA reported his concern on 20 May that Mr Y is becoming unkempt and his flat is becoming untidy and dirty. This change coincided with Mr Y acquiring some new friends whom he sees regularly. The PA also believes that he spends less money on food than he used to, and is worried that he is giving money to these new friends.*

Heading	**Summary**
Consent by the adult, or capacity assessment	*Mr Y initially indicated that he would not consent to an enquiry, but subsequently agreed after speaking to an independent advocate. Mr Y has substantial difficulty in involvement, but does not lack the capacity to make the decision to consent or to make the decisions that are the subject of the enquiry.*
Chronology of the abuse or neglect	*20 May – PA reports his concerns to the social worker who undertook the last review of his care and support plan.*
Category of abuse/ neglect	*Financial abuse and self neglect.*
Decision making prior to enquiry	*22–28 May – Social worker explores the situation with Mr Y's father who acts as the appropriate person at Mr Y's annual review. Mr Y's father talks to the PA. Agreed that Mr Y senior will visit his son and talk to him.* *30 May – Visit takes place and Mr Y senior reports that his son says that there is no problem and he doesn't need any help. Mr Y senior was shocked about how unkempt his son is and annoyed that his son refused to show him his bank statements.* *1 June – Team Manager authorises a section 42 enquiry because of suspected financial abuse and specifies that the enquiry also investigates the deterioration in Mr Y's wellbeing that appears to be linked to alleged self-neglect. Enquiry to be led by the social worker who knows Mr Y. As there are indications that Mr Y may refuse to consent to the enquiry, an independent advocate is to be appointed to ensure effective involvement of Mr Y in this decision.* *25 June – Mr Y visited by the independent advocate and Mr Y agrees to participate in the enquiry.*
Account given by the person at risk or their representative	*1 July – Independent advocate and social worker visit Mr Y. Mr Y admits that he has been under pressure from his friends to withdraw money from his account and wants advice about this.*
Views and wishes of the adult (and family) including risk and desired outcomes	• *Mr Y wants to maintain contact with his new friends.* • *Family want to have more control over Mr Y's bank account, as they are not convinced that he will resist pressure to withdraw money.*
Enquiry findings and analysis	*Financial abuse is taking place insofar as there is pressure on Mr Y to withdraw money from his bank account that he is uncomfortable with. There is also concern from Mr Y's family that the changes to his lifestyle that are linked with the association with his new friends, is having a negative impact on Mr Y's wellbeing – although Mr Y has not expressed any concern.*
Conclusion about whether abuse/ neglect has occurred	*Mr Y is at risk of financial abuse. There are some indicators of self-neglect and psychological abuse (linked to the financial abuse).*

Heading	**Summary**
Determination of extent to which the adult has achieved their desired outcome	*Mr Y's desired outcomes have shifted in the course of the investigation, although he has consistently maintained that he wants to remain in contact with these new friends.*
Determination of extent to which the adult feels safer	*Mr Y is reassured that he will get some help to address his concern about being under pressure from his friends to withdraw money from his account.*
Recommendations for the next step or safeguarding plan	• *Mr Y to be offered a reassessment of his care and support needs, to consider whether the way he has developed personal relationships is having a significant impact on his wellbeing. Whether or not his eligible needs have changed, consideration is to be given to revising his care and support plan to better meet needs that are already agreed.* • *Independent advocate to be retained for this reassessment.* • *Family to be advised of this plan, if Mr Y agrees.*

Comment and analysis

What follows considers the versions of the cases set out in the section 42 enquiry record.

Readers should note that what is set out in this section and the previous section is intended to show how the statutory guidance might be applied, and in doing so, what would be complex situations in real life have had to be simplified.

Details of the safeguarding concern

In many circumstances the safeguarding concern will be reported to the local authority by staff in an organisation outside of the local authority, and the reporting organisation may not be asked to undertake the subsequent enquiry. However, there are circumstances where the professional from the organisation who identified the concern then leads the coordination of the enquiry, as in the case of Mrs J. In all cases the local authority is responsible for agreeing to the outcomes of the enquiry.

People who report safeguarding concerns can often be involved in the initial stages of determining whether there should be a safeguarding enquiry, by helping to obtain further information about the adult, especially where there is uncertainty about whether the section 42 criteria are met and when there might need to be a mental capacity assessment.

Decision to undertake a safeguarding enquiry

It may not always be clear at the outset that all three of the section 42 criteria are met. There is often uncertainty with organisational abuse, as was the case with Mrs B, because the adult's physical condition may have been caused by circumstances other than abuse, and in these circumstances medical opinion is required.

Mrs B's case illustrates the difficulties of making judgements about when not to undertake an enquiry. If there was evidence of Mrs B being left on a hard stretcher for hours, or poor transfers from one bed to another had taken place, this may have been considered to be organisational abuse. Organisational abuse is described as including "neglect and poor care practice within an institution.... (and) may range from one off incidents to on-going ill-treatment" (paragraph 14.17), but on the other hand the statutory guidance envisages that where there is "poor, neglectful care or practice" by staff employed in health or social care, "then an employer-led disciplinary response may be more appropriate" (paragraph 14.42).

Mr Y's case highlighted that although the category of self-neglect did not apply for a section 42 enquiry because there was no evidence that he could not 'protect' himself.

In all of the four cases the adults met the first criteria of having care and support needs. In all cases but Mr P, their care and support needs had already been established. However, if the adult does not have care and support needs but nevertheless appears to be experiencing abuse or neglect – there would be no duty to undertake a safeguarding enquiry. For example, if Mrs J did not have a mental illness or any other physical or mental impairment, then she would not meet the criteria. Although it might be argued that there is a case for the local authority to use its power to undertake an enquiry on the grounds that this could prevent further abuse and promote her wellbeing.

The local authority will often undertake the enquiry, but in Mrs J's case it was decided that the Mental Health Trust would be 'caused' by the local authority to undertake the enquiry. In agreeing that the CPN be the lead professional, this would be because she has been trained to undertake this task.

Views and wishes of the adult and their family

It is essential to ascertain the adult's views, wishes, feelings and beliefs, because these must be taken into account in deciding on any action. This applies both to the process of the enquiry, as well as having regard to the desired outcomes of the adult in deciding on the safeguarding plan. There is a requirement to handle enquiries in a sensitive way and minimise distress. Also the adult's wishes ought always to be at the forefront in making the professional judgement to intervene. This can be particularly challenging where personal relationships with the perpetrator need to be balanced against the risk to the individual, eg in the case of Mrs J (and in her case there are also the needs of her children to consider).

The Social Care Institute of Excellence (SCIE) publication *Adult Safeguarding – practice questions*[2] proposes that the views of the adult's family are also considered where appropriate, but there is no such requirement in the statutory guidance.

The consent of the adult to an enquiry taking place ought to be obtained wherever practicable. This is in line with paragraph 14.95 which states that "consent of the adult before taking action" should be sought, and goes on to make reference to consent being in relation to undertaking an enquiry. The statutory guidance identifies that consent can be set aside where the individual lacks capacity and it is in their best interests to undertake an enquiry, or if other people are at risk or a criminal offence has occurred. In considering consent it is not made explicit what is meant by 'wherever practicable', so setting aside consent in circumstances other than those provided for in the statutory guidance is a matter for local policy and/or professional judgement.

Where consent to a care and support assessment is being refused by someone who has capacity, it must nevertheless go ahead where they are experiencing or are at risk of abuse and neglect. This means that in a situation where the individual will not give consent to a section 42 enquiry and there are no grounds to set consent aside, a care and support assessment must still be undertaken even if the individual refuses to participate, so far as this is possible.

Some adults will need additional support to be able to express their views, wishes, feelings and beliefs. If it is concluded that they have substantial difficulty in involvement, as with Mr Y and Mrs B, then an appropriate person or an independent advocate must be appointed. (See Chapter 10 for more information on substantial difficulty and mental capacity, and the role of independent advocates in safeguarding enquiries.)

Where there are difficulties in gaining access to the person who is experiencing abuse or neglect to ascertain their views, as in the case of Mrs J, there are a range of options set out in other legislation and guidance. These are summarised in the Social Care Institute for Excellence (SCIE) guidance, *Gaining access to an adult suspected to be at risk of neglect or abuse: A guide for social workers and their managers in England.*[4]

Assess the needs of the adult for protection, support and redress and how they might be met, in accordance with the wishes of the adult

Where there is physical injury it is often relatively straightforward to establish the facts, although it may not be easy to conclude whether or not abuse or neglect has taken place. This is particularly the case with organisational abuse, as with Mrs B.

With other types of abuse, such as domestic abuse, the facts may be more intangible. In such cases it may be necessary to refer to the expertise of colleagues and managers who have some experience in understanding the significance of controlling, coercive and threatening behaviour associated with domestic abuse. For more information on the definition of domestic abuse and domestic violence see paragraph 14.20 of the statutory guidance.

In the case of Mr Y there was relatively little evidence of abuse or neglect having taken place, although there were important indicators that financial abuse might take place in the future.

But whatever the facts are, the most important considerations are how they are perceived by the adult and the extent to which they want protection, support and/or redress.

With Mr P, getting him some help and support to reduce the risk of him falling could address the unintentional physical abuse that took place. This would be achieved through an assessment of Mr P's care and support needs and Mrs P's support needs, and meeting their agreed needs through a care and support plan for Mr P and support plan for Mrs P.

For Mr Y, addressing his care and support needs is also the means of minimising the risk of financial abuse and preventing his self-neglect. In his case it is a matter of reassessing his care and support needs and/or revising his existing care and support plan. He does not want any redress; in fact he wants to retain the friendship of the people he might be at risk from.

Although Mrs J does have care and support needs, the means of reducing the risk of domestic abuse would be through making use of the resources of a voluntary organisation, ie Refuge. She does not want to leave her husband and go to a refuge, because she has concluded for the time being that taking such a step would be too much of a threat to her mental health.

In Mrs B's case it was concluded that organisational abuse had not taken place. The circumstances that were most likely to have caused the pressure ulcer were no longer present, so the risk has been removed.

In all three of the cases where the enquiry established that abuse or neglect had taken place, the adult's desired outcomes changed over the course of the enquiry. Initially Mr P was reluctant to accept any involvement from social services, but he subsequently agreed that both he and Mrs P would like more help. Mrs J initially indicated that she wanted support with leaving her husband, but having had the opportunity to reflect on the options she has decided to stay with him for the time being. Mr Y was clear throughout the enquiry that he didn't want to lose the people he regards as friends, although the enquiry process enabled him to express an anxiety about withdrawing money from his bank account and agree to get help with managing this.

Make decisions as to what follow-up action should be taken with regard to the person or organisation responsible for the abuse or neglect

The enquiry has resulted in Mrs P acknowledging that she may have support needs. She has said that she would value being able to go out by herself and not have to worry about her husband having an accident or being alone if he had another stroke. So the follow-up action will be to undertake a carer's assessment.

The bruising on Mr P was as a result of unintentional harm by Mrs P. Harm is referenced in one of the stated aims for safeguarding as a whole, which is to "prevent harm and reduce the risk of abuse or neglect to adults with care and support needs" (paragraph 14.11). There are no detailed descriptions of what is meant by 'harm' and it is not defined, whereas there are such descriptions of 'abuse' and 'neglect', although the terms themselves are not defined (see paragraphs 14.17–25).

The perpetrator of the abuse is not always aware that a safeguarding enquiry is taking place. At the conclusion of the enquiries into the abuse of Mrs J and Mr Y, both Mr J and the friends of Mr Y do not know of the allegations against them. In both cases the person experiencing the abuse did not want them to be confronted in the enquiry. While it might be considered good practice to adhere to the adult's preferences, there is nothing in the statutory guidance that says that the local authority (or any other organisation) must or should do so. If a criminal offence is alleged this will be a matter for the police to decide.

Enable the adult to achieve resolution and recovery

Mr P is likely to be satisfied with the outcome of the enquiry to provide help with meeting his care and support needs. Mr P says he will feel safer once he has received advice about what is reasonable for him to aim to do for himself, and has a care and support plan.

Mr Y will also probably be satisfied that he is going to receive more help and he can make his own decisions about his friends. He is reassured that he will get some help to address his concern about being under pressure from his friends to withdraw money from his account.

Mrs J's situation is unresolved. She will still be experiencing domestic abuse, although she will probably feel less stressed about it, as she now has a number of ways that she can express her feelings and explore future options.

Although in Mrs B's case the enquiry concluded that no abuse took place, the matter is unresolved for her relatives. They believe that there were grounds for making a complaint against the hospital in relation to the care of Mrs B while in A & E, and intended to do so.

Safeguarding plan

Mr P and Mr Y will have safeguarding built into their care and support plans. In determining Mr P's eligibility and reassessing Mr Y's eligibility, consideration will be given to the significance of the impact of their needs on their wellbeing in relation to protection from abuse and neglect.

The statutory guidance makes reference to the assessing of care and support needs being undertaken both in parallel with a safeguarding enquiry, and as part of a safeguarding plan. For both Mr P and Mr Y their respective assessments and reassessments took place as part of the safeguarding plan.

Although Mrs J has care and support needs and these have been included in her Care Programme Approach Plan, it is not proposed to reassess her needs. Her plan focuses on her getting advice and support from a domestic abuse specialist organisation.

Although Mrs B will not have a safeguarding plan as no enquiry took place, the statutory guidance encourages poor, neglectful care or practice to be reported where it believed that this has occurred.

Conclusion

As with all of the statutory guidance very little is said about social work practice, and rightly so. The guidance sets out where professional judgement is required in undertaking safeguarding enquiries, but does not say how this judgement is to be exercised. The policies and procedures developed by local Safeguarding Adults Boards go into more detail than the statutory guidance, and while these are useful in providing summaries of what may need to be considered and pointers from case law, they too are only there to provide the context within which professional judgement is exercised.

But social workers do more than just make judgements within the framework of the legislation and statutory guidance. For some adults the agreeing of a safeguarding plan isn't the end of the safeguarding for them; it is often just the beginning of a relationship with a social worker that may continue for some time, especially where the individual has chosen to remain in a situation where abuse is ongoing.

The particular skillset of social workers is recognised in relation to safeguarding in paragraph 14.149, which states that "a social worker's ability to understand the individual within complex social networks and other systems makes social work input a vital component". It is this set of skills that is essential to achieving outcomes for adults that balance safety with wellbeing.

It is recognised that support and training is needed "to enable staff to work confidently and competently with difficult and sensitive situations" (paragraph 14.228). The support that is stated as essential is "regular face-to-face supervision and reflective practice" (paragraph 14.228). Paragraph 14.225 specifies that there should be "specialist training for those who will be undertaking enquiries" and "advanced training for those who work with more complex enquiries and responses". Training should "be updated regularly to reflect current best practice" (paragraph 14.226).

Safeguarding enquiries can often involve social workers working with a number of agencies, and while this has been referred to in this chapter, a fuller exploration of multi-agency working takes place in Chapter 12 of this book.

References

1. www.local.gov.uk/documents/10180/5852661/Making+Safeguarding+Personal+-+Guide+2014/4213d016-2732-40d4-bbc0-d0d8639ef0df
2. www.scie.org.uk/care-act-2014/safeguarding-adults/adult-safeguarding-practice-questions/
3. www.gov.uk/government/uploads/system/uploads/attachment_data/file/192572/2900774_InfoGovernance_accv2.pdf
4. www.scie.org.uk/care-act-2014/safeguarding-adults/adult-suspected-at-risk-of-neglect-abuse/

9 Safeguarding – types of abuse, SABs and SARs

Introduction

This chapter reproduces sections from the statutory guidance in relation to the following:

- A list and description of types of abuse and neglect
- The new powers and duties in relation to Safeguarding Adults Boards
- The new powers and duties in relation to Safeguarding Adults Reviews.

The types of abuse and neglect

Paragraphs 14.17–25 list what are described as "the different types and patterns of abuse and neglect and the different circumstances in which they may take place" (paragraph 14.16). Please note that all of the material set out in this section is as it appears in the statutory guidance.

The caveat is added that it "is not intended to be an exhaustive list but an illustrative guide as to the sort of behaviour which could give rise to a safeguarding concern".

Physical abuse including:

- assault
- hitting
- slapping
- pushing
- misuse of medication
- restraint
- inappropriate physical sanctions

Domestic violence including:

- psychological
- physical
- sexual
- financial
- emotional abuse
- so called 'honour' based violence

Sexual abuse including:

- rape
- indecent exposure
- sexual harassment
- inappropriate looking or touching
- sexual teasing or innuendo
- sexual photography
- subjection to pornography or witnessing sexual acts
- indecent exposure
- sexual assault
- sexual acts to which the adult has not consented or was pressured into consenting

Psychological abuse including:

- emotional abuse
- threats of harm or abandonment
- deprivation of contact
- humiliation
- blaming
- controlling
- intimidation
- coercion
- harassment
- verbal abuse

- cyber bullying
- isolation
- unreasonable and unjustified withdrawal of services or supportive networks

Financial or material abuse including:

- theft
- fraud
- internet scamming
- coercion in relation to an adult's financial affairs or arrangements, including in connection with wills
- property, inheritance or financial transactions
- the misuse or misappropriation of property, possessions or benefits

Modern slavery encompasses:

- slavery
- human trafficking
- forced labour and domestic servitude
- traffickers and slave masters using whatever means they have at their disposal to coerce, deceive and force individuals into a life of abuse, servitude and inhumane treatment

Discriminatory abuse including forms of:

- harassment
- slurs or similar treatment because of:
  - race
  - gender and gender identity
  - age
  - disability
  - sexual orientation
  - religion

Organisational abuse

Including neglect and poor care practice within an institution or specific care setting such as a hospital or care home, for example, or in relation to care provided in one's own home. This may range from one-off incidents to on-going ill-treatment. It can be through neglect or poor professional practice as a result of the structure, policies, processes and practices within an organisation.

Neglect and acts of omission including:

- ignoring medical, emotional or physical care needs;
- failure to provide access to appropriate health, care and support or educational services;
- the withholding of the necessities of life, such as medication, adequate nutrition and heating.

Self-neglect

This covers a wide range of behaviour, neglecting to care for one's personal hygiene, health or surroundings and includes behaviour such as hoarding. It should be noted that self-neglect might not prompt a section 42 enquiry. An assessment should be made on a case-by-case basis. A decision on whether a response is required under safeguarding will depend on the adult's ability to protect themselves by controlling their own behaviour. There may come a point when they are no longer able to do this, without external support.

Domestic abuse

The cross-government definition of domestic violence and abuse is: any incident or pattern of incidents of controlling, coercive, threatening behaviour, violence or abuse between those aged 16 or over who are, or have been, intimate partners or family members regardless of gender or sexuality. The abuse can encompass, but is not limited to:

- psychological;
- sexual;
- financial;
- emotional.

A new offence of coercive and controlling behaviour in intimate and familial relationships was introduced into the Serious Crime Act 2015. The offence will impose a maximum five years' imprisonment, a fine or both.

Financial abuse

Financial abuse is the main form of abuse investigated by the Office of the Public Guardian both among adults and children at risk. Financial recorded abuse can occur in isolation, but as research has shown, where there are other forms of abuse, there is likely to be financial abuse occurring. Although this is not always the case, everyone should also be aware of this possibility.

Potential indicators of financial abuse include:

- change in living conditions;
- lack of heating, clothing or food;
- inability to pay bills/unexplained shortage of money;
- unexplained withdrawals from an account;
- unexplained loss/misplacement of financial documents;
- the recent addition of authorised signers on a client or donor's signature card;
- sudden or unexpected changes in a will or other financial documents.

This is not an exhaustive list, nor do these examples prove that there is actual abuse occurring. However, they do indicate that a closer look and possible investigation may be needed.

Further information

These links are listed in the text of this section of the statutory guidance:

(www.gov.uk/government/uploads/system/uploads/attachment_data/file/328096/Modern_slavery_booklet_v12_WEB 2_.pdf)

(www.gov.uk/government/publications/statutory-guidance-framework-controlling-or-coercive-behaviour-in-an-intimate-or-family-relationship)

(www.cpa.org.uk/information/reviews/financialabuse240408%5B1%5D.pdf)

Safeguarding Adults Boards (SABs)

"Each local authority must set up a Safeguarding Adults Board (SAB). The main objective of a SAB is to assure itself that local safeguarding arrangements and partners act to help and protect adults in its area who meet the criteria set out at paragraph 14.2." (paragraph 14.133).

The SAB's duties are set out in paragraph 14.139 as follows:

- identify the role, responsibility, authority and accountability with regard to the action each agency and professional group should take to ensure the protection of adults;
- establish ways of analysing and interrogating data on safeguarding notifications that increase the SAB's understanding of prevalence of abuse and neglect locally that builds up a picture over time;
- establish how it will hold partners to account and gain assurance of the effectiveness of its arrangements;
- determine its arrangements for peer review and self-audit;

- establish mechanisms for developing policies and strategies for protecting adults which should be formulated, not only in collaboration and consultation with all relevant agencies but also take account of the views of adults who have needs for care and support, their families, advocates and carer representatives;
- develop preventative strategies that aim to reduce instances of abuse and neglect in its area;
- identify types of circumstances giving grounds for concern and when they should be considered as a referral to the local authority as an enquiry;
- formulate guidance about the arrangements for managing adult safeguarding, and dealing with complaints, grievances and professional and administrative malpractice in relation to safeguarding adults;
- develop strategies to deal with the impact of issues of race, ethnicity, religion, gender and gender orientation, sexual orientation, age, disadvantage and disability on abuse and neglect;
- balance the requirements of confidentiality with the consideration that, to protect adults, it may be necessary to share information on a 'need-to-know basis';
- identify mechanisms for monitoring and reviewing the implementation and impact of policy and training;
- carry out safeguarding adult reviews and determine any publication arrangements;
- produce a strategic plan and an annual report;
- evidence how SAB members have challenged one another and held other boards to account;
- promote multi-agency training and consider any specialist training that may be required. Consider any scope to jointly commission some training with other partnerships, such as the Community Safety Partnership.

The following requirements for SABs set out in paragraph 15.151 will be of particular interest to social workers:

Policies and procedures

- The SAB must develop clear policies and processes that have been agreed with other interested parties, and that reflect the local service arrangements, roles and responsibilities.
- Policies will state what organisations and individuals are expected to do where they suspect abuse or neglect.

Training

- It will promote multi-agency training that ensures a common understanding of abuse and neglect, appropriate responses and agree how to work together.
- The SAB should also consider any specialist training that is required.

Prevention

- A key part of the SAB's role will be to develop preventative strategies and aiming to reduce instances of abuse and neglect in its area.

Safeguarding Adults Reviews (SARs)

"SABs must arrange a SAR when an adult in its area dies as a result of abuse or neglect, whether known or suspected, and there is concern that partner agencies could have worked more effectively to protect the adult" (paragraph 14.162).

"SABs must also arrange a SAR if an adult in its area has not died, but the SAB knows or suspects that the adult has experienced serious abuse or neglect. In the context of SARs, something can be considered serious abuse or neglect where, for example the individual would have been likely to have died but for an intervention, or has suffered permanent harm or has reduced capacity or quality of life (whether because of physical or psychological effects) as a result of the abuse or neglect. SABs are free to arrange for a SAR in any other situations involving an adult in its area with needs for care and support" (paragraph 14.163).

"The SAB should be primarily concerned with weighing up what type of 'review' process will promote effective learning and improvement action to prevent future deaths or serious harm occurring again. This may be where a case can provide useful insights into the way organisations are working together to prevent and reduce abuse and neglect of adults. SARs may also be used to explore examples of good practice where this is likely to identify lessons that can be applied to future cases" (paragraph 14.164).

Paragraph 14.167 sets out the principles that should be applied by SABs and their partner organisations to all reviews:

- There should be a culture of continuous learning and improvement across the organisations that work together to safeguard and promote the wellbeing and empowerment of adults, identifying opportunities to draw on what works and promoting good practice.
- The approach taken to reviews should be proportionate according to the scale and level of complexity of the issues being examined.
- Reviews of serious cases should be led by individuals who are independent of the case under review and of the organisations whose actions are being reviewed.
- Professionals should be involved fully in reviews and invited to contribute their perspectives without fear of being blamed for actions they took in good faith.
- Families should be invited to contribute to reviews. They should understand how they are going to be involved and their expectations should be managed appropriately and sensitively.

"SARs should seek to determine what the relevant agencies and individuals involved in the case might have done differently that could have prevented harm or death. This is so that lessons can be learned from the case and those lessons applied to future cases to prevent similar harm occurring again. Its purpose is not to hold any individual or organisation to account. Other processes exist for that, including criminal proceedings, disciplinary procedures, employment law and systems of service and professional regulation, such as CQC and the Nursing and Midwifery Council, the Health and Care Professions Council, and the General Medical Council" (paragraph 14.168).

"It is vital, if individuals and organisations are to be able to learn lessons from the past, that reviews are trusted and safe experiences that encourage honesty, transparency and sharing of information to obtain maximum benefit from them. If individuals and their organisations are fearful of SARs their response will be defensive and their participation guarded and partial" (paragraph 14.169).

Part III Involvement – difficulties and disputes

Many people with care and support needs struggle to express their wishes and feelings and it has always been a core task for social work to help people with this. Much of the change brought about by the Act, the regulations and the statutory guidance is designed to improve the way that this is done, particularly with the emphasis on wellbeing and the requirement to incorporate the individual's views, wishes and feelings into assessment and care and/or support planning.

Paragraph 6.30 makes it clear that local authorities "must involve the person being assessed in the process".

This duty is considered in each of the chapters in Part III of this book. The main purpose of Chapter 10 is to consider what is required when adults and carers experience particular difficulties with involvement in decisions about their care and/or support. Chapter 11 considers disputes about the care and/or support plan, and how these can be minimised by effective involvement.

To provide context for the following chapters in this part of the book, what follows is a summary of the requirements in relation to involvement.

A. The first of the eight key principles listed in section 1 (3) of the Care Act 2014 is "the importance of beginning with the assumption that the individual is best-placed to judge the individual's wellbeing". The statutory guidance adds that "the local authority should assume that the person themselves knows best their own outcomes, goals and wellbeing" (paragraph 1.14 a).

B. The statutory guidance states: "Local authorities must involve people in decisions made about them and their care and support or where there is to be a safeguarding enquiry or SAR" (paragraph 7.6).

C. Involvement in decisions about particular aspects of the care and support function is specified in section 67 (3) of the Care Act 2014, as follows:

- carrying out a needs assessment or carer's assessment;
- preparing a care and support plan or support plan;
- revising a care and support plan or support plan;
- carrying out a child's needs assessment, a child's carer's assessment or a young carer's assessment.

D. Paragraphs 7.6 sets out the key elements of involvement as comprising of the following:

- the local authority helping people to understand how they can be involved;
- how they can contribute and take part and sometimes lead or direct the process;
- people should be active partners in the key care and support processes of assessment, care and support and support planning, review and any enquiries in relation to abuse or neglect;
- no matter how complex a person's needs, local authorities are required to involve people, to help them express their wishes and feelings, to support them to weigh up options, and to make their own decisions.

The approach taken in this book differs from the way this material is presented in the statutory guidance, where there is a chapter on independent advocacy that makes references to mental capacity and substantial involvement.

10 Substantial difficulty in involvement

Introduction

The purpose of this chapter is to bring together the information about involvement of people in decisions about their care and support where they are experiencing substantial difficulty in being involved, and to understand how this applies where a person also lacks capacity. This chapter draws on the references to substantial difficulty and mental capacity in the statutory guidance from first contact through to review, and also safeguarding.

The Care Act requires local authorities to ensure that individuals with care and support needs who have substantial difficulty in being involved in decision making receive support from an appropriate person, or from an independent advocate when there is nobody who can fulfill the role of the appropriate person.

A significant proportion of people with care and support needs will not have substantial difficulties with involvement. The government's impact assessment[1] in preparation for the implementation of the Care Act estimated that only 7 per cent of people assessed or who received a review would be eligible for independent advocacy and would take up the offer. However, the purpose of this was to estimate the costs of providing independent advocacy, so no estimate was made of the number of people who would be supported by an appropriate person.

There are similarities and differences between substantial difficulty in involvement and circumstances where a person lacks capacity to make specific decisions. Where people lack capacity to consent to decisions in relation to assessment, care and support planning and safeguarding, the Mental Capacity Act 2005 provides a framework for addressing this. This chapter considers lack of capacity as defined in the Mental Capacity Act 2005; however, its application is a specialist area of social work practice and thus is not considered in detail in this book.

The role of independent advocate has some similarities with the role of the independent mental capacity advocate established by the Mental Capacity Act 2005. This chapter describes how advocates are intended to enhance the voice of people with care and support needs, and considers the implications for the social work role.

The chapter headings are as follows:

- **Advocacy arrangements prior to April 2015**
- **Key definitions in the legislation**
- **Similarities between lack of capacity and substantial difficulty**
- **Substantial difficulty in involvement**
- **Lack of mental capacity**
- **Support for people who lack capacity and/or have substantial difficulty**
- **The role of the independent advocate**
- **Applying the guidance using case examples**
- **Conclusion.**

There are circumstances where a detailed consideration of the application of substantial difficulty and lack of capacity is best undertaken alongside other content, eg deferred payment agreements.

Advocacy arrangements prior to April 2015

The role of the independent advocate was newly created by the Care Act 2014.

The statutory guidance issued in 2010 in *Prioritising Need in the Context of Putting People First: A Whole System Approach to Eligibility for Social Care* stated in paragraph 88 that local authorities "should help people prepare for the assessment process and find the best way for each individual to state their views", and that advocates "can be critical in this regard". The guidance did not specify the role of the advocate and there was only a general requirement that local authorities "should make sure that they are able to draw on sufficient expertise to understand and support people with a range of needs so that specific groups of people are not marginalised by the assessment process".

Key definitions in the legislation

In any of the circumstances where the local authority is required to involve a person with care and/or support needs, sections 67 (2), (4) and (5) of the Care Act 2014 apply as follows:

67 (2): The authority must, if the condition in subsection (4) is met, arrange for a person who is independent of the authority (an “independent advocate”) to be available to represent and support the individual for the purpose of facilitating the individual’s involvement; but see subsection (5).

67 (4): The condition is that the local authority considers that, were an independent advocate not to be available, the individual would experience substantial difficulty in doing one or more of the following –

(a) understanding relevant information;

(b) retaining that information;

(c) using or weighing that information as part of the process of being involved;

(d) communicating the individual’s views, wishes or feelings (whether by talking, using sign language or any other means).

67 (5): The duty under subsection (2) does not apply if the local authority is satisfied that there is a person –

(a) who would be an appropriate person to represent and support the individual for the purpose of facilitating the individual’s involvement, and

(b) who is not engaged in providing care or treatment for the individual in a professional capacity or for remuneration.

Section 2 (1) of the Mental Capacity Act 2005 defines a person who lacks capacity as follows:

> *For the purposes of this Act, a person lacks capacity in relation to a matter if at the material time he is unable to make a decision for himself in relation to the matter because of an impairment of, or a disturbance in the functioning of, the mind or brain.*

Section 3 (1) of the Mental Capacity Act 2005 defines inability to make decisions as follows:

> *For the purposes of section 2, a person is unable to make a decision for himself if he is unable –*

(a) to understand the information relevant to the decision,

(b) to retain that information,

(c) to use or weigh that information as part of the process of making the decision, or

(d) to communicate his decision (whether by talking, using sign language or any other means).

Similarities between lack of capacity and substantial difficulty

A comparison of section 67 (4) of the Care Act 2014 with Section 3 (1) of the Mental Capacity Act 2005 shows that the four areas listed are described in the same way. This is recognised in paragraph 7.17 of the statutory guidance in the following statement: "Both the Care Act and the Mental Capacity Act recognise the same areas of difficulty, and both require a person with these difficulties to be supported and represented, either by family or friends, or by an advocate in order to communicate their views, wishes and feelings."

In the Mental Capacity Code of Practice 2015, paragraph 4.15 states that the first three of these areas, ie (a), (b) and (c) in section 3 (1) of the Mental Capacity Act 2005 "should be applied together" and if "a person cannot do any of these three things, they will be treated as unable to make the decision". The statutory guidance for the Care Act does not require this combining of the conditions, and clearly states: "The Care Act defines 4 areas in any one of which a substantial difficulty might be found" (paragraph 7.10).

The four areas of substantial difficulty

Substantial difficulty	Description (from paragraphs 7.11–14)
Understanding relevant information	"Many people can be supported to understand relevant information, if it is presented appropriately and if time is taken to explain it."
Retaining information	"If a person is unable to retain information long enough to be able to weigh up options and make decisions, then they are likely to have substantial difficulty in engaging and being involved in the process"
Using or weighing the information	"A person must be able to weigh up information, in order to participate fully and express preferences for or choose between options. For example, they need to be able to weigh up the advantages and disadvantages of moving into a care home or terminating an undermining relationship."
Communicating their views, wishes and feelings	"A person must be able to communicate their views, wishes and feelings whether by talking, writing, signing or any other means, to aid the decision process and to make priorities clear."

The four areas of mental capacity

Mental capacity	Description taken from the Mental Capacity Code of Practice (paragraphs 4.16–25)
Understanding relevant information	"Relevant information includes: • the nature of the decision • the reason why the decision is needed, and • the likely effects of deciding one way or another, or making no decision at all."

Mental capacity	Description taken from the Mental Capacity Code of Practice (paragraphs 4.16–25)
Retaining information	"The person must be able to hold the information in their mind long enough to use it to make an effective decision."
Using or weighing the information	"For someone to have capacity, they must have the ability to weigh up information and use it to arrive at a decision."
Communicating their views, wishes and feelings	"If a person cannot communicate their decision in any way at all, the Act says they should be treated as if they are unable to make that decision."

Substantial difficulty in involvement

The Care and Support (Independent Advocacy Support) (No. 2) Regulations 2014 set out what must be taken into account in making the judgement about substantial difficulty. The statutory guidance also provides more detail about the circumstances where the local authority is required to consider whether an individual has substantial difficulty in involvement.

Making the judgement about substantial difficulty

In making the judgement about substantial difficulty, local authorities must have regard to any of the following that applies to the individual:

- health condition;
- learning difficulty;
- disability;
- the degree of complexity of the individual's circumstances, whether in relation to the individual's needs for care and support or otherwise;
- where an assessment has previously been refused;
- where there is, or risk of, abuse or neglect.

These requirements are set out in section 3 of the Care and Support (Independent Advocacy Support) (No. 2) Regulations 2014, but they are not referred to in the statutory guidance.

Circumstances where a substantial difficulty judgement must be made

Paragraph 7.18 of the statutory guidance specifies "the local authority must judge whether a person has substantial difficulty in involvement with the assessment, the care and support planning or review processes". Paragraph 7.19 clarifies that this includes safeguarding.

Some examples

The statutory guidance provides two 'case study' examples of people who have substantial difficulty in involvement but do not lack capacity. These are summarised as follows:

- An assessment of care and support needs is being planned for a person with a brain injury sustained in a fall. The social worker has an initial conversation with the individual and concludes that he is articulate and can converse well about plans for the future, but lacks insight which means he may have trouble estimating his true care and support needs. The individual doesn't want his mother to be the appropriate person, so an independent advocate with expertise in brain injury is appointed. (See after paragraph 7.16.)
- A safeguarding enquiry is initiated for a person with learning disabilities who lives in a care home. The individual cannot express herself easily, so the advocate uses communication techniques including using photos. After the enquiry a protection plan is put in place but the independent advocate subsequently judges it to be insufficient, and sets this out in a report. (See after paragraph 7.28.)

Lack of mental capacity

It is essential to appreciate that assessments of capacity must always be made in relation to the specific decision to be made. The Mental Capacity Code of Practice 2015 clarifies this as follows:

- a person lacks capacity if "the impairment or disturbance means that they are unable to make a specific decision at the time it needs to be made" (paragraph 4.3);
- assessment of a person's capacity must not be based on "their ability to make decisions in general" (paragraph 4.4);
- "a person may also lack capacity to make a decision about one issue but not about others" (paragraph 4.5).

An illustration of the capacity test is given in paragraph 19.19, which states "it is not necessary for a person to understand local authority funding arrangements to be able to decide where they want to live".

Circumstances where a mental capacity judgement must be made

This section outlines the circumstances identified in the statutory guidance where capacity must be considered in assessment, care and support planning and safeguarding. However, consideration of how to make judgements about lack of capacity, as set out in the Mental Capacity Code of Practice 2015, is outside of the scope of this book.

Assessment

A capacity assessment must be carried out where an individual is "unable to request an assessment" or struggles "to express their needs" (paragraph 6.11). This applies at all stages of assessment including first contact and staff in first contact teams "must also be able to identify a person who may lack mental capacity and to act accordingly" (paragraph 6.25).

Where an adult lacks capacity and "carrying out a needs assessment would be in the adult's best interests" (paragraph 6.20) an assessment must take place and the adult cannot exercise the choice to refuse an assessment in these circumstances.

A telephone assessment is not appropriate where an adult might lack capacity. Paragraph 6.20 states: "Where there is concern about a person's capacity to make a decision... a face-to-face assessment should be arranged."

Paragraph 6.49 states: "Before offering a supported self-assessment local authorities must ensure that the individual has capacity to fully assess and reflect their own needs."

Care and support plans

Paragraph 10.59 makes reference to person-centred planning being "particularly important for people with the most complex needs" and the fact that "many people receiving care and support have mental impairments, such as dementia or learning disabilities, mental health needs or brain injuries". This paragraph states that where a person lacks capacity, "the principles and requirements of the Mental Capacity Act 2005" will apply. Section 39 of the Mental Capacity Act 2005 requires that an IMCA (Independent Mental Capacity Advocate) be appointed where

> *a local authority propose to make arrangements –*
>
> (a) for the provision of residential accommodation for a person ("P") who lacks capacity to agree to the arrangements, or
>
> (b) for a change in P's residential accommodation,
>
> *and are satisfied that there is no person, other than one engaged in providing care or treatment for P in a professional capacity or for remuneration, whom it would be appropriate for them to consult in determining what would be in P's best interests.*

The MCA Regulations provide for IMCAs to be involved in care reviews.

In circumstances where a local authority has a duty to protect the property of an adult with care and support needs who is being cared for away from home, they require the prior consent of the adult to enter their home. Where "the adult lacks the capacity to give consent to the local authority entering the property, consent should be sought from a person authorised under the Mental Capacity Act 2005 to give consent on the adult's behalf" (paragraph 10.90).

Where an adult lacks capacity to request a direct payment "an authorised person can request the direct payment on the person's behalf" (paragraph 12.16) and manage the direct payment on behalf of the adult. More details about how this applies are provided in Chapter 6.

Safeguarding

Paragraph 14.58 states: "The requirement to apply the MCA in adult safeguarding enquiries challenges many professionals and requires utmost care, particularly where it appears an adult has capacity for making specific decisions that nevertheless places them at risk of being abused or neglected."

Paragraph 10.2 of the Mental Capacity Code of Practice 2015 notes that the MCA Regulations provide for IMCAs to be involved in "adult protection cases".

Young persons

Paragraph 16.37 states the following in relation to a young person or young carer who may lack capacity to agree to an assessment of their potential care and/or support needs: "Where a young person or carer lacks mental capacity or is not competent to agree, the local authority must be satisfied that an assessment is in their best interests."

Support for people who lack capacity and/or have substantial difficulty

Any adult with care and support needs, or a carer with support needs, who has substantial difficulty in involvement must have someone designated to help them. If no appropriate person is available, then an independent advocate must be appointed.

Where an adult with care and support needs also lacks capacity to make particular decisions, an IMCA may need to be appointed. If there is someone who is willing and able to support the adult this will mostly not be required.

The combined mental capacity and substantial difficulty pathway

Where someone has a mental impairment such as dementia or learning disability, mental health needs or brain injuries, the mental capacity route has to be followed. It may be that initially there are no decisions to be made by the individual where the individual lacks capacity, and the individual only needs help in relation to their substantial difficulty in involvement. But if at a later stage a care home is being considered for example, then the individual may lack capacity to make the decision about taking this step.

Substantial difficulty will always need to be considered where lack of capacity has been established in relation to a particular decision. The fact that there is lack of capacity means that it is highly likely that there will also be substantial difficulty in involvement.

Where someone both lacks capacity and experiences substantial difficulty in involvement, this could result in them requiring both an independent advocate and an independent mental capacity advocate. Consequently "regulations have been designed to enable independent advocates to be able to carry out both roles" (paragraph 7.63).

Where someone does not have a mental impairment the pathway is more straightforward, as only the substantial difficulty in involvement route need be considered.

Figure 10.1 outlines the sequence of decision taking where someone may lack capacity and/or have substantial difficulty in involvement.

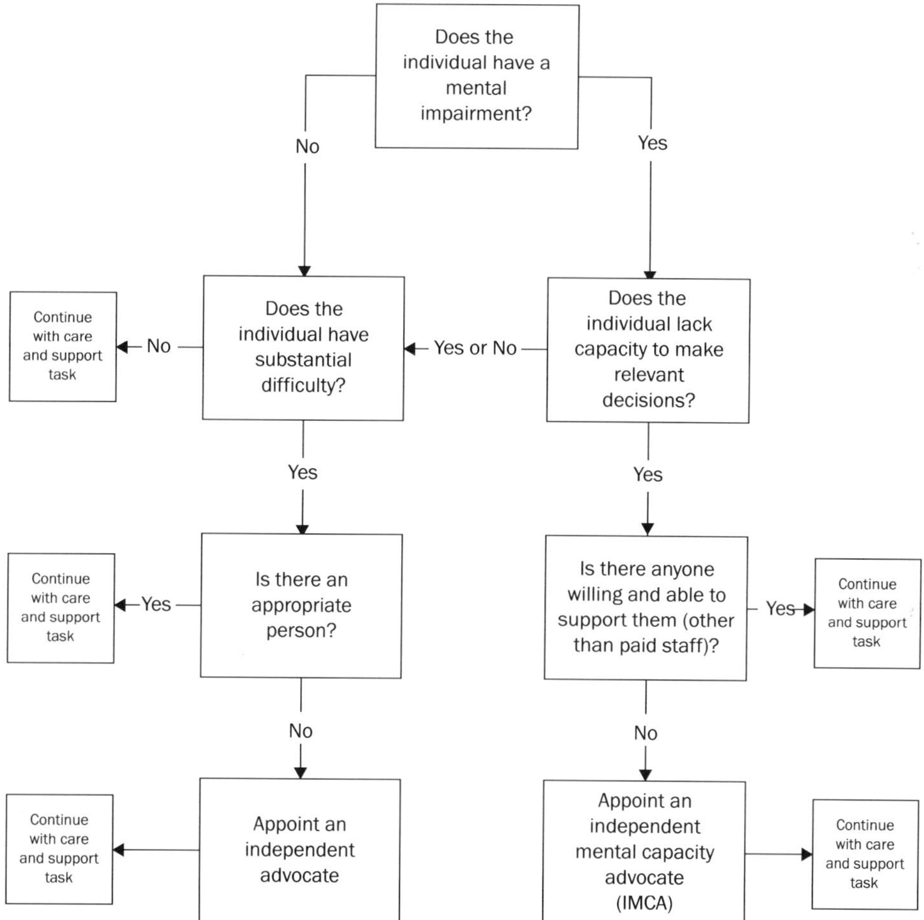

Figure 10.1 *Substantial difficulty and mental capacity*

Independent advocate or appropriate person

Where a person with care and/or support needs is judged to have substantial difficulty in being involved in specified aspects of the care and support journey, someone has to be appointed to support and represent them. The first consideration is whether an appropriate person is available, and where there is no such person the local authority must appoint an independent advocate. This same requirement applies to adults who are subject to a safeguarding enquiry or a Safeguarding Adults Review (SAR), where the adult has substantial difficulty in involvement.

The following conditions apply to the appointment of an appropriate person:

- The appropriate person has to be someone "who is not engaged in providing care or treatment for the individual in a professional capacity or for remuneration" (section 67 (5) (b) of the Care Act 2014).
- Consent is required from the person being represented, or "where the individual lacks capacity or is not competent so to consent, the local authority is satisfied that being represented and supported by that person would be in the individual's best interests" (section 67 (6) of the Care Act 2014).

Paragraphs 7.35 and 7.36 of the statutory guidance describe the types of circumstances where people would be unsuited to the role of 'appropriate person', as follows:

- a family member who lives at a distance and who only has occasional contact with the person;
- a spouse who "finds it difficult to understand the local authority processes";
- a friend who expresses strong opinions of her own prior to finding out those of the individual concerned;
- a housebound parent;
- where they are implicated in any enquiry of abuse or neglect or have been judged by a SAR to have failed to prevent an abuse or neglect.

Examples are also given, as follows:

- The cared-for person wants her daughter to advocate for her, but as she receives a payment from her mother for providing personal care she is prohibited from taking on this role. (See after paragraph 7.33.)
- Prior to the determination of substantial difficulty the individual already has an advocate who can become the appropriate person. (See after paragraph 7.34.)
- A young adult with a moderate learning disability wants to leave home and her parents are opposed to this. In these circumstances it would be inappropriate for the parents to act as the appropriate person. (See after paragraph 7.35.)
- An elderly man with advancing dementia and who is receiving support at home is having a review. His daughter is judged as not being suitable as the appropriate person because she has had little contact and there is a conflict of interest as she will inherit his house. (See after paragraph 7.35.)

Paragraph 7.40 makes it clear that it is "the local authority's decision as to whether a family member or friend can act as an appropriate person to facilitate the individual's involvement", and it is also the responsibility of the local authority to "communicate this decision to the individual's friends and family".

Regulation 4 of the Care and Support (Independent Advocacy Support) (No. 2) Regulations 2014 sets out specific circumstances where a person is eligible for an independent advocate even though an appropriate person has been appointed. They are described succinctly in paragraph 7.42 of the statutory guidance, and are as follows:

- Where the exercising of the assessment or planning function might result in placement in NHS funded provision in either a hospital for a period exceeding 4 weeks or in a care home for a period of 8 weeks or more and the local authority believes that it would be in the best interests of the individual to arrange an advocate.
- Where there is a disagreement, relating to the individual, between the local authority and the appropriate person whose role it would be to facilitate the individual's involvement, and the local authority and the appropriate person agree that the involvement of an independent advocate would be beneficial to the individual.

The statutory guidance provides additional examples of occasions where there can be both an appropriate person and an independent advocate, as follows:

- Where an appropriate person comes onto the scene after an independent advocate has been appointed and all agree "it would be beneficial for the advocate to continue their role" (paragraph 7.37);
- "The family member can provide a lot of information but not enough support" (paragraph 7.38).

The role of the independent advocate

The Care and Support (Independent Advocacy Support) (No. 2) Regulations 2014 set out how "independent advocates are to carry out their functions" in regulations 6, 7 and 8. The following references in this section are taken from the statutory guidance, as the requirements are expressed in a more straightforward manner.

In carrying out their role the independent advocate "will decide the best way of supporting and representing the person they are advocating for, always with regard to the wellbeing and interest (including their views, beliefs and wishes) of the person concerned" (paragraph 7.46).

Supporting the individual

Paragraph 7.48 sets out the responsibilities of an independent advocate. The content is set out in full in this section with formatting and drafting amendments to improve clarity.

1) In assisting a person to understand the assessment, care and support planning and review and safeguarding processes –
    - this requires advocates to understand:
        - local authority policies, and other agencies' roles, and processes

  - the available assessment tools, the planning options, and the options available at the review of a care or support plan
  - good practice in safeguarding enquiries and SARs.
- it may involve advocates spending considerable time with the individual, considering their communications needs, their wishes and feelings and their life story, and using all this to assist the person to be involved and where possible to make decisions.

2) a) Assisting a person to communicate their views, wishes and feelings to the staff who are carrying out an assessment or developing a care or support plan or reviewing an existing plan, or

   b) Communicate their views, wishes and feelings to the staff who are carrying out safeguarding enquiries or reviews.

3) Assisting a person to understand how their needs can be met by the local authority or otherwise – understanding for example how:
   - a care and support and support plan can be personalised
   - it can be tailored to meet specific needs
   - it can be creative, inclusive
   - how it can be used to promote a person's rights to liberty and to family life.

4) Assisting the person to make decisions about their care and support arrangements – assisting them to weigh up various care and support options and to choose the ones that best meet the person's needs and wishes.

5) Assisting the person to understand their rights under the Care Act –

   a) To have an assessment which considers:
      - their wishes and feelings
      - the views of other people

   b) Their right to have their eligible needs met, and to have a care or support plan that reflects their needs and their preferences.

   c) In relation to safeguarding, understanding their right to have their concerns about abuse taken seriously and responded to appropriately.

   d) Also assisting the person to understand their wider rights, including their rights to liberty and family life.

   e) A person's rights are complemented by the local authority's duties, for example to involve the person, to meet needs in a way that is least restrictive of a person's rights.

6) Assisting a person to challenge a decision or process made by the local authority – and where a person cannot challenge the decision even with assistance, then to challenge it on their behalf.

Paragraph 7.49 adds that in relation to safeguarding advocates must also assist an individual with the following:

a) decide what outcomes/changes they want;

b) understand the behaviour of others that are abusive/neglectful;

c) understand which actions of their own may expose them to avoidable abuse or neglect;

d) understand what actions that they can take to safeguard themselves;

e) understand what advice and help they can expect from others, including the criminal justice system;

f) understand what parts of the process are completely or partially within their control;

g) explain what help they want to avoid reoccurrence and also to recover from the experience.

The independent advocate has the power to examine and take copies of records kept on the person that they are supporting and representing. This is addressed in paragraph 7.47, as follows:

- Where a person has capacity the advocate should ask and obtain their written consent to look at their records and to talk to their carer, family, friends, care or support worker and others who can provide information about their needs and wishes, their beliefs and values.
- Where a person does not have capacity to decide whether an advocate should look at their relevant records or talk to their family and friends, then the advocate should consult the records and the family and others as appropriate, but consulting the family and others only where the advocate considers this is in the person's best interests.

It should be noted that in representing the individual in developing a care and support plan (or a support plan for a carer), paragraph 10.80 states that the independent advocate "should not be asked to sign off the plan" by the local authority.

Challenging decisions on behalf of the individual

In addition to supporting the individual with involvement, there are circumstances where an advocate "may have concerns about how the local authority has acted or what decision has been made or what outcome is proposed" (paragraph 7.51), where the individual:

- does not have capacity, or is not otherwise able, to challenge a decision (paragraph 7.51)
- has been assisted and supported and nevertheless remains unable to make their own representations or their own decisions (paragraph 7.52).

In these circumstances where the individual is unable to challenge the decision of the local authority, the independent advocate must do this for them "where they believe the decision is inconsistent with the local authority's duty to promote the individual's wellbeing" (paragraph 7.51).

In making representations on behalf of individuals with care and/or support needs who are unable to do so for themselves, the aim of the independent advocate "is to secure a person's rights, promote the individual's wellbeing and ensure that their wishes are taken fully into account" (paragraph 7.52). In this paragraph the circumstances are listed where advocates can legitimately put the individual's case as they see it, in the following circumstances:

a) if they do not appear to meet all eligible needs;

b) do not meet them in a way that fits with the person's wishes and feelings; or

c) are not the least restrictive of the person's life.

This may result in the independent advocate having "to challenge local authority decisions where necessary" (paragraph 7.52).

The relationship between the local authority and the independent advocate

In recognising that it is an advocate's duty "to support and represent a person who has substantial difficulty" the local authority "should understand that the advocate's role incorporates 'challenge' on behalf of the individual" (paragraph 7.53).

The local authority has obligations to independent advocates and vice versa. The local authority "should take reasonable steps to assist the independent advocate" (paragraph 7.56). Advocates are required to comply with "reasonable requests (from the local authority)... for information or for meetings" (paragraph 7.57) about the individual they represent.

The way that representations must be made initially from the advocate is through a written report "outlining their concerns for the local authority" (paragraph 7.52). The local authority should then "convene a meeting with the advocate to consider the concerns and provide a written response to the advocate following the meeting" (paragraph 7.52).

The IMCAs

There are many similarities between the roles of independent advocates under IMCAs, and there will be many circumstances where an individual will require both types of advocacy. In these circumstances the statutory guidance suggests that it would be better for the individual and for the local authority, if these roles could be combined.

Paragraph 7.55 states that "frequently a person will be entitled to an advocate under the Care Act and then, as the process continues it will be identified that there is a duty to provide an advocate (IMCA) under the Mental Capacity Act". The example given in this paragraph is where "it is identified that a decision needs to be taken about the person's long-term accommodation" during the process of assessment or care and support planning, and in these circumstances "it would be better that the advocate who is appointed in the first instance is qualified to act under the Mental Capacity Act (as IMCAs) and the Care Act".

Applying the guidance using case examples

This section illustrates and analyses some of the key elements of the processes described in this chapter that are of particular relevance for social workers.

Mr K has previously appeared in the care and support journey chapters. In addition Mrs B and Mr Y from the safeguarding chapter are also considered. The examples illustrate the following:

- **where substantial difficulty is not clearly evident;**
- **lack of capacity;**
- **the decision about whether a relative can be the appropriate person;**
- **the role of the independent advocate.**

Mr K

Mr K has COPD (Chronic Obstructive Pulmonary Disease) and arthritis. His daughter (Ms K) has been cooking meals for him but is no longer willing to do so, although she is willing to do her father's shopping.

Mr K feels strongly that he should continue to have a home-cooked meal every day to replace what his daughter has been doing. At the outset of the assessment, a judgement would need to be made as to whether this strongly expressed view is an indication of him having substantial difficulty in weighing up information in order to be able to choose between options.

In deciding whether someone has substantial difficulty, the consideration isn't specific to a particular decision. So the determination of substantial difficulty in involvement doesn't need to focus on his views about having a home-cooked meal. Other more neutral issues could be used to determine substantial difficulty, eg by asking him how he decides what he wants to eat.

It was concluded that Mr K was able to weigh up information about options and did not have substantial difficulty in involvement. He recognised that it might be costly to employ someone to provide him with a home-cooked meal everyday, but because he was being encouraged to say what he wanted – that's what he was doing.

Mrs B

Mrs B (aged 95) has Alzheimer's disease and is physically frail and lives in a nursing home. She was admitted to hospital for treatment for a UTI (urinary tract infection) and a chest infection. It was subsequently identified that she had developed a pressure ulcer in the process of admission. A safeguarding enquiry concluded that abuse had not taken place, and she was discharged back to the nursing home after treatment. (See Chapter 8 for more details of the safeguarding enquiry.)

Although Mrs B was aware of the pain and discomfort from the pressure ulcer and had some awareness of how long it had been going on, it was concluded that Mrs B did not have the capacity to consent to the safeguarding enquiry because of her inability to weigh up the significance of this information. A decision was taken that it was in her best interests that a safeguarding enquiry take place. A relative, who had previously supported her with decisions where she lacked capacity, was involved in this decision.

Because she would not be able to retain information long enough to weigh up what had happened to her, it was decided that she had substantial difficulty in being involved in the enquiry process itself, so an appropriate person would need to be appointed (and failing that, an independent advocate). The same relative who has supported her with capacity decisions has also previously acted as the appropriate person, and could undertake this role on this occasion.

As Mrs B lacks the capacity to consent to any relative who might act as the appropriate person, the local authority has to be satisfied that being represented and supported by that person continues to be in her best interests.

Any relative acting as the appropriate person has to be able to distinguish between what are Mrs B's desired outcomes (as best as they can be established) and what they think is best for her, and put Mrs B's wishes first. If the local authority did not think that this relative was able to do this, and there was no other appropriate person, then an independent advocate would be appointed.

It could be the case that the relative acting as the appropriate person wants Mrs B to remain in hospital because she/he is not happy with the outcome of the medical investigation and wants a second opinion, but the social worker who has assessed her needs believes that it would be best for her to return to the nursing home as soon as possible. If it is believed that the relative remains capable of being the appropriate person, a way of resolving the disagreement would be for an independent advocate to be appointed – if the appropriate person agrees.

If there is to be an independent advocate, the decision about appointing one needs to be made as early as possible to ensure that her discharge is not delayed.

Mr Y

Mr Y is a young adult with a learning disability who lives in supported living accommodation. He has a personal assistant (PA), funded through a direct payment, who comes to his flat twice a week to help him to plan his activities, organise his shopping and ensure that he adheres to the conditions of his tenancy. His parents live in a town 20 miles away but they are in close contact. His father is the nominated person for the direct payment, and he has also been appointed as the appropriate person to help Mr Y to be involved in the review process. There have been no circumstances where Mr Y is thought to lack capacity to make decisions.

A safeguarding enquiry was undertaken following concerns that Mr Y was increasingly unkempt and his flat has started to become untidy and dirty. These changes coincided with Mr Y acquiring some new friends who he sees regularly, and there was concern that he might be giving money to these new friends. It was concluded that financial abuse is taking place because there is pressure on Mr Y to withdraw money from his bank account that he is uncomfortable with. Concern was also expressed by Mr Y's family that the changes to his lifestyle that are linked with the association with his new friends is having a negative impact on Mr Y's wellbeing, although Mr Y has not expressed any concern. See Chapter 8 for more information.

An independent advocate was appointed to assist with Mr Y's involvement in the safeguarding enquiry because the social worker decided his father would not be able to be sufficiently objective, given the strong views being expressed about Mr Y's new friends.

In the subsequent review and revision of Mr Y's care and support plan the independent advocate continues to assist Mr Y, in part because Mr Y doesn't want his father to do this. In the description of the meeting to revise Mr Y's care and support plan (see Chapter 7), the role of the independent advocate is relatively straightforward because Mr Y wants help in resisting pressure from his friends to withdraw money from his bank account. However, it could have been more challenging if Mr Y had wanted to go ahead with withdrawing money and was resisting advice. In these circumstances the independent advocate has a duty to assist Mr Y in understanding that the behaviour of his friends is potentially abusive, and she/he would also play a role in helping Mr Y to consider the offer of help from the social worker – with the aim of helping him to resist pressure to spend his money in this way. But at the same time the independent advocate also has to assist the individual to communicate their views, wishes and feelings – however unwise they may be.

If it had been the case that Mr Y had raised no objections to his father acting as the appropriate person at the meeting to revise his care and support plan, the local authority would want to be confident that the fallout from their last meeting wouldn't disqualify him from this role. During the period of the safeguarding enquiry Mr Y had been visited by his father and the note on file says: "Mr Y senior reports that his son says that there is no problem and he doesn't need any help. Mr Y senior was shocked about how unkempt his son is and annoyed that his son refused to show him his bank statements." In these circumstances there would be a tension between the role of Mr Y senior as a father and that of the appropriate person, and it may be better for all concerned if Mr Y senior concentrated on his role as a father and did not act as the appropriate person.

Comment and analysis

Each of the examples illustrates a different facet of substantial difficulty in involvement, and also that the determination of this takes place at different points in the care and support journey.

From what readers will have seen in other chapters Mr K does not appear to have substantial difficulty in involvement, but in his case, as in all circumstances, there is a duty to explicitly address this. The statutory guidance says that this should be considered at first contact (see paragraph 6.23), although in practice it may not be evident that there is substantial difficulty until a more detailed assessment takes place. The statutory guidance doesn't say anything about how this should be recorded, but most local authority assessment formats ensure that communication difficulties are considered at an early stage and require the decision to be recorded.

Mrs B is an example of someone who, because she lacks capacity, also has substantial difficulty in involvement. In such circumstances the resolving of the two sets of statutory guidance can seem a little tortuous on paper. If a relative is supporting her with capacity decisions, this person could also be the 'appropriate person' in accordance with the statutory guidance on substantial difficulty in involvement. If there was no such relative then the IMCA ought to be someone who can act as an independent advocate under the Care Act. In practice making these arrangements is relatively straightforward, although there can be complications such as where the local authority does not agree that a relative who is being consulted on capacity issues can be the 'appropriate person' for the purposes of addressing substantial difficulty in involvement.

Mr Y demonstrated that the independent advocate has a role that goes beyond simply helping the individual communicate their views, wishes and feelings, and that in relation to safeguarding they are also responsible for assisting adults to understand what actions they can take to safeguard themselves.

Conclusion

Making this judgement about whether an individual has substantial difficulty in involvement is new to social work, and while there are situations where the difficulty is very evident, there will be many where it will not be clear whether the criteria apply. Over time guidance will hopefully emerge to support social workers in making this judgement, but until the research into the application of this new duty has taken place and been analysed, social workers must rely solely on their individual professional skills to interpret the Act, regulations and statutory guidance.

The role of the independent advocate is also new and because of a degree of overlap with the role of social worker, both in terms of the general duty to promote involvement and the specific activity of advocacy, guidance may be needed to clarify the role relationship.

Arguably the promotion of involvement is integral to everything that social workers do, for as paragraph 7.6 states "people should be active partners in the key care and support processes of assessment, care and support and support planning, review and any enquiries in relation to abuse or neglect... (and) no matter how complex a person's needs, local authorities are required to involve people, to help them express their wishes and feelings, to support them to weigh up options, and to make their own decisions". Where someone has substantial difficulty in involvement, this requirement does not diminish, and a social worker will continue to be responsible for achieving as much involvement as possible – with the help of an independent advocate (or an appropriate adult).

However, tensions may emerge where advocacy is concerned. Social workers have a role in advocating on behalf of people, both in the general sense of helping adults and carers to achieve their desired outcomes as much as possible through their care and/or support plan, but also in specific circumstances such as ensuring that the personal budget is sufficient to meet the individual's needs. But there can be circumstances where an independent advocate challenges decisions made by a local authority which the social worker may be party to. The professional skill is in being able to adopt the role that is appropriate to the circumstances.

The value of meaningful involvement is the increased likelihood that care and/or support plans will meet needs in a way that achieves the outcomes that matter most to people. An additional benefit from people being fully involved in decision making is that it should limit the number and nature of disputes that result in complaints. The statutory guidance sets out some clarifications in relation to disputes, and these are summarised in the next chapter.

Reference

1. www.gov.uk/government/uploads/system/uploads/attachment_data/file/317817/ConsultationIA.pdf

11 Disputes

Introduction

The purpose of this chapter is to summarise the references to disagreement, disputes, complaints and appeals in the statutory guidance in relation to care and/or support plans.

The statutory guidance outlines the importance of the role played by effective involvement in minimising disputes about care and support plans. Reference is also made to circumstances where a dispute takes the form of non-payment of financial contributions.

Effective involvement

Effective involvement has an important role to play in limiting disputes about care and/or support plans between the local authority and people with care and/or support needs. Paragraph 10.54 sets out what "genuine involvement" can achieve in relation to care and/or support plans, as follows:

- aid the development of the plan;
- increase the likelihood that the options selected will effectively support the adult in achieving the outcomes that matter to them;
- may limit disputes as people involved will be fully aware and have agreed to decisions made.

Managing disagreements

There will be occasions where even though there has been full involvement, the plan cannot be agreed with the individual or their representative. To resolve the disagreement this "may require going back to earlier elements of the planning process" (paragraph 10.86).

Whatever the reasons for the lack of agreement "the local authority should state the reasons for this and the steps which must be taken to ensure that the plan is signed-off" (paragraph 10.86).

The statutory guidance recognises that decisions about personal budgets can result in disagreement if they are not managed carefully. Paragraph 11.47 exhorts local authorities to "take all reasonable steps to limit disputes regarding the personal budget allocation", and suggests the following:

- effective care and support planning;
- transparency in the personal budget allocation process;
- informing people of the timescales that are likely to be involved in different stages of the process.

Complaints

If a dispute cannot be resolved "and the local authority feels that it has taken all reasonable steps to address the situation" (paragraph 10.86), and the individual remains dissatisfied with a decision made by the local authority, he/she can make a complaint about the decision and have that complaint handled by the local authority.

At present local authorities are required to make arrangements for dealing with complaints in accordance with the Local Authority Social Services and NHS Complaints Regulations 2009.

Unarticulated disagreement

People with care and support needs get into debt in relation to financial contributions they have been assessed to make towards their personal budget for a range of reasons. In some cases this may be because of an unarticulated disagreement with the local authority about how their care and support needs are being met, or it could be a reflection of needs not being met satisfactorily. It is recognised in Annex D, section 14 that such debts may be because "a person may be unhappy about being placed in a care home and wish to return home, or could be depressed, have mental health needs or dementia".

Appeals

At present the only option open to individuals who are unable to resolve a dispute with the local authority about their care and/or support plan is to use the complaints procedure. This may change in the future as paragraph 17.73 states that an "appeals system will come into force in April 2020".

The scope of decisions that could be appealed against has yet to be specified, but consideration will be given about "whether decisions made by local authorities on care planning and personal budgets will be eligible for appeal" (paragraph 17.73).

Conclusion

The statutory guidance suggests that more effective involvement "may limit disputes" (paragraph 10.54). However, this ought to be seen as a by-product of the principle policy objective of better involvement.

The statutory guidance gives particular emphasis to the importance of social workers developing skills in effective involvement, not just for complaints but for all aspects of their work. Paragraph 10.54 states that local authorities "should ensure that staff have appropriate learning and development opportunities in order to be able to facilitate involvement in the development of the plan".

Part IV Co-operating with partner organisations

The Care Act 2014 specifies that local authorities must co-operate with each of its relevant partners, and each relevant partner must also co-operate with the local authority, in the exercise of their functions relevant to care and support. In addition there is a duty on local authorities to ensure the integration of care and support provision with health provision and health-related provision.

Section 6 of the Act specifies the 'relevant partners' who have a reciprocal responsibility to co-operate, as the following local organisations:

- other local authorities;
- NHS bodies;
- local offices of the Department for Work and Pensions, eg Job Centre Plus;
- police services;
- prisons and probation services.

Co-operation in relation to care and/or support functions is intended to be a general principle, and should inform organisations about how they exercise their day-to-day functions. In addition the Care Act sets out particular requirements in section 7 that apply to individual cases, as follows:

- cooperation must be provided as requested "unless doing so would be incompatible with their own duties or have an adverse effect on the exercise of their functions" (paragraph 15.26).
- where an organisation decides not to co-operate with a request "then they must write to the other, setting out reasons for not doing so" (paragraph 15.28).

The integration duty applies to the NHS and housing, and this is considered in Chapter 12 of this book. This chapter also considers the boundary between the NHS and local authorities, and how the NHS and local authorities are required to work together in relation to NHS Continuing Healthcare and people being discharged from hospital.

There are particular sets of circumstances where the legislation specifies modifications and additions, ie people who are in prison and young people in transition to adult care. The different ways that the legislation applies to these groups of people is considered in Chapter 13.

Co-operation with police services is most often in relation to safeguarding enquiries and this is considered in Chapter 8 of this book.

12 Working with the NHS and housing

Introduction

The interface between health and social services, and the impact of this on social work, has been subject to review and revision ever since the establishment of lady almoners in the early twentieth century.

The creation of Social Services Departments in 1970, and the subsequent transfer of what were hospital-employed almoners to employment by local authorities as hospital social workers in 1974, helped to establish the distinctive nature of the social work role in relation to health. The NHS and Community Care Act 1990 sought to establish a closer working relationship through the mechanism of care management, and in the late 1990s the policy aim was for people who had both health and social care needs to receive 'seamless' services, which subsequently led to the organisational integration of community-based services for people with learning disabilities and mental ill-health. More recently 'integration' appeared for the first time in legislation in the Health and Social Care Act 2012, through the requirement for the NHS to provide health services in an integrated way with social services.

The Care Act 2014 means that local authorities now also have an integration duty which aims "to eliminate the disjointed care that is a source of frustration to people and staff, and which often results in poor care, with a negative impact on health and wellbeing" (paragraph 15.1). This chapter focuses on:

- **The implications for assessment;**
- **Care and/or support planning.**

In addition this chapter also considers those sections of the Act, regulations and statutory guidance that clarify the relationship between local authorities and the NHS and providers of health-related services, as follows:

- **boundaries between local authorities and the NHS and housing;**
- **how the NHS and local authorities are required to work together in relation to:**
  - **NHS Continuing Healthcare;**
  - **people being discharged from hospital.**

Working with the NHS and housing prior to April 2015

Section 47 (3) of the NHS and Community Care Act 1990 required local authorities to notify the relevant housing or health authority where an assessment identified a possible housing or health need, but there was no obligation on the receiving organisation to respond.

The regulations set out in the *National Framework for NHS Continuing Healthcare and NHS-funded Nursing Care* published in 2012 are unchanged by the Care Act.

Hospital discharge previously took place under the Community Care (Delayed Discharges etc.) Act 2003, which has now been repealed and arrangements are now set out in the Care Act. The practical changes are relatively minor but the opportunity has been taken to improve the description of how the process applies.

Key terms and definitions

The following have been selected because they appear in either the Care Act and/or the Regulations.

Key term	Care Act 2014	The Care and Support Regulations 2014	The Care and Support Statutory Guidance (revised 2017)
Integration	Local authorities must ensure the "integration of care and support provision with health provision and health-related provision", as follows: • to promote the wellbeing of adults and carers • to contribute to the prevention of needs for care and/or support • to improve the quality of care and/or support (see section 3 (1))	No relevant regulations	Paragraph 15.7 gives the following examples of integration: • integrating an assessment with information and advice about housing options on where to live, and adaptations to the home • a local area could introduce a single care plan for an individual spanning health, care and housing • a housing assessment should form part of any assessment process, in terms of suitability, access, safety, repair, heating and lighting (eg efficiency)

Key term	Care Act 2014	The Care and Support Regulations 2014	The Care and Support Statutory Guidance (revised 2017)
Provision of health services	Local authorities cannot provide services that the NHS is required to provide, unless – a) doing so would be merely incidental or ancillary to doing something else to meet needs under those sections, and b) the service or facility in question would be of a nature that the local authority could be expected to provide. (see section 22 (1))	The Care and Support (Provision of Health Services) Regulations 2014 clarify that local authorities are permitted to arrange for the provision of accommodation together with nursing care.	The statutory guidance clarifies that the purpose of Section 22 is to ensure that "all partners involved are clear about their own responsibilities, and how they fit together" (paragraph 15.30)
Health-related services	These are "services which may have an effect on the health of individuals" but are not provided by the NHS, eg housing (see section 3 (4) and (5))	No relevant regulations	Housing is described as "a crucial health-related service which is to be integrated with care and support and health services to promote the wellbeing of adults and carers and improve the quality of services offered" (paragraph 15.50)
NHS continuing healthcare	Section 12 (1) (g) states that in relation to assessment that the regulations may "specify circumstances in which the local authority must refer the adult concerned for an assessment of eligibility for NHS continuing healthcare".	The Care and Support (Assessment) Regulations 2014 clarify that where it appears that an individual may be eligible for NHS continuing healthcare the local authority must refer the individual to the relevant body.	Paragraph 6.80 states: "Where it appears that a person may be eligible for NHS Continuing Healthcare, local authorities must notify the relevant Clinical Commissioning Group."

Key term	Care Act 2014	The Care and Support Regulations 2014	The Care and Support Statutory Guidance (revised 2017)
Hospital discharge	Where the NHS considers "that it is not likely to be safe to discharge the patient unless arrangements for meeting the patient's needs for care and support are in place", then it must give the local authority an assessment notice (see Schedule 3 1 (1)).	The Care and Support (Discharge of Hospital Patients) Regulations 2014 outline how assessment notices and discharge notices are to be applied.	More detail is given on the application of the Regulations in Annex G.

The care and support journey

Paragraph 6.78 outlines the key elements of working in partnership for the benefit of people with both health needs and care and support needs. Local authorities should undertake the following:

- shape the process around the person, involve the person and consider their experience when co-ordinating an integrated assessment;
- work with other professionals to ensure the person's health and care services are aligned;
- link together various care and support plans to set out a single, shared care pathway.

The general requirement for local authorities to "carry out their care and support responsibilities with the aim of joining-up the services or other actions taken with those provided by the NHS and other health-related services (for example, housing or leisure services)" (paragraph 15.3) is considered in this section in relation to the following:

- **prevention;**
- **assessment;**
- **eligibility determination;**
- **care and/or support planning.**

Prevention

The statutory guidance recommends joint commissioning of "advice services covering healthcare and housing, and services like housing-related support that can provide a range of preventative interventions alongside care" (paragraph 15.7 b)).

In the section on tertiary prevention (delaying needs) in the statutory guidance, reference is made to "interventions aimed at minimising the effect of disability or deterioration for people with established or complex health conditions", and local authorities "must provide or arrange services, resources or facilities that maximise independence for those already with such need" and this will include "the use of joint case-management for people with complex needs" (paragraph 2.9).

There are also people who can benefit from prevention at an earlier stage and this could include "adaptions to housing to improve accessibility" (paragraph 2.8).

The importance of housing is emphasised in paragraph 15.50, which states "the setting in which a person lives, and its suitability to their specific needs can have a major impact on the extent and means to which their care and support needs can be met, or prevented, over time".

Some types of preventative support "may be more effectively provided in partnership with other local partners (e.g. rehabilitation or falls clinics provided jointly with the local NHS), and further types may be best provided by other organisations (e.g. specialist housing providers or some carers' services)" (paragraph 2.24).

Assessment

The aim is that "where more than one agency is assessing a person, they should all work closely together to prevent that person having to undergo a number of assessments at different times, which can be distressing and confusing" (paragraph 6.77).

The statutory guidance describes the relationship between an adult's needs assessment or a carer's assessment, and assessments being undertaken by other organisations, as follows:

> JOINT ASSESSMENT
> This is "where relevant agencies work together to avoid the person undergoing multiple assessments" (paragraph 6.3).
>
> INTEGRATED ASSESSMENT
> In some circumstances it can be important to make changes to the assessment process itself so that it is more suited to the needs of the individual. Paragraph 6.76 gives local authorities the power to "integrate or align assessment processes" to achieve this.
>
> COORDINATED ASSESSMENT
> This applies where the individual has both health and care and support needs. Paragraph 6.78 states that "local authorities and the NHS should work together effectively to deliver a high quality, coordinated assessment".

The only reference to the relationship between assessments in the Care Act is where it states that the local authority can carry out an assessment "on behalf of ... the body responsible for carrying it out" (section 12 (7)). The statutory guidance provides a slight clarification in paragraph 6.79 in the statement that "the local authority may carry out the care and support assessment jointly with any other assessment, and can also undertake the other assessment on behalf of the other body, where this is agreed". However, no examples are given of the circumstances where this power might be applied.

Eligibility determination

The health of an individual is a factor in determining eligibility in a number of ways, and in some circumstances social workers will want to obtain input from health practitioners.

In deciding whether an adult has a physical impairment, mental impairment or illness it is not necessary to obtain a diagnosis. However, it may be helpful to get input from health practitioners about the following:

- the nature of pain an adult is experiencing in trying to achieve any of the specified outcomes;
- the extent to which a carer's physical or mental condition is deteriorating;
- the impact on the individual's wellbeing in relation to their physical health or mental health, of their inability to achieve any of the specified outcomes.

(Various references taken from paragraphs 6.100–134)

A specific component of wellbeing is the 'suitability of living accommodation', and is thus a consideration in determining eligibility for care and/or support. Paragraph 15.58 also points out the importance of housing in other areas of wellbeing, as follows:

- access to a safe settled home underpins personal dignity;
- a safe suitable home can:
  - contribute to physical and mental wellbeing;
  - provide control over day-to-day life;
  - provide protection from abuse and neglect.
- a home or suitable living accommodation can enable participation in:
  - work or education;
  - social interactions;
  - family relationships.

Care and/or support planning

Paragraph 10.74 states that "the local authority should attempt to establish where other plans are present, or are being conducted and seek to combine plans, if appropriate", and it gives two different types of examples as follows:

- where the plan can be combined with a plan being developed to meet other needs;
- where a plan might usefully be combined with that of a carer, or family member.

The example given of combining plans for someone who is receiving both local authority care and support and NHS healthcare is where an individual has a "mental disorder who meets the criteria for care and support under the multi-agency Care Programme Approach" (paragraph 10.79).

The statutory guidance uses the terminology of 'combining plans'. This is to take place where "it is vital to avoid duplicating process or introducing multiple monitoring regimes" (paragraph 10.80). Where plans are combined, "local authorities should work alongside health and other professionals (such as housing)... to establish a 'lead' organisation who [*sic*] undertakes monitoring and assurance of the combined plan". This may also involve deciding on someone to be the "lead professional and detailing this in the plan so the person knows who to contact when plans are combined".

Where such a combining of plans is being contemplated the following applies, as set out in paragraph 10.74:

- the plan should only be combined if all parties to whom it is relevant agree and understand the implications of sharing data and information;
- it is the responsibility of the local authority to obtain consent from all parties involved.

Paragraph 10.79 describes using personal health budgets in health alongside personal budgets in social care "to enable integrated health and care provision which focuses on what matters most to the person". Direct payments for social care can also be combined with personal health budget direct payments, and this could result in a local authority agreeing with the NHS "that the monitoring is performed solely by one organisation, reporting to the other as appropriate" (paragraph 12.34).

Paragraph 15.7 (c) makes reference to the possibility of "a single care plan for an individual spanning health, care and housing that is owned and directed by that person".

"Local authorities should... seek to work with health colleagues to combine health and care plans wherever possible" (paragraph 10.79). This paragraph also states people should be provided with information about "the benefits of combining health and social care support".

Boundaries between local authorities and the NHS and housing

In rephrasing section 22 (1) of the Care Act, the statutory guidance states that where "the NHS has a clear legal responsibility to provide a particular service, then the local authority may not do so" (paragraph 15.31). It goes on to state "this general rule is intended to provide clarity and avoid overlaps, and to maintain the existing legal boundary".

Similarly, section 23 of the Care Act "clarifies the existing boundary in law between care and support relevant housing legislation" (paragraph 15.51), ie where people have accommodation needs, local authorities must apply the Housing Act 1996.

NHS

Although it is not lawful for local authorities to meet needs by providing or arranging services that are legally the responsibility of the NHS, "the local authority may provide or arrange healthcare services where they are incidental or ancillary to doing something else to meet needs for care and support and the service or facility in question is of a nature that a local authority could be expected to provide" (paragraph 6.79).

Examples of healthcare that the local authority cannot provide are given in paragraph 15.32, as follows:

- nursing care provided by registered nurses;
- services that the NHS has to provide because the individual is eligible for NHS Continuing Healthcare.

The only example given of what could be considered 'incidental or ancillary' is in relation to eligibility, where it states that "local authorities do not have responsibility for the provision of NHS services such as patient transport, however they should consider needs for support when the adult is attending healthcare appointments" (paragraph 6.106 i).

Housing

Paragraph 15.51 states "the Care Act is clear that suitable accommodation can be one way of meeting care and supports needs" and "where housing forms part of the solution to meeting a person's needs for care and support, or preventing needs for care and support, then a local authority may include this in the care or support plan even though the housing element itself is provided under housing legislation".

This boundary between social services and housing "does not prevent joint working, and it does not prevent local authorities in the care and support role from providing more specific services such as housing adaptations, or from working jointly with housing authorities" (paragraph 15.52).

NHS Continuing Healthcare

There is nothing new in the Care Act about NHS Continuing Healthcare (CHC) other than establishing the duty to refer, and also making recommendations about the use of independent advocacy. The statutory guidance is helpful in outlining the key features of CHC from a social care perspective, but it does not describe the criteria or how they are applied.

Paragraph 15.33 outlines the CHC criteria as follows:

- it is for individuals outside a hospital setting who have complex ongoing healthcare needs that have arisen as a result of disability, accident or illness;
- these healthcare needs are of a type or quantity such that they meet the criteria for a 'primary health need';

- this is not dependent on a person's condition or diagnosis, but is based on their specific physical or mental health needs.

Where someone has a 'primary health need' paragraph 15.34 states "it is the responsibility of the health service to meet all assessed health and associated care and support needs, including suitable accommodation, if that is part of the overall need".

The relevant regulations and guidance on their application are set out in the revised version of the *National Framework for NHS Continuing Healthcare and NHS-funded Nursing Care* published in 2012.

The key features of the application of Continuing Healthcare for social workers are set out in paragraphs 6.80 of the statutory guidance, as follows:

- It is a package of on-going care that is arranged and funded solely by the NHS.
- There are no limits on the settings in which the package of support can be offered and may be provided in a nursing or care home, or in a person's own home.
- There are no limits on the type of service delivery and could be by way of joint personal budget.

Paragraph 6.82 outlines circumstances where there can be part-funding if a person is not found to be eligible for NHS Continuing Healthcare, because "the NHS may still have a responsibility to contribute to that person's health needs – either by directly commissioning services or by part-funding the package of support. Where such a package of support is "commissioned or funded by both a LA and a Clinical Commissioning Group (CCG), this is known as a 'joint package' of care", and could include any of the following characteristics:

- NHS-funded nursing care and other NHS services that are beyond the powers of a local authority to meet;
- the CCG could be commissioning part of the package;
- it may be provided in a nursing or care home, or in a person's own home, and could be by way of joint personal budget.

Paragraph 15.35 gives the example of "funding provided by the NHS to care homes providing nursing, to support the provision of nursing care by a registered nurse".

Paragraph 6.83 refers to the local disputes resolution process to resolve cases where there is a dispute between local authorities and the CCG about the following:

- eligibility for NHS Continuing Healthcare;
- the apportionment of funding in joint funded care and support packages;
- the operation of refunds guidance.

It is important that "disputes should not delay the provision of the care package, and the (local) protocol should make clear how funding will be provided pending resolution of the dispute" (paragraph 6.83).

Paragraph 7.22 notes in reference to NHS Continuing Healthcare and joint packages of care that "these processes and arrangements have historically been difficult for individuals, their carers, family or friends, to understand and be involved in". This is not a reference to people who have substantial difficulty in involvement, but a reference to the difficulty inherent in the process itself. Nevertheless, the statutory guidance proposes that local authorities "consider the benefits of providing access to independent advice or independent advocacy for those who do not have substantial difficulty and/or those who have an appropriate person to support their involvement" (paragraph 7.22).

Hospital discharge

Discharge of hospital patients with care and support needs takes place under Schedule 3 of the Care Act and the Care and Support (Discharge of Hospital Patients) Regulations 2014. Paragraph 15.38 of the statutory guidance states that Schedule 3 covers the following:

- the scope of the hospital discharge regime and the definition of the patients to whom it applies;
- the notifications which an NHS body must give a local authority where the NHS considers that it is not likely to be safe to discharge the patient unless arrangements for meeting the patient's needs for care and support are put in place;
- the period for which an NHS body can consider seeking reimbursement from a local authority, where that local authority has not fulfilled its requirements to assess or put in place care and support to meet needs, or (where applicable) to meet carers' needs for support, within the time periods set such that the patient's discharge from hospital is delayed.

These discharge provisions apply only to hospital patients with care and support needs who are receiving acute care. Section 7 (7) of Schedule 3 states that the following do not fall within the scope of acute care:

(a) care of an expectant or nursing mother

(b) mental healthcare

(c) palliative care

(d) a structured programme of care provided for a limited period to help a person maintain or regain the ability to live at home

(e) care provided for recuperation or rehabilitation.

Also "the Discharge of Hospital provisions do not apply to patients who have given an undertaking to pay for their care in an NHS hospital or who are accommodated at an independent hospital under private arrangements" (paragraph 15.45).

Paragraph 15.40 notes that the statutory guidance "does not address the wider practice issues associated with planning safe and effective discharge which apply to all cases of hospital discharge regardless of they whether they fall within the scope of these provisions or not". Nevertheless, this paragraph goes on to state that "in relation to all cases, both NHS and local authorities should, using the best evidence available, develop and apply local protocols that ensure that all patients receive appropriate and safe discharge procedures".

This section considers the following in more detail:

- **assessment notices and discharge notices;**
- **delayed transfers of care.**

Assessment notices

Annex G of the statutory guidance sets out what is required from assessment notices and discharge notices, and how these are to be applied.

The NHS must not issue an assessment notice "without having satisfied itself that there is a reasonable prospect that there may be a need for care and support for which arrangements may need to be made in order to ensure a safe discharge" (Annex G, section 6).

Before a notice is issued, section 8 specifies that both of the following must take place:

a) the patient and carer (where applicable) must be consulted so that unnecessary assessments are avoided, eg where the patient wishes to make private arrangements for care and support without the involvement of the local authority;

b) an assessment of the potential Continuing Health Care needs of the patient and if applicable a decision made on what services the NHS will be providing.

Section 12 of Annex G clarifies that "the information contained in an assessment notification is intended to be minimal, both to reflect patient confidentiality requirements and to minimise bureaucracy – it is only the trigger for assessment and care planning". In addition to confirming that the patient may require care and support on discharge, it must include the following:

a) if given before the patient's admission, the expected date of admission and the name of the hospital in which the patient is being accommodated;

b) an indication of the patient's discharge date, if known.

After the assessment notice has been given, the NHS organisation responsible "must consult the authority before deciding what it will do for the patient in order for discharge to be safe" (section 2 (1) (a) of Schedule 3 of the Care Act).

Section 17 of Annex G specifies that "on receiving an assessment notice, the local authority must carry out a needs assessment" (and a carer's assessment where applicable). Having decided "how it proposes to meet any (if at all) of those needs", the local authority must then "inform the NHS of the outcome of its assessment and decisions".

Section 23 sets out the circumstances when the NHS must withdraw an assessment notice, as follows:

- The NHS body considers that it is likely to be safe to discharge the patient without arrangements being put in place for the meeting of the patient's needs for care and support or (where applicable) the carer's needs for support.
- The NHS body considers that the patient's on-going need is for NHS Continuing Health Care.
- Following the decision as to which (if any) services the relevant local authority will make available to the patient or (where applicable) carer, the NHS body still considers that it is unlikely to be safe to discharge the patient from hospital unless further arrangements are put in place for the meeting of the patient's care and support needs or (where applicable) the carer's needs for support.
- The patient's proposed treatment is cancelled or postponed.
- The NHS body has become aware that the relevant authority is not required to carry out any assessment because the patient has refused a needs assessment, or (where applicable) the carer has refused a carer's assessment.
- The NHS body becomes aware that either one of the following applies:
  - the patient's ordinary residence has changed since the assessment notice was given;
  - the notice was given to a local authority other than the one in whose area the patient is ordinarily resident.

Discharge notices

Section 26 states that the purpose of a discharge notice "is to confirm the discharge date as it either may not have been previously known at the time of the issue of the assessment notice or may have subsequently changed since the assessment notice was issued". A discharge date may have been identified in the assessment notice, but regardless of this a discharge notice must be issued.

Section 25 states "patients and carers should be informed of the discharge date at the same time as or before the local authority".

Timescales

Requirements and guidance on timescales is set out in sections 9–11, 17–21 and 29–33 of Annex G. The key principles and requirements are as follows:

Advance notice

- The NHS should seek to give the local authority as much notice as possible of a patient's impending discharge.
- An assessment notice must not be issued more than seven days before the patient is expected to be admitted into hospital.
- There is no upper limit for advance warning of a discharge date.

Minimum periods

- The local authority must carry out a needs assessment and put in place any arrangements for meeting such needs that it proposes to meet before 'the relevant day'.
- The relevant day is either the date upon which the NHS proposes to discharge the patient or the minimum period, whichever is the later.
- The minimum period is two days after the local authority has received an assessment notice or is treated as having received an assessment notice.
- The minimum discharge notification allowed is at least one day before the proposed discharge date.

The process of assessment notices and discharge notices is summarised in Figure 12.1 based on the minimum periods.

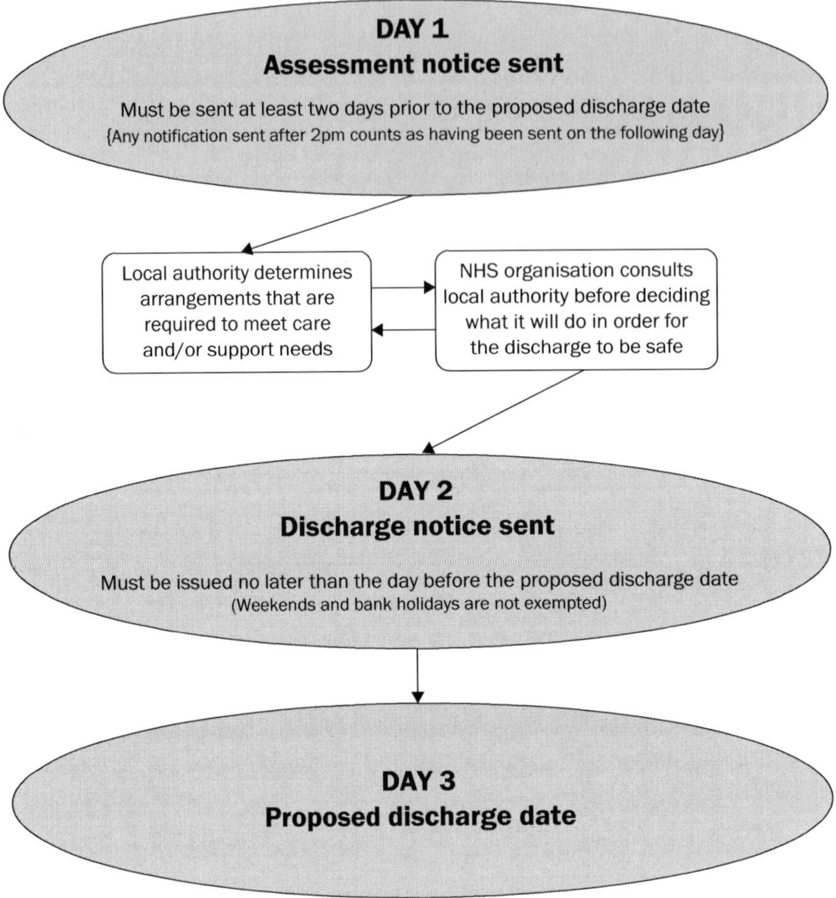

Figure 12.1 *Assessment and discharge notices*

Delayed transfer of care (DTOC)

The Care and Support (Discharge of Hospital Patients) Regulations 2014 enable the NHS to seek reimbursement from local authorities, but "the recovery of any reimbursement has now been placed on a discretionary rather than mandatory footing" (paragraph 15.37).

Section 40 specifies that the NHS is able to seek reimbursement from the local authority arising from a delayed transfer of care in the following circumstances:

a) the NHS has first sent both an assessment notice and a discharge notice to the local authority;

b) the local authority has then either –

- not carried out an assessment; or
- not put arrangements in place for the meeting of care and/or support needs which it proposes to meet, by the end of the relevant day.

It is emphasised that "while reimbursement remains available for use by the NHS body, they and local authorities are encouraged to use the provisions on the discharge of hospital patients (such as the issue of assessment and discharge notices) to seek to focus on effective joint working so as to improve the care of those people whose needs span both NHS and local authority care settings" (section 39).

Applying the guidance using case examples

This section illustrates and analyses some of the key elements of the processes described in this chapter that are of particular relevance for social workers.

Case examples used in previous chapters are revisited to illustrate hospital discharge, boundary issues and integrating assessments. NHS CHC is not included as this would require the reader having a good understanding of the *National Framework for NHS Continuing Healthcare and NHS-funded Nursing Care.*

Mr K

Background

Mr K has COPD (Chronic Obstructive Pulmonary Disease) and arthritis. His daughter (Ms K) has been cooking meals for him but is no longer willing to do so, although she is willing to do her father's shopping. He is now purchasing meals from the home meals service. Mr K has a direct payment to pay for someone to help with the cleaning and laundry. He cannot use public transport, but receives help from friends and his daughter. Following a recent review Ms K agreed to have a carer's assessment but this has not yet been completed.

Acute episode

Mr K was admitted to hospital by ambulance. He was having difficulty breathing and he called his neighbour. She noticed that his lips had turned blue and called an ambulance. Following treatment and medical re-assessment, he will be ready for discharge home once arrangements have been made for him to be provided with oxygen and the hospital is satisfied that Mr K knows how to use it. He is also being referred for respiratory physiotherapy to commence as soon as possible after he goes home.

Assessment, eligibility and care and support planning

The ward staff know that he has care and support needs because they are aware that social services are involved. It is decided that it will not be safe to discharge him home unless the existing arrangements in place for meeting his needs are reinstated. To make sure that this takes place an assessment notice is sent in accordance with the local protocol.

The assessment notice gives an indicative discharge date that is in five days' time. By this time it is anticipated that his treatment will have been completed and oxygen can be made available for him at home. A decision has been made that there are no indications that he meets the criteria for NHS Continuing Healthcare.

As Mr K already has a care and support plan, his previous needs assessment can be used by the hospital social work team to review his needs and decide whether any changes might be required to his care and support plan.

The only change to his plan is in relation to arrangements for Mr K to be accompanied to his physiotherapy appointments following discharge. This is seen as a non-eligible need. Ms K says she will accompany her father.

The locally agreed protocol requires notification of any anticipated delayed transfer. The hospital social worker is confident that services can be reinstated at short notice. This is helped by the indicative discharge date being on a Wednesday, ie there is time to plan this within the working week.

This information is passed to the person designated by the hospital to coordinate discharge. It is decided that it is safe to discharge and the formal discharge notice is sent to the local authority.

His care and support plan now reads as follows:

My desired outcomes	***Needs that the local authority has agreed / not agreed it will ensure are met D – duty P – power N – not meeting***	***Needs being met by the carer***	***Needs to be met through friends, family and community resources***	***Personal budget and payment method***	***Evaluation of extent to which my desired outcomes are achieved***
I want someone to come in every day and prepare me a home-cooked meal in the way that my daughter has been doing.	*The effect of me being unable to cook for myself has a significant impact on my physical wellbeing and also control over my day-to-day life (D).*	*My daughter, Ms K, is willing to do my shopping and cook me a Sunday dinner.*		*I have opted to purchase meals from the home meals service.*	*Moderately satisfied.*

My desired outcomes	**Needs that the local authority has agreed / not agreed it will ensure are met** **D – duty** **P – power** **N – not meeting**	**Needs being met by the carer**	**Needs to be met through friends, family and community resources**	**Personal budget and payment method**	**Evaluation of extent to which my desired outcomes are achieved**
Cleaning and laundry – I find this very time consuming and I would rather employ someone to do this.	*The effect of me being unable to do cleaning and laundry has a significant impact on my physical wellbeing and also control over my day-to-day life (D).*			*£... to pay for ... hours of cleaning and laundry. Direct payment of £ ... to Ms K.*	*I've got several people coming from an agency. They're not as good as my neighbour was.*
Attending the local jazz club.	*Not being able to go to the jazz club has a significant impact on my wellbeing in relation to participation in recreational activities (D).*		*Friends and acquaintances who attend the jazz club give me a lift and my daughter says she will take me if nobody can do it.*		*I was worried about having to rely on people to go to the jazz club, but that is working out OK so far.*
Support to attend physiotherapy for the next six weeks.	*I get NHS transport to get there, but I get a bit anxious if I have to rely on porters to get me to the right department (N).*	*My daughter, Ms K, will come with me.*			*I'm pleased that my daughter can come with me.*

Given that Mr K has health needs as well as care and support needs, it could be useful for him to have a combined plan. This would not be necessary for the purposes of ensuring a safe discharge, but it is something that could be developed subsequently.

Alternative scenarios

If Mr K did not already have a care and support plan and the situation is as it was before an assessment of needs had been requested, ie his meals were being cooked by his daughter and there was a private arrangement with a neighbour to do the cooking and cleaning, two alternative routes are possible.

(a) *It is possible that an assessment notice would not be issued if Mr K is clear that that he wishes to continue with making private arrangements without the involvement of the local authority. In these circumstances the hospital would need to be satisfied that these private arrangements supported a safe discharge.*

(b) *If Mr K was not opposed to local authority involvement, an assessment notice would be issued because it appears that he has care and support needs and the current arrangements may not be meeting his needs in such a way as to facilitate a safe discharge.*

We saw in Chapter 2 that Mr K's assessment was not completed until he had received reablement, but this cannot take place while he is in hospital. The needs assessment is thus initiated in hospital and would then be completed after Mr K is discharged. In responding to the assessment notice, the focus for the hospital social worker would be on arranging any additional care and support to meet those needs that are essential to ensure his safe discharge. A carer's assessment would be offered, but as before Ms K may well decline this.

The likely conclusion would be that Mr K has sufficient support to enable him to be discharged safely, and that his needs assessment be completed after a period of reablement. This information would then be passed to the person designated by the hospital to coordinate discharge, who would then send the formal discharge notice to the local authority (assuming that the discharge plan is accepted).

Ms W

Background

Ms W (aged 40) has psychotic depression and is socially isolated. When her care and support plan was recently reviewed she expressed her disappointment that social services would not pay for her to continue to attend a gym regularly. The NHS had been paying for exercise on prescription, but this had now ceased.

Assessment, eligibility and care and support planning

Ms W had taken the lead herself in coordinating plans to meet both her health and care and support needs, with support from a social worker. She had seen her GP and obtained exercise on prescription for a 12-week period. The GP readily agreed to this as she met the criteria because of her depression and her evident motivation. She had hoped to be able to get agreement for a further period of exercise because she said it made her feel more positive about life.

The intention of such exercise programmes is that participants will be motivated to continue exercising after the 12-week period so that the health benefits can be maintained. But Ms W says that the intensity of exercise that she finds beneficial can only be obtained from the equipment that is available in a gym, eg the cross-trainer, and she can't afford to buy the domestic versions of this type of equipment.

It was thought that by going to the gym Ms W might engage with fellow gym members and this might have a positive impact, increasing her social networks and thus reducing her social isolation, but this objective was not achieved. As Ms W recorded in her review, "people just keep to themselves".

If there was no other means of reducing her social isolation, then other ways of making use of gym attendance to achieve this could be considered by the local authority. But she has recently started volunteering and this is successfully achieving this objective.

Mrs J

Mrs J has a history of psychotic illness and is supported by a Community Psychiatric Nurse (CPN) who visits her fortnightly and administers her depot injections. Mrs J is married with two young children, aged nine and seven years old. Since the birth of her youngest child, she has had a history of psychotic illness, including periods of voluntary admission to hospital.

She is experiencing domestic abuse and as a result of this there was a safeguarding enquiry (see Chapter 8 of this book for more details).

Mrs J wants to have more freedom and responsibility, and when the children are older she would like to go back to work. She can't see her husband changing his controlling behaviour, so the only way she can see of achieving her desired outcomes is to leave him and start a new life. But she doesn't think she can go through with it, because she is worried that the stress of it would mean that she would end up back in hospital.

Assessment, eligibility and care and support planning

Mrs J's circumstances present a challenge to professionals in integrating procedures and minimising bureaucracy, because of the variety of assessments that apply to her circumstances, as follows:

- *the plan to meet her mental health needs is set out in a Care Programme Approach plan;*
- *when she disclosed to the CPN that she was experiencing domestic abuse, a safeguarding enquiry took place and a safeguarding plan was developed;*

- *she may accept specialist help from a voluntary organisation to help her review her circumstances and decide what is best for her and the children;*
- *if she decides to leave her husband she may want help with travel costs to get to a women's refuge, and as she will also become homeless she will need help with housing;*
- *if she decides to remain with her husband it may be necessary to assess the needs of her children.*

If Mrs J does decide to leave her husband, Mrs J will have housing needs and additional care and support needs. In these circumstances a coordinated assessment should take place and a combined plan developed. Given this degree of complexity a social worker may be appointed to undertake this coordination.

Comment and analysis

Hospital discharge

The example of Mr K illustrates that a needs assessment is often not finalised until after the individual is discharged from hospital.

It should be noted that there is no reference in the statutory guidance to planning discharges where someone already has a care and support plan. It is likely that it was anticipated that this level of detail would be addressed in the recommended local protocols (see Annex G, section 7).

In the example of Mr K, no new care and support has to be arranged to ensure a safe discharge. But where this is required this can sometimes result in a delayed transfer of care, because the service that is needed is not immediately available, eg homecare.

Joining-up assessments and combining plans

Where there are several strands to a person's needs that each fall within the scope of different assessment and planning regimes, as is the case with Mrs J, the challenge in achieving a holistic response from the agencies involved is to join things up without creating additional unnecessary bureaucracy. In complex situations such as Mrs J's where there is assessment of her mental health needs, safeguarding needs, care and support needs and the needs of her children – at the very least the relevant agencies could work together to minimise the extent to which she is asked to repeat her story.

What is probably most useful in such situations is to focus on pulling all the strands together in a combined plan, and if possible identifying a lead person. In Mrs J's case this can probably be achieved through the Care Programme Approach, with either the existing CPN continuing to lead or possibly passing the lead role to a social worker in the mental health team. However, it is important to remember that it is the responsibility of the local authority to obtain the consent of all parties to the combining of the plan.

Another way of cutting through the bureaucracy associated with the different regimes for assessing and meeting needs may be to encourage the use of paragraph 15.7 (c), which envisages "a single care plan for an individual spanning health, care and housing that is owned and directed by that person". This could certainly be a useful next step for Ms W, and possibly for Mr K.

Boundary issues with the NHS

Mr K's wish to have someone support him while he attends physiotherapy is an example of a potential health-related ancillary need. In deciding that this was a non-eligible need, consideration would have been given as to whether the anxiety that Mr K experiences in having to rely on a porter being found to take him from outpatient's reception to his physiotherapy has a significant impact on his control over day-to-day life. It was concluded that the impact would not be significant, and in any event his daughter was willing to undertake this task.

Ms W's gym membership was something that could potentially meet both a health need and a care and support need. But as it turned out, attending the gym did not achieve any benefit in helping Ms W to develop her social network. If it had, then the local authority might pay for the continuation of gym membership and the health benefit could be regarded as incidental. Clearly the local authority cannot pay for the gym membership to continue the health benefit, as this is a NHS responsibility.

Conclusion

The particular value for social workers in the sections of the Care Act, the Regulations and the statutory guidance described in this chapter is in the clarification provided on the key aspects of the relationship between local authorities and the NHS and housing. In addition there are particular points to note about the following:

- **NHS Continuing Healthcare;**
- **integration.**

The sections on what integration might mean for day-to-day practice are helpful in providing the basis for operational clarity, but much of the statutory guidance would have to be further developed in local policies and procedures.

NHS Continuing Healthcare

It has been noted that the sections on NHS Continuing Healthcare and hospital discharge do not introduce many new duties and powers. Nevertheless there have been some minor changes that have implications for social workers.

The new duty to refer people who it is thought may be eligible for NHS Continuing Healthcare is of significance because, as with all duties that social workers are required to undertake, the Care Act states that they must have to have the necessary skills, knowledge and competence to do this. In carrying out assessments under the Care Act, social workers need to know enough about eligibility for NHS Continuing Healthcare to make a competent referral.

In addition to making referrals, social workers will sometime be called upon to participate in the multi-disciplinary team assessment that contributes towards determining eligibility for NHS Continuing Healthcare, and also planning joint packages of care for individuals whose needs fall short of the NHS Continuing Healthcare criteria. This is a complex area of work, so making available independent advice and advocacy for adults with these needs, as recommended in the statutory guidance, will be welcomed by social workers.

Integration

Any major piece of legislation and its accompanying regulations and statutory guidance will, as well as settling some matters, aim to shape future practice and policy development. The latter is particularly evident with the Care Act in what is sometimes described as the 'integration agenda'.

With care and/or support planning, the statutory guidance states that local authorities 'should' do the following:

- "link together various care and support plans to set out a single, shared care pathway" (paragraph 6.78);
- "seek to work with health colleagues to combine health and care plans wherever possible" (paragraph 10.79);
- "work alongside health and other professionals (such as housing) where plans are combined to establish a 'lead' organisation who undertakes monitoring and assurance of the combined plan (this may also involve appointing a lead professional and detailing this in the plan so the person knows who to contact when plans are combined)" (paragraph 10.80).

In addition, the future direction of travel is indicated in the following suggestions about what local authorities 'could' do:

- "agree with the NHS that the social care and health direct payments are combined and that the monitoring is performed solely by one organisation, reporting to the other as appropriate" (paragraph 12.34);
- "introduce a single care plan for an individual spanning health, care and housing that is owned and directed by that person" (paragraph 15.7 (c)).

The sections on assessment are less explicit about future development, and are more about setting out terminological definitions. Assessment is described variously as being 'joint', 'integrated' or 'coordinated'. A joint assessment appears to be the generic term, with the other two being sub-variants. It could be argued that an example of the use of the power to "integrate or align assessment processes" (paragraph 6.76) is evident in the hospital discharge process and the Care Programme Approach, and that an example of a coordinated assessment occurs within the safeguarding enquiry process as set out in paragraphs 14.93–111.

What is interesting about hospital discharge arrangements is that the protocol for the integrating of assessments is set out as a statutory requirement. It goes beyond the general power of local authorities to integrate assessment processes, and sets out how it must be done. Not only are timescales specified, but also the communication stages between NHS staff and local authority staff are precisely specified in relation to how decisions are reached about safe discharge.

What next?

Given that the relationship between health and social care is subject to ongoing revision, it is likely that soon after this book is published there will be further changes. At the time of writing, the stated government target of integrated health and social care across England by 2020 is being called into question, and there may also be developments that derive from the precarious state of public sector funding.

13 Modifications and additions for young people and prisoners

Introduction

The aim of this chapter is to summarise how the legislation applies in different ways to people in the following circumstances:

- young people in transition to adult care;
- prisoners and persons in approved premises.

Young people in transition to adult care

The Care Act and the statutory guidance applies to young people, young carers and the carers of young people in the same way as it does for adults – but with some additional requirements in relation to assessment.

Where it appears to a local authority that a young person is "likely to have needs for care and support after becoming 18" (section 58 (1)), or a young carer appears "likely to have needs for support after becoming 18" (section 63 (1)), an assessment must take place where the following two additional requirements are both met:

a) the local authority is satisfied that it would be of significant benefit to the individual;

b) the consent condition is met.

For a carer of a young person to receive an assessment of whether they have needs for support, the local authority must be "satisfied that it would be of significant benefit to the carer to do so" (section 60 (1)).

It should be noted that the sections in both the Care Act and the statutory guidance have been written so that they can be understood as stand-alone sections, hence detail is replicated about the application of all of the key processes.

Definitions

The statutory guidance "uses the term 'young person' for people under 18 with care and support needs who are approaching transition, rather than the legal term 'child' contained in the Care Act itself" (paragraph 16.6).

Significant benefit

The decision about significant benefit is in relation to the timing of the assessment, and "will generally be at the point when their needs for care and support as an adult can be predicted reasonably confidently" (paragraph 16.6).

Paragraph 16.10 states that "when considering whether it is of significant benefit to assess, a local authority should consider factors which may contribute to establishing the right time to assess (including but not limited to the following)":

- the stage they have reached at school and any upcoming exams
- whether the young person or carer wishes to enter further/higher education or training
- whether the young person or carer wishes to get a job when they become a young adult
- whether the young person is planning to move out of their parental home into their own accommodation
- whether the young person will have care leaver status when they become 18
- whether the carer of a young person wishes to remain in or return to employment when the young person leaves full-time education
- the time it may take to carry out an assessment
- the time it may take to plan and put in place the adult care and support
- any relevant family circumstances
- any planned medical treatment.

Consent

For young people the consent condition is specified as being met in sections 58 (3) of the Care Act:

a) the child has capacity or is competent to consent to a child's needs assessment being carried out and the child does so consent, or

b) the child lacks capacity or is not competent so to consent but the authority is satisfied that carrying out a child's needs assessment would be in the child's best interests.

It is similarly specified for young carers in section 63 (3):

a) the young carer has capacity or is competent to consent to a young carer's assessment being carried out and the young carer does so consent, or

b) the young carer lacks capacity or is not competent so to consent but the authority is satisfied that carrying out a young carer's assessment would be in the young carer's best interests.

Where a young person or a young carer refuses an assessment, sections 58 (4) and 63 (4) specify that "the local authority must nonetheless carry out the assessment if the child (or young carer) is experiencing, or is at risk of, abuse or neglect".

Prisoners and persons in approved premises

The Care Act and the statutory guidance emphasise that "people in custody or custodial settings who have needs for care and support should be able to access the care they need, just like anyone else" because "in the past, the responsibilities for meeting the needs of prisoners have been unclear, and this has led to confusion between local authorities, prisons and other organisations" (paragraph 17.1).

Definitions

References to prison include "a reference to a young offender institution, secure training centre or secure children's home" (section 76 (11) (a) of the Care Act).

Approved premises "are usually supervised hostel-type accommodation" providing "supervision and rehabilitation of offenders, and for people on bail" (from 'Definitions' following paragraph 17.13).

Ordinary residence

Sections 76 (1–3) of the Care Act are stated succinctly in paragraph 17.5 of the statutory guidance as follows: "Adults detained or residing in a custodial setting are treated as if they were ordinarily resident in the area where the custodial setting is located."

On an individual's release from prison they are not deemed to have been ordinarily resident in the area of the prison. The 'deeming provisions' in section 39 do not apply (see paragraph 17.48). The key determinant is where the individual plans to live upon release. Paragraph 17.50 states that where "their place of ordinary residence is unclear and/ or they express an intention to settle in a new local authority area, the local authority to which they plan to move should take responsibility for carrying out the needs assessment".

Where a person requires the type of accommodation that is specified in paragraph 19.39 (eg residential care), paragraph 17.48 states that "local authorities should start from a presumption that they remain ordinarily resident in the area in which they were ordinarily resident before the start of their sentence".

Exceptions

All aspects of the legislation apply to adults in custody or custodial settings, but there are some exceptions and the most important of these are set out in this section.

Preference for accommodation

The legislation requiring that the local authority "must provide for the person's preferred choice of accommodation, subject to certain conditions" (paragraph 8.36) does not apply while individuals are in prison or approved premises. This is set out in the Care Act in section 76 (4).

Direct payments

Section 76 (5) specifies that direct payments "do not apply in the case of an adult who, having been convicted of an offence, is –

a) detained in prison, or

b) residing in approved premises".

Paragraph 17.40 clarifies that adults "in bail accommodation and approved premises who have not yet been convicted are entitled to direct payments, as they would have been whilst in their own homes".

Safeguarding

Paragraph 17.61 states that the "local authority will not have the legal duty to lead enquiries in any custodial setting." This reflects section 76 (7) that states "sections 42 and 47 (safeguarding: enquiry by local authority and protection of property) do not apply". However, "prison and probation staff may approach the local authority for advice and assistance in individual cases" (paragraph 17.61).

Limitations

It is recognised that it may not always be possible to put people in control of their care and for them to be actively involved and influential throughout the planning process, so the care and support plan must include "how, if applicable, the custodial regime limited the individual's choice and control" (paragraph 17.33).

Where equipment or adaptations are required, paragraph 17.35 states "local authorities should make it clear to individuals that the custodial regime may limit the range of care options available". Guidance on relative responsibilities for provision are set out in paragraph 17.35, but these should be agreed locally.

Conclusion: Implications for professional judgement

Introduction

The statutory guidance sets out where professional judgement is required and the parameters of the decisions to be taken – but as would be expected it does not say how social work expertise should be applied. It states what social workers must and should consider in applying their professional knowledge and skills in making these judgements, and provides detail about what is lawful, but it does not give guidance on professional standards or ethical social work practice and it has very little to say about how social workers might use their skills to meet the needs of individuals.

There are numerous references to judgements to be made by local authorities in the statutory guidance, and in discharging its duty to provide information and advice on the care and support system, paragraph 3.23 states that an outline should be provided that includes "judgements that may need to be made".

This final chapter considers the distinctions between what the statutory guidance states local authorities 'must do', what they 'should do' and what they 'could do' – and how this applies to social workers. This is followed by a consideration of how the statutory guidance mandates and shapes the professional judgements of social workers.

Duties, powers and suggestions

The intention of the statutory guidance is to set out "how a local authority should go about performing its care and support responsibilities" (paragraph 1.1).

One of the ways that the statutory guidance does this is by building on the duties of local authorities (what they 'must do' and 'must not do') and powers (what they 'may do'), by stating what they 'should do'. These duties and powers mostly derive from the Act and the regulations, but there are some examples of duties and powers that appear only in the statutory guidance. The statutory guidance also makes suggestions about what local authorities 'might do' or 'could do'.

A duty is "something that the law says that someone (in this case, usually a local authority) must do, and that if they do not follow may result in legal challenge" (glossary in the statutory guidance). Some of the duties set out in the Act, regulations and the statutory guidance are applicable in all circumstances, eg in preparing a care and support plan "the local authority must involve... the adult for whom it is being prepared" (section 25 (3)), whereas other duties are specifying circumstances where a judgement has to be made, eg about whether it "appears... that an adult may have needs for care and support" (section 9 (1)).

The status of the statutory guidance was clarified in the introduction to the draft issued in June 2014, as follows: "Local authorities are required to act under the guidance, which means that they must follow it, unless they can demonstrate legally sound reasons for not doing so."

It should be noted that the statutory guidance does not use the term 'good practice' very often. One of the few examples where this term is used that is of relevance to social workers is in a reference to the sharing of safeguarding information about an individual with professional colleagues, which states: "It is good practice to inform the adult that this action is being taken unless doing so would increase the risk of harm" (paragraph 14.92).

What follows explores the differences between some of the duties, powers and 'suggestions' in relation to professional judgements made by social workers, and the relationships between them.

Care Act duties

The duties that are of particular relevance to social workers are set out in the Care Act in sections 1–36 (the care and support journey), 42–47 (safeguarding), 58–66 (transition of children) and 66–68 (independent advocacy).

A good example that demonstrates how the implementation of a Care Act duty is supported by statutory guidance on what 'should' be done is in relation to section 25 (3). This states: "In preparing a care and support plan, the local authority must involve... the adult for whom it is being prepared." Paragraph 10.2 of the statutory guidance restates this duty by saying that the "person must be genuinely involved and influential throughout the planning process", and this paragraph then gives some details about how this duty should apply:

- [The individual] should be given every opportunity to take joint ownership of the development of the plan with the local authority if they wish, and the local authority agrees.
- There should be a default assumption that the person, with support if necessary, will play a strong pro-active role in planning if they choose to.

- It should be made clear that the plan "belongs" to the person it is intended for, with the local authority role being to ensure the production and sign-off of the plan to ensure that it is appropriate to meet the identified needs.

Duties specified in the regulations

There are 21 sets of regulations and most of them are of relevance to social workers. What follows is a consideration of one of these, the Care and Support (Eligibility Criteria) Regulations 2014, to demonstrate the following:

- the relationship of the Regulations with the Care Act and the statutory guidance;
- the distinction between 'must' and 'should'.

The Care Act states in section 13 (1): "Where a local authority is satisfied on the basis of a needs or carer's assessment that an adult has needs for care and support or that a carer has needs for support, it must determine whether any of the needs meet the eligibility criteria." The Care and Support (Eligibility Criteria) Regulations 2014 set out the conditions that must be met for the needs of an adult or carer to meet the eligibility criteria, which in the case of adults is specified in section 2 (1) as follows:

a) the adult's needs arise from or are related to a physical or mental impairment or illness;

b) as a result of the adult's needs the adult is unable to achieve two or more of the outcomes specified in paragraph (2); and

c) as a consequence there is, or is likely to be, a significant impact on the adult's wellbeing.

In providing further detail the statutory guidance adds definition to what is meant by 'physical or mental impairment or illness' by stating: "Local authorities must consider at this stage if the adult has a condition as a result of either physical, mental, sensory, learning or cognitive disabilities or illnesses, substance misuse or brain injury" (paragraph 6.104). In this case the statutory guidance is specifying what local authorities 'must consider', ie adding an additional requirement.

But when it comes to what is meant by 'outcomes' the statutory guidance is slightly less prescriptive. It demonstrates what is meant by this term by giving examples. Paragraph 6.106 states that the statutory guidance is providing "examples of how local authorities should consider each outcome set out in the Eligibility Regulations (which do not constitute an exhaustive list) when determining the adult's eligibility for care and support". The key word here is 'should' rather than 'must'.

Very little statutory guidance is provided about the final condition of 'significant impact on wellbeing'. 'Wellbeing' is set out in section 1 (2) of the Care Act and this is not further defined in the statutory guidance. There is a brief description of how 'impact' might apply, but the term 'significant' is not defined – and as stated in paragraph 6.109 it "must therefore be understood to have its everyday meaning".

Duties specified in the statutory guidance

Duties are mostly specified in the Care Act and the Regulations, but there are a few examples of duties being specified in the statutory guidance. One such example is in relation to 'sufficiency' of the personal budget.

Paragraph 11.10 of the statutory guidance states: "The personal budget must always be an amount sufficient to meet the person's care and support needs, and must include the cost to the local authority of meeting the person's needs which the local authority is under a duty to meet, or has exercised its power to do so." This significant formulation does not appear in the Act or the regulations in any form.

Detailed guidance is provided in paragraphs 11.24–28 about how the duty of 'sufficiency' of the personal budget should be applied, and examples are given of how to balance this duty with the duty to include the 'cost to the local authority', including the following:

- "Consideration should therefore be given to local market intelligence and costs of local quality provision to ensure that the personal budget reflects local market conditions" (paragraph 11.25);
- "In all circumstances, consideration should be given to the expected outcomes of each potential delivery route" (paragraph 11.27).

There is statutory guidance on how 'sufficiency' could be applied, as follows:

- "There may be concern that the 'cost to the local authority' results in the direct payment being a lesser amount than is required to purchase care and support from the local market due to local authority bulk purchasing and block contract arrangements. However, by basing the personal budget on the cost of quality local provision, this concern should be allayed" (paragraph 11.25).
- An example is given in the following paragraph 11.27 which describes how an hourly rate for a care worker from a particular agency is agreed that is higher than the usual rate, to ensure that the individual receives the same care worker on each occasion as this has been decided to be essential to meet this individual's particular needs.

Powers

The legislation confers on local authorities the power to take action in certain circumstances, should it wish to do so, ie the Act, regulations and statutory guidance state what local authorities 'may do'. Sometimes a power is a significant addition to local authorities' options but it can also be simply a clarification of the scope of a duty.

An example of a power that is a significant addition to what local authorities may do is that which allows local authorities to meet non-eligible needs. Section 19 (1) states: "A local authority, having carried out a needs assessment ... may meet an adult's needs for care and support." The Care Act makes no reference to what these needs might be, but this is to be found in the statutory guidance in paragraph 10.28, which states these needs "may include... needs which are not 'eligible' (for example, those which do not meet the eligibility criteria) or meeting eligible needs in circumstances where the duty does not apply (for example, where the person is ordinarily resident in another area)". Although a local authority can choose whether it will meet an individual's needs, nevertheless two important duties apply, as follows:

- "Where the local authority exercises such a power to meet other needs, the same duties would apply regarding the next steps" (paragraph 10.28);
- "If the local authority decides not to use its powers to meet other needs, it must give the person written explanation for taking this decision" (paragraph 10.29).

An example of where a power is clarifying the scope of what a local authority may do is in section 8 (1) of the Care Act, which gives "examples of what may be provided to meet needs under sections 18 to 20". Where there is a duty to meet needs, local authorities may meet them by providing the following:

- accommodation in a care home or in premises of some other type;
- care and support at home or in the community;
- counselling and other types of social work;
- goods and facilities;
- information, advice and advocacy.

Sometimes the co-operation of other organisations is required to apply a power, such as those that relate to integrated assessments. Paragraph 6.76 sets out that a local authority has the following powers:

- to carry out a needs or carer's assessment jointly with another body carrying out any other assessment in relation to the person concerned;
- to integrate or align assessment processes in order to better fit around the needs of the individual;
- working together with relevant professionals on a single assessment;
- putting processes in place to ensure that the person is referred for other assessments such as an assessment for after-care needs under the Mental Health Act 1983.

The statutory guidance is proposing ways that the integration duty can be delivered, but achieving the objectives contained within these powers requires local policies and procedures to be developed.

Suggestions in the statutory guidance about applying duties and powers

The statutory guidance also includes suggestions about what local authorities 'might do' or 'could do' in applying a duty or a power.

For example, in undertaking an assessment local authorities have a duty to "consider the person's own strengths or if any other support might be available in the community to meet those needs" (paragraph 6.6). Paragraphs 6.63–64 suggest how this duty might and could be applied as follows:

- Strengths-based approaches might include co-production of services with people who are receiving care and support to foster mutual support networks.
- Encouraging people to use their gifts and strengths in a community setting could involve developing residents' groups and appropriate training to support people in developing their skills.
- Local authorities might also consider the ways a person's cultural and spiritual networks can support them in meeting needs and building strengths.

Another example of a 'suggestion' is the advice given on the application of the duty to "have regard to where the direct payment can be integrated with other forms of public funding, such as personal health budget direct payments" (paragraph 12.34). This paragraph goes on to state "the local authority could agree with the NHS that the social care and health direct payments are combined and that the monitoring is performed solely by one organisation, reporting to the other as appropriate".

The mandate for social work and professional judgement

Local authorities do not have a duty to employ or otherwise commission social workers to undertake the duties required by the Care Act, but they may do so under section 8 (1).

The statutory guidance sets out which roles social workers should and could undertake, but there are no circumstances where local authorities are under a duty to deploy social workers to particular tasks and activities.

This section outlines the range of roles that are deemed appropriate for social workers. This is followed by a consideration of those tasks and activities where a significant level of professional judgement by social workers is required. They are as follows:

- **preventing, reducing, or delaying needs for care and support;**
- **significant impact on wellbeing;**
- **meeting non-eligible needs;**
- **sufficiency of the personal budget;**
- **substantial difficulty in involvement.**

Roles that social workers should and could undertake

The statutory guidance identifies relatively few roles that are to be undertaken exclusively by social workers. Mostly social workers are referred to alongside occupational therapists or included within the generic term of 'professional'.

The most significant reference to social workers having an exclusive role is in relation to safeguarding. Paragraph 14.81 of the statutory guidance states:

- It is likely that many enquiries will require the input and supervision of a social worker, particularly the more complex situations.
- Where abuse or neglect is suspected within a family or informal relationship it is likely that a social worker will be the most appropriate lead.

Social workers are identified in this paragraph as having the skills to handle "enquiries in a sensitive and skilled way to ensure distress to the adult is minimised".

Following the initial stages of an enquiry, social workers have an important role in discussing with the adult what action could be taken, in terms of the options available and how these can best reflect their wishes. Paragraph 14.105 states: "Social workers must be able to set out both the civil and criminal justice approaches that are open and other approaches that might help to promote their wellbeing, such as therapeutic or family work, mediation and conflict resolution, peer or circles of support." The only other references to activities that are identified as exclusively for social workers are as follows:

- recovering debt incurred as a result of charges levied for the provision of care and support (see Annex D, sections 12 and 14);
- with reference to transition assessments paragraph 16.16 states: "Social workers will often be the most appropriate lead professionals for complex cases."

Social workers are referred to alongside other professionals, as follows:

- Paragraph 2.22 refers to professionals "who are effective at preventing, reducing, or delaying needs for care and support... (including) consideration of a person's strengths and their informal support networks as well as their needs and the risks they face".
- Paragraph 6.7 states: "Registered social workers and occupational therapists can provide important support and may be involved in complex assessments which indicate a wide range of needs, risks and strengths that may require a coordinated response from a variety of statutory and community services. Or they may be involved at the point of first contact to advise on whether preventative services would be more appropriate at that time."
- Paragraph 6.27 states: "Staff who are involved in this first contact must have the appropriate training and should have the benefit of access to professional support from social workers, occupational therapists and other relevant experts as appropriate, to support the identification of any underlying conditions or to ensure that complex needs are identified early and that people are signposted appropriately."

- Paragraph 6.84 states: "Assessments can be carried out by a range of professionals including registered social workers, occupational therapists and rehabilitation officers."
- It is recognised in paragraph 10.33 that "one-to-one support from a paid professional, such as a social worker" is one of the choices available to a person to meet their needs.
- Where a care and/or support plan is being developed by someone other than a social worker "the local authority should ensure… that there is… access to social work advice" (paragraph 10.35).
- Paragraph 10.41 states that local authorities "should have regard to how universal services and community-based and/or unpaid support could contribute to the factors in the plan, including support that promotes mental and emotional wellbeing and builds social connections and capital", and this "may require additional learning and development skills and competencies for social workers and care workers".
- In agreeing the level of involvement of the individual in developing their care and/or support plan, paragraph 10.50 states: "Social workers or other relevant professionals should have a discussion with the person to get a sense of their confidence to take a lead in the process and what support they feel they need to be meaningfully involved."
- Paragraph 13.16 states: "There should be a range of review options available, which may include… face to face reviews with a social worker or other relevant professional."
- In relation to reviews where "a person is recorded as having a mental impairment and lacking capacity to make some decisions… making appropriate use of a social worker as the lead professional should be encouraged" (paragraph 13.17).

There are specific references to social workers having a role in all stages of the care and support journey except for eligibility determination, deciding on whether there is a duty to meet needs and charging and financial assessment. However, as the professional who completed the assessment usually determines eligibility and the duty to meet needs, as well as initiating the financial assessment, this apparent omission is mostly of no consequence.

There are additional references in the statutory guidance to the role of social workers in assessing whether an individual lacks capacity, but this pertains to the Mental Capacity Act 2005 and not the Care Act.

The most frequent reference to social workers is where there is complexity. This can be where an individual's needs are complex and/or their circumstances are complex. What follows is a recap of those areas of the care and support journey where there is a level of complexity where social work expertise is particularly applicable.

Preventing, reducing, or delaying needs for care and support

There are three interrelated aspects of prevention where social work knowledge and skills are particularly applicable, as follows:

- *strengths and capabilities;*
- *support from the individual's wider network and community;*
- *developing social capital.*

These elements of prevention are to be taken account of in the assessment stage, eligibility determination and in developing the care and/or support plan.

Paragraph 6.2 states an assessment can "help people to understand their strengths and capabilities, and the support available to them in the community and through other networks and services". This is seen as a "critical intervention in its own right" (paragraph 6.2). The purpose of assisting people to develop this understanding at the assessment stage is twofold:

- "Identify needs that could be reduced, or where escalation could be delayed, and help people improve their wellbeing by providing specific preventive services" (paragraph 6.61);
- "Consider what else other than the provision of care and support might assist the person in meeting the outcomes they want to achieve" (paragraph 6.63).

Eligibility determination is "based on the remaining needs" (section 6.62) which have not been met through preventive interventions, so it is important that any benefits of prevention are realised where possible before considering whether the person has any eligible care and/or support needs.

In developing a care and/or support plan the statutory guidance states that "needs may be met through types of care and support which are available universally, including those which are not directly provided by the local authority" (paragraph 10.41). The intention is to signal the importance of what this paragraph describes as "support that promotes mental and emotional wellbeing and builds social connections and capital".

There is very little detail in the statutory guidance about what applying a strengths-based approach involves. This has been recognised by the Social Care Institute of Excellence (SCIE) and it has produced a thorough guide to the strengths-based approach in March 2015. This guide[1] makes suggestions about good practice for social workers in relation to prevention in general, as well as the specifics of the strengths-based approach. In addition, in March 2016 Think Local Act Personal (TLAP) published *Developing a Wellbeing and Strengths-Based Approach to Social Work Practice: Changing Culture*,[2] which sets out the case for strengths-based social work and community-based development.

Significant impact on wellbeing

Social workers play a vital role in interpreting the eligibility framework. The essential features of the framework are relatively straightforward to understand, but the circumstances of adults and carers to which it is applied are complex. The skill of the social worker lies in ensuring that the complexities of an individual's circumstances are reflected in the application of the framework.

In making the judgement about whether an individual has eligible needs there is a considerable amount of detail set out in the Act, regulations and statutory guidance that social workers need to know how to interpret and apply. But when it comes to the final stage of eligibility determination, deciding on whether there is consequential significant impact on wellbeing, the statutory guidance is necessarily imprecise. This is in part because the term 'significant' cannot be defined in law and as paragraph 6.109 states it "must therefore be understood to have its everyday meaning", but it is also reasonable to assume that it was concluded that good practice can only develop over time and that any further statutory guidance would have been too constraining.

SCIE provided some suggestions about how significant impact could be interpreted in January 2015.[3]

Meeting non-eligible needs

The statutory guidance has little to say about how non-eligible needs should be met, except to specify that the requirements and constraints that apply to eligible needs mostly apply to non-eligible needs. As a consequence most local authorities have developed a local policy to provide guidance on how they will exercise their power to meet care and support needs that are not eligible, and anecdotally these appear to vary considerably in how much scope there is for professional judgement.

Sufficiency of the personal budget

Social workers have a key role in ensuring that the personal budget is sufficient to meet the individual's care and support needs. But they are also expected to represent the interests of the local authority in ensuring that ways of meeting needs at no cost to the local authority are fully utilised, as well as helping people to understand that the local authority can only pay what is the 'cost to the local authority' to meet agreed needs.

The professional skill is in being able to achieve a balanced approach where there is tension between these requirements. Sometimes this will involve advocating for the individual where the indicative budget is not sufficient to meet their needs, but it can also mean helping individuals to understand and accept a plan that is less (both in scope and funding) than they had hoped for.

Substantial difficulty in involvement

Making the judgement about whether an individual has substantial difficulty in involvement is new to social work, and while there are situations where the difficulty is very evident, there will be many where it will not be clear whether the criteria apply.

The implementation of this new requirement introduces a number of important areas of activity where it will take time for good practice to emerge, as follows:

- *the new role of independent advocate;*
- *determining where it is inappropriate for someone to be the 'appropriate adult';*
- *where the individual also lacks capacity.*

The statutory guidance gives no indication about where to draw the line in making this judgement about whether a person is experiencing substantial difficulty. It could be argued that there are some similarities in the challenge of judging what is 'substantial' to that of judging what is 'significant' (as is in 'significant impact on wellbeing'), in that good practice can only develop over time and that any further statutory guidance would have been too constraining.

Conclusion

The Care Act 2014 and the associated Regulations and the Care and Support Statutory Guidance provide a policy framework that embraces and supports the development of modern social work. This framework has consolidated much of previously established good practice into duties and powers. But as with any major piece of legislation and its accompanying regulations and statutory guidance, as well as settling some matters, it introduces new sets of circumstances that will require practice and policy development.

There are many areas where the framework is very robust, such as eligibility determination, but there are also many areas of practice that need further development – as have been outlined in this chapter. Both the well-developed aspects of the system and the necessary uncertainties are leading to a reshaping of the way that local authorities meet care and/or support needs, and this will in turn have an impact on the roles that social workers undertake.

This reshaping is evolving in a number of different ways, eg earlier in this book reference was made to the different approaches being developed at first contact for steering individuals towards alternatives to a needs assessment. Some local authorities see the exploration of how people can make best use of their own resources, and other resources that they may not be aware of, as being best undertaken by a social worker. The thinking behind this is that the knowledge and skills of social workers are required to ensure that at this early stage there is an effective conversation with people about helping them to help themselves. However, a different approach has been adopted by other local authorities, whereby people are encouraged to make their own arrangements to use what is available in the community and in their own networks before requesting an assessment of care and support needs.

Social workers play a vital role in interpreting the Act, regulations and statutory guidance for people with care and/or support needs. Much of the legislation is complex, and the circumstances of the adults and carers to whom it is being applied are also complex. The skill of the social worker lies in ensuring both that the complexities of an individual's circumstances are addressed in accordance with a local authority's duties and powers, and making sure that the individual experiences the relevant processes as straightforwardly as possible. To achieve this social workers must rely on their professional knowledge and skills to interpret the Act, regulations and statutory guidance.

At the time of writing the main source of additional guidance is in the materials produced by SCIE. There were a number of publications from this organisation in early 2015 that provided suggestions about how the statutory guidance could be interpreted, and reference is made to these in this book, and more recently there have been publications that include good practice in applying the Care Act such as *A manual for good social work practice – Supporting adults who have dementia.*[4] As yet there has been no published research on how social workers are applying their knowledge, skills and values to the professional judgements they are making, but projects are underway that will enable social workers to learn more about how the Act is being implemented locally and to share learning about what works.

Good practice guidance is only one of the sources that social workers will use to enhance their knowledge, skills and capabilities. As part of maintaining their registration, social workers are required to evidence their continuing professional development. Training can help social workers develop their knowledge and this is recognised in the statutory guidance specifically in relation to assessment, safeguarding and care and/or support planning as follows:

- "Local authorities must ensure that assessors are appropriately trained and competent whenever they carry out an assessment" (paragraph 6.86);
- "Training should be... updated regularly to reflect current best practice" (paragraph 14.226);
- "Applying the requirement that local authorities "should have regard to... support that promotes mental and emotional wellbeing and builds social connections and capital... may require additional learning and development skills and competencies for social workers and care workers" (paragraph 10.41).

The core aims of this book have been to provide the following:

1. *a solid foundation for social work students in developing a critical understanding of the Care Act and its application;*
2. *the material to help experienced social workers with developing the critical reflection necessary to develop professional judgement;*

3. *a source of reference which social workers can use to evaluate their local systems and their associated policies and procedures.*

In addition to achieving these core aims, the author also hopes that this book can provide a useful resource both for those who are planning to evaluate the implementation of the Care Act and those who are developing good practice guidance.

References

1. www.scie.org.uk/care-act-2014/assessment-and-eligibility/strengths-based-approach
2. www.thinklocalactpersonal.org.uk/_assets/Resources/TLAP/BCC/TLAPChangingSWCulture.pdf
3. www.scie.org.uk/care-act-2014/assessment-and-eligibility/eligibility/
4. socialwelfare.bl.uk/subject-areas/services-client-groups/adults-mental-health/departmentofhealth/1762400ffice_Dementia_Practice_Guide_Accessible_pdf.pdf

Index

Feedback and praise for this book

It's an excellent guide that will give students a comprehensive background to a complex field.

Graham Ixer, University of Winchester

A very comprehensive and helpful guide to the legislation.

Alexandra Summer, University of Sunderland

The case examples are particularly useful.

Stan Henshaw, Buckinghamshire New University

I like the manner in which the provisions of the Care Act are set out as a journey which students could conceptualise travelling through with a service user. I also found the tables listing the key terms and definitions particularly relevant and useful … the book spoke particularly well around the interface with the Mental Capacity Act.

Kathryn Blake-Holmes, University of East Anglia

I found the book to be helpful in its intuitive logic – it will … make good sense to students in following the client 'journey', both chronologically and in terms of their care. The safeguarding section is also particularly helpful for social work students, and is written approachably.

Luke Tibbits, Warwick University

I like how it goes through each section of the Care Act 2014 giving extensive details of what is involved within the Care Act. I will be able to … direct students to publications like this one for them to gain more in-depth knowledge.

Gary Parle, New College Durham